Learning and Tea[illegible]g

At the Interface

Volume 60
A volume in the *At the Interface* series
'The Idea of Education'

Probing the Boundaries

Learning and Teaching in a Metropolis

Edited by

Lynn Ang, John Trushell and Patricia Walker

Rodopi

Amsterdam - New York, NY 2010

The paper on which this book is printed meets the requirements of "ISO 9706:1994, Information and documentation - Paper for documents - Requirements for permanence".

ISBN: 978-90-420-2795-4
E-Book ISBN: 978-90-420-2796-1

Printed in the Netherlands

Acknowledgements

The editors would like to acknowledge the work of all contributors to this book, whose unwavering belief and perseverance in the genesis and development of the project has made this collective enterprise a reality. We would also like to thank all colleagues in the Cass School of Education, who have in one way or another contributed ideas, information, and support for the production of this book.

Particular acknowledgement and thanks must also go to the practitioners, teachers, teacher educators, and members of the community who have provided valuable ideas, time and insights into the educational practice and research that have contributed to this text.

We would also like to thank Rodopi for their support in the development of this book over the past two years, especially to the commissioning editor, Dr. Rob Fisher, for his staunch belief in the value of this publication.

This book is written for all the highly motivated and dedicated professionals in education, the children, students and families with whom they work, and from whom we continue to learn so much.

We hope that this book will allow all those who come across it to reflect on their beliefs and practice, to articulate their views and act as advocates for education across the spectrum.

Lynn Ang, John Trushell, and Patricia Walker
Editors

Table of Contents

Foreword

I am delighted to write the Foreword to this book. *Learning and Teaching in a Metropolis* is a celebration of the work of the editors and contributors in making possible the publication of this collaborative, multi-professional volume. The book is written by a team of colleagues at the Cass School of Education, all of whom have been on a journey which started more than two years ago. The journey has involved much discussion, sharing of knowledge, peer mentoring and, where necessary, the challenging of established norms of practice to ensure that core values and principles about teaching and learning are shared by each contributing member, irrespective of the area of education.

All successful edited publications involve collegiate commitment and dedicated planning and that is certainly true of this book. The text demonstrates some of the key strengths of the Cass School of Education, including the breadth and mix of professional expertise, the innovative and often practice-based research undertaken by members of staff, and the high levels of engagement with professionals in the University of East London's local communities. The book shows how, with effort and shared vision, individuals can collaborate to find common ground in their research and practice, building and sustaining an inclusive culture of research-informed teaching. The book shows the enormous potential of a diverse learning and teaching community to create innovative and powerful practice, research and educational experiences.

The key question asked by the book is whether there are new ways in which we can transform how we teach and learn in order to enhance our practice. Students, teacher educators, practitioners and academics in the field of education have a duty to reflect on their beliefs and practices, to research their teaching and to communicate their work in order to maximise its relevance in enhancing the learning of the communities around them. This book will help.

Ann Slater
Dean of School
Cass School of Education
University of East London

Learning and Teaching in a Metropolis: Introduction

Lynn Ang and John Trushell

"London is the place for strange rencounters."
George Borrow, *Lavengro* (1851)[1]

1. Diversity in Education

A recent publication of the Greater London Authority, alluding to the cultural and linguistic diversity to be found in London, was entitled *London – the World in a City*.[2] This title has two implications. The first and more obvious implication is that London is extraordinary: historic, revelatory and significant. The second and less obvious implication is that, in a city where an entire world of languages and cultures may be encountered, the exotic has become esoteric, and strange rencounters can be everyday occurrences or infraordinary.[3]

The metropolis and the metropolitan are towards one pole on a demographic continuum, and from 23rd May 2008 the majority of the world's population had moved towards this pole: 3.3 billion people, more than half of the global population, live in urban areas now.[4] The world has changed, particularly in the last decade, and our lives have become different and diverse. Advances in science and technology – particularly in communications and informatics – have stimulated new economies, paralleled by increased geographical mobility including diasporas, migration and other international travel. These trends have meant that the dawn of the twenty-first century has witnessed new styles of living and ways of thinking, with a higher degree of cosmopolitanism and internationalism.

The ever-increasing mobility of individuals and communities across the world has achieved diversity and heterogeneity rather than homogeneity, and our identities are continually being constructed by the interplay of considerations such as class, culture, disability, gender, ethnicity, race and sexuality. Globally, we are in the midst of one of the most significant changes of all time - technologically, socio-economically and politically – and this change deeply implicates education - one of the most fundamental aspects of society, education - in the way that it profoundly affects our capacity for learning and meaning-making.

Indeed, education in a twenty-first century metropolis highlights the need for us to rethink our curricula and pedagogies in light of the impact that new knowledge, skills and understandings can have on our learning. As Giroux asserts, education in contemporary society necessitates the expansion of 'the relevance of the curriculum and pedagogy to include the richness and diversity of students'.[5] However, in London and Britain, such diversity and richness often 'remain objectives rather than reality'[6] and this is despite neoliberal reforms to education which envisage a 'future of a knowledge economy, high skills, innovation and creativity and a meritocracy within which social boundaries are erased' in a 'world that is flexible and fluid, within which identities can be continually remade'.[7]

2. Devolution of Education

Neoliberalism is a deceptively 'solid' sounding term that actually represents a loose aggregation of points of view.[8] These various perspectives share two common tenets: first, discontent with government intervention, perceived as directivist and economically misguided; and, second, celebration of market mechanisms to ensure economic prosperity and the maximization of individual freedom.[9] Neoliberalism envisages communities, families, individuals and private enterprises as self-regulating and free to maximize their own personal benefits - and to prioritise their own agendas - with minimal intervention from the government and state. The neoliberal ideal is that all communities and individuals should be included and respected within society - regardless of class, culture, disability, gender, ethnicity and race and sexuality – and this ideal is associated with notions of equal opportunity, inclusion, participation and social justice. However, fundamental to the introduction of market mechanisms into society is the acceptance that 'all markets have losers (even victims) as well as winners' and that the operation of market forces will create 'not a more equal society but one that is more "acceptably" unequal'.[10] Thus, while there is an assumption, within neoliberal discourse, that most individuals and social groups will ultimately benefit from the effects of economic liberty and a market driven economy, in reality neoliberal agendas may serve to reinforce economic and social inequalities in society. The decreased commitment of neoliberal governments to take responsibility for education, health and social welfare services often means that disadvantaged groups in society are most likely to be adversely affected as their ability to access these services becomes increasingly compromised.

In education, neoliberalism has been criticized as potentially 'disastrous for the children of the poor and disenfranchised'.[11] The notion of education in a neoliberal society remains a contested concept. In his text *The Education Debate*,[12] Ball raises concerns for the individualisation and fragmentation of the current educational system in Britain. He argues that education is often regarded as an economic product, 'as a crucial factor in ensuring economic productivity and competitiveness in the context of "information capitalism"'.[13] Education in our contemporary society is seen primarily as a business opportunity and economic necessity, delivered for the benefit of the individual and global economy.

In London and Britain, the operation of market forces in education has been facilitated by reforms that have devolved education: the autonomy of educational institutions has been increased; educational provision is marked by attempts at diversification or specialization of institutions to increase contestability;[14] educational institutions are encouraged to engage in competition; and students and parents are reconceptualised as customers who have the choice of institutions. Apple has argued that, within a neoliberal discourse, the idea of the consumer is fundamental.[15] The world is like a massive supermarket in which essential public sector services such as education, health, housing and welfare are subject to the for-profit market and are socially engineered to become self-regulating. The problem with a market model which privileges choice for the distribution of education as a commodity is that this achieves optimal average benefits for all but with wide disparities: there will inevitably be disproportionate acquisition of education by the most advantaged and disproportionate non-acquisition of education by the least advantaged.[16] Outcomes of these disparities are greater inequity and increased socio-economic segregation.[17] Notably, Allen and Vignoles contend that school segregation has risen faster in London where school choice is most developed.[18]

This utilitarian model does not necessarily acknowledge inequity or social disadvantage but characterizes those individuals, families and communities whose lives are marred by social inequalities such as poverty and unemployment as experiencing social exclusion, attributable to individual, family and community inadequacies.[19] The state must intervene for those who are disadvantaged to control their dislocation and potential risk[20] - but without fostering a dependency culture or removing incentive – by the provision of a minimum safety net.[21] One such safeguard is the 'Every Child Matters' [ECM] policy statement[22] which was introduced subsequent to the death of Adjo Victoria Climbié.

The public haste to respond to extraordinary and untoward events rather than to infraordinary circumstances was noted by Perec who remarked:

> 'Social problems' aren't 'a matter of concern' when there's a [tragedy], they are intolerable twenty-four hours out of twenty-four, three hundred and sixty-five days a year.[23]

Adjo Victoria Climbié was an eight year old from the Ivory Coast who died in Tottenham, London, on 25th February 2000 from hypothermia, malnutrition and physical abuse at the hands of her aunt and her cohabitee. Her death provoked public outcry and a public inquiry and was the catalyst for the formulation of the ECM initiative, embedded in the neoliberal rhetoric of combating social exclusion.[24] Nevertheless, the ECM agenda was welcomed by many people engaged in education, especially in London where social problems are pronounced:

> London was seen as prime territory for the development of a policy with a strong focus on the needs of each and every child, particularly the most vulnerable, and in addition it was seen as precisely what was required in the London context as a means of enhancing the capacity to learn and thus to raise standards.[25]

However, in the final analysis of the case, Adjo Victoria Climbié's death was tragic, but the intolerable circumstances of the situation were exacerbated by those which placed her at risk.

3. Learning and Teaching as Infraordinary

Social justice, as an ideal, appears uncontentious and incontestable. However, there are tensions between the positions of social justice in egalitarian (welfare) and neoliberal (post-welfare) contexts. An egalitarian position prioritises social justice and redistributes benefits by limiting individual choice to achieve welfare for all[26] while a neoliberal position balances a concern for social justice with the right for individual autonomy[27] and the exercise of choice.[28]

An egalitarian position in education would support the redistribution of educational opportunities for reasons such as (1) avoidance of collective social 'evils', (2) an investment in a positive public good and (3) an altruistic obligation to social justice.[29] Arguably, educators share an altruistic social justice agenda and commitments to the moral ideal of equal opportunity and to providing an educational provision that is fair and just, valuing diversity and ensuring that participation is equitable.

Education is often seen as a means by which the disadvantaged are able to overcome their deprived circumstances and to better their economic and social futures. The role of educators is to be concerned with organizing learning opportunities and guiding the learning process[30] to enable learners not only to acquire skills that will be relevant to their lives but also to encourage curiosity and creativity so that the foundations for lifelong learning are established. Education in contemporary society is about finding optimal ways in which educators can promote meaningful and useful learning in educational institutions across compulsory and post-compulsory sectors. This requires educators to be alert to the ways in which educational provision may exacerbate the discursive inequality and power relations between those who are advantaged and disadvantaged, and to be sensitive to the widening gaps between the wealthy and the poor. Educators should be committed to an infraordinary moral ideal of equal opportunity, where individuals are perceived as active agents, capable of realising their personal potential, through all available educational means. The assertions of William Temple concerning education and welfare in 1944 still reverberate among educationists today:

> you can have no justice at the basis of your social life until education has done its full work... and... if you want human liberty you must have educated people.[31]

4. Learning and Teaching in a Metropolis

This book contests neoliberal orthodoxy in education and raises questions concerning education in an urban context. Contemporary commentators have observed that urban education provides a territory where the purposes of education are contested and in London, as a particularly large metropolis, these purposes are hotly contested. [32] The contributions provide both empirical research and theoretical debates concerning teaching, learning and education. Collectively, the essays demonstrate the diversity of education experiences that the authors bring to their work in a higher educational institution in London.

This is a book in which the writers articulate their professional ideas and values relating to learning and teaching, putting these into perspective in contemporary society and bringing these to life in their everyday practice. The contributions of the writers to this book pose pertinent questions. What does education actually entail? How can lecturers and teacher-educators who work on a daily basis with a diverse student body provide an inclusive education provision? How can teacher trainers, trainees and newly qualified teachers be empowered in their teaching and learning experiences in schools and the wider community? How can education be delivered, at any level, when the circumstances and backgrounds of learners are so very diverse and changeable? What kinds of pedagogical strategies are there in place to recognise such diversity? How can the delivery of education be adapted to take account of diversity and are these strategies sufficient to address issues of inequality? These questions are enormously difficult to answer but the writers make concerted attempts so to do, thereby reinforcing the centrality of teaching, learning and the learner's autonomy in the pursuit of educational goals.

The strength of this publication lies in its perspective on education from the standpoint of school practitioners and higher education educators. The distinguishing feature of this publication is as a collation of essays on the theme of education and diversity, each with its own distinct illustration of what it is like to teach and learn in a culturally diverse community such as East London. The contributors to this book write in the full knowledge that education is a pivotal subject for all who pass through compulsory and post-compulsory systems, but that learners have diverse and unique learning experiences. The writers share common ground in their work with undergraduate and postgraduate students in the Cass School of Education at the University of East London. The University attracts non-traditional students, many from mixed local communities with non-traditional academic backgrounds, at times with low formal educational participation, particularly in higher education. The discussions in the contributions demonstrate that education in the contemporary context takes on many new complex forms, and, in the midst of such diversity, there is an urgent need to address educational inequalities. This is especially the case in a neoliberal society where educators and educational institutions have to negotiate a precarious relationship between education and the economy. The most pressing issues of learning and teaching in a diverse institution such as UEL arise precisely from this context.

Recent publications in this area have tended to stress the perspectives and voice of recipients or users of education. However, this book stresses the position of those who deliver education, the challenges, issues and rewards of teaching and learning in a metropolis.

5. The Contributions

Research in higher education is dominated by relatively small-scale, evaluative case studies, typically of learning and/or teaching or of educational provision at the levels of programme, institution, or authority.[33] The contributions to this book are such case studies. The essays which follow this introduction concern the formation of teachers, learning and teaching with children in the primary and secondary compulsory sectors and issues in the post-compulsory higher education sector.

The earliest contributions concern the formation of teachers, from initial teacher-training to early teaching experiences. Herrington, Brennan and Wright provide an account of the factors to be taken into consideration when establishing initial teacher training [ITT] provision. While it is widely accepted that 'teacher supply and retention has always been a chronic and sometimes acute feature of London schools',[34] East London boroughs probably encounter the greatest challenges. Herrington et al describe the manner in which the secondary ITT programme at the University of East London works in partnerships with these boroughs.

Teachers in London, as a matter of course, have to cope with 'changing identities, diversity and mobility' and, while this is a "taken-for-granted skill of London teachers", this skill has to be acquired.[35] Cudworth and Cudworth examine learning and teaching encounters between Gypsy/Traveller children and teachers and intending teachers.

Dorrington, Morris and Trushell report studies concerning intending teachers on the primary ITT programme in the Cass School of Education. Morris and Trushell examine differentials in information and communication technology resources available to primary teacher-trainees on school placements in boroughs of East London which have 'incomes lower than the national average and higher rates of poverty and deprivation'.[36] Dorrington and Trushell report on teacher trainees' perceptions of scientists, collected by an exercise intended to raise intending teachers' awareness of potential stereotypical views of scientists that, unwittingly, may be communicated to pupils.

Czerniawski examines the post-ITT experiences of London-based newly qualified teachers [NQTs], and the value positions and perspectives that these NQTs have identified as central to their professional identity. In her chapter on special educational needs in London, Mackenzie considers the effects of policy and perceptions upon staff working on a daily basis with children with special educational needs - from special educational needs coordinators to teaching assistants - and how working with children with special educational needs in London presents particular challenges.

The contributions from Chakrabarty, Hassan, Kenworthy, McCalman and Preston examine educational provision in diverse settings and authorities in London. McCalman explores the provision of steel pan workshops for pupils and adults with special educational needs and considers the contribution that such provision may make to social inclusion. Hassan investigates those factors which Muslim pupils at secondary schools in East London report as affecting their sense of group identity. Chakrabarty and Preston consider the role of drama in secondary classrooms, particularly the tensions that exist between performance and posturing. Kenworthy provides an account of the establishment of a discovery centre in East London, which emphasizes consultation with children concerning that establishment and its engagement with children.

The final contributions concern post-compulsory higher education provision. Walker reviews the expansion of higher education – widening participation – and the implications for the University of East London as a former polytechnic/post-92 university. Masterton considers the effects of the Special Educational Needs and Disability Act upon higher education institutions, especially the effects that greater inclusivity have had for academic and administrative staff. Perumal investigates the potential of entry level undergraduates to the Cass School of Education to demonstrate autonomy in their studies and tentatively identifies variables that apparently enhance or restrict that potential.

Each contribution is distinct in its discussion of education with its unique illustration of what it is like to teach and learn in a culturally diverse community. Some essays provide snapshots of current pedagogical practice. Others discuss critical questions concerning the shape and direction of contemporary education. Collated in this book, these contributions provide a contemporary picture of learning and teaching in a diverse community such as East London.

Notes

[1] G Borrow, *Lavengro*, Dent and Sons, London, 1961, p.250.
[2] M Mackintosh, *London – the World in a City*, Greater London Authority Data Management and Analysis Group, London, 2005.
[3] G Perec, "Approaches to what?", in *Species of Spaces and Other Pieces*, Perec, G with Sturrock, J (trans. and ed.), Penguin Books, London, 1997, pp. 209-211, p. 210: Perec defines the term as 'the banal, the quotidian, the obvious, the common, the ordinary, the infraordinary, the background noise, the habitual'.
[4] United Nations Population Fund [UNFPA], State of the World Population 2007: Unleashing the Potential of Urban Growth, [http://www.unfpa.org/swp/2007/english/introduction.html, accessed 5th May, 2008].
[5] H Giroux, 'Education in unsettling times: public intellectuals and the promise of Cultural Studies', in *Power/Knowledge/Pedagogy: The Meaning of Democratic Education in Unsettling Times*, D Carlson and M Apple (ed.), Westview Press, Boulder, Col., 1998, pp.41-60, p. 49.
[6] G Whitty, *Making Sense of Education Policy*, Paul Chapman, London, 2002, p. 99.
[7] S Ball, *The Education Debate*, Policy Press, University of Bristol, 2008, p. 205.
[8] P Trowler, *Education Policy*, 2nd ed., Routledge, London, 2003, p. 104.
[9] M Olssen, J Codd and A-M O'Neill, *Education Policy: Globalization, Citizenship and Democracy*, Sage, London, 2004, p. 137.
[10] Whitty, op. cit., p. 80.
[11] M Apple, 'Preface to the 1995 edition', *Education and Power*, Routledge: London, 1995, pp. vii-xxii, p. xxi.
[12] Ball, op. cit.
[13] Ibid, p. 3.
[14] F Coffield and R Steer, 'The UK government's model of public service reform' in *Public Sector Reform: Principles for Improving the Education System*, F Coffield, R Steer, R Allen, A Vignoles, G Moss and C Vincent, Bedford Way Papers, Institute of Education, University of London, 2007, pp. 8-18, p. 13., 1999.
[15] M Apple, 'Whose values? Whose education? – Legitimating educational inequalities in conservative times', in Proceedings from the 2nd International Conference *Values in Education Across Boundaries*, B Widerstedt (ed) National Centre for Values Education, Umeå University, Sweden, pp. 15-46, p. 19.
[16] Olssen et al, pp. 216 ff.
[17] Coffield and Steer, op. cit.,, p. 15.

[18] R Allen and A Vignoles, 'Market incentive in schools, in *Public Sector Reform: Principles for Improving the Education System*, F Coffield, R Steer, R Allen, A Vignoles, G Moss and C Vincent, Bedford Way Papers, Institute of Education, University of London, 2007, pp. 34-41, p. 38.
[19] See Ball, op. cit., p. 153.
[20] X Bonal, 'The neoliberal education agenda and the legitimation crisis', *British Journal of Sociology of Education*, Vol. 24-2, 2003, pp. 159-175, p. 167
[21] Whitty, op. cit.
[22] Department for Education and Skills (DfES), *Every Child Matters: Change for Children*, DFES 1081-2004, DFES, Nottingham, 2004.
[23] Perec, op. cit., p. 209.
[24] P Garrett, 'How to be modern: New Labour's neoliberal modernity and the *Change for Children* programme', *British Journal of Social Work*, Vol. 38-2, pp. 270-289, p. 272.
[25] J Mokades, 'Does every London child matter? The new agenda for children in London', in *Education in a Global City: Essays from London*, T Brighouse and L Fullick (eds.), Bedford Way Papers, Institute of Education, University of London, 2007, pp. 122-146, p. 132.
[26] Olssen et al, op. cit., p. 216.
[27] P Fitzsimons, 'Third Way: values for education?', *Theory and Research in Education*, Vol. 4-2, 2006, pp. 151-171, p. 154.
[28] Olssen et al, op. cit..
[29] J Codd, 'Neo-liberal education policy and the ideology of choice', *Educational Philosophy and Theory*, Vol. 25-2, 2007, pp. 31-48, p.43.
[30] T Husén, *The School in Question*, Oxford University Press, Oxford, 1979, p. 168.
[31] R Butler, *The Art of Memory: Friends in Perspective*, Hodder and Stoughton, London, 1982, pp. 144-145.
[32] S Gray and G Whitty, 'Comprehensive schooling and social inequality in London: past, present and possible future, in *Education in a Global City: Essays from London*, T Brighouse and L Fullick (eds.), Bedford Way Papers, Institute of Education, University of London, 2007, pp. 95-121, p. 95.
[33] See M Tight, *Researching Higher Education*, Open University Press, Buckingham, 2003.
[34] T Brighouse, 'The London Challenge – a personal view', in *Education in a Global City: Essays from London*, T Brighouse and L Fullick (eds.) Bedford Way Papers, Institute of Education, University of London, 2007, pp.71-94, p. 80.
[35] J McKenley, 'Ethnic diversity in London schools', in *Education in a Global City: Essays from London*, T Brighouse and L Fullick (eds.) Bedford Way Papers, Institute of Education, University of London, 2007, pp. 197-220, p. 216.

[36] R Lupton and A Sullivan, 'The London Context' in *Education in a Global City: Essays from London*, T Brighouse and L Fullick (eds.) Bedford Way Papers, Institute of Education, University of London, 2007, pp. 8-17, p. 16.

Bibliography

Allen, R. and A. Vignoles, 'Market incentive in schools, in *Public Sector Reform: Principles for Improving the Education System*, F. Coffield, R. Steer, R. Allen, A. Vignoles, G. Moss and C. Vincent, Bedford Way Papers, Institute of Education, University of London, 2007, pp. 34-41.

Apple, M., 'Preface to the 1995 edition', *Education and Power*, Routledge: London, 1995, pp. vii-xxii.

Apple, M., 'Whose values? Whose education? – Legitimating educational inequalities in conservative times', in Proceedings from the 2nd International Conference *Values in Education Across Boundaries*, B Widerstedt (ed) National Centre for Values Education, Umeå University, Sweden, pp. 15-46.

Ball, S., *The Education Debate*, Policy Press: University of Bristol, 2008.

Bonal, X., 'The neoliberal education agenda and the legitimation crisis', *British Journal of Sociology of Education*, Vol. 24-2, 2003, pp. 159-175.

Borrow, G., *Lavengro*, Dent and Sons, London, 1961.

Brighouse, T., 'The London Challenge – a personal view', in *Education in a Global City: Essays from London*, T. Brighouse and L. Fullick (eds.) Bedford Way Paper, Institute of Education, University of London, 2007, pp.71-94.

Butler, R., *The Art of Memory: Friends in Perspective*, Hodder and Stoughton, London, 1982

Codd, J., 'Neo-liberal education policy and the ideology of choice', *Educational Philosophy and Theory*, Vol. 25-2, 2007, pp. 31-48.

Coffield, F. and R. Steer, 'The UK government's model of public service reform' in *Public Sector Reform: Principles for Improving the Education System*, F. Coffield, R. Steer, R. Allen, A. Vignoles, G. Moss and C. Vincent, Bedford Way Papers, Institute of Education, University of London, 2007, pp. 8-18.

Department for Education and Skills (DfES), *Every Child Matters: Change for Children*, DFES 1081-2004, DFES, Nottingham, 2004.

Fitzsimons, P., 'Third Way: values for education?', *Theory and Research in Education*, Vol. 4-2, 2006, pp. 151-171.

Garrett, P., 'How to be modern: New Labour's neoliberal modernity and the *Change for Children* programme', *British Journal of Social Work*, Vol. 38-2, pp. 270-289.

Giroux, H., 'Education in unsettling times: public intellectuals and the promise of Cultural Studies', in *Power/Knowledge/Pedagogy: The Meaning of Democratic Education in Unsettling Times*, D Carlson and M Apple (ed.), Westview Press: Boulder, Col., 1998, pp.41-60

Gray, S. and G Whitty, 'Comprehensive schooling and social inequality in London: past, present and possible future, in *Education in a Global City: Essays from London*, T Brighouse and L Fullick (eds.), Bedford Way Papers, Institute of Education, University of London, 2007, pp. 95-121.

Husén, T., *The School in Question*, Oxford University Press, Oxford, 1979.

Lupton, R. and A. Sullivan, 'The London Context' in *Education in a Global City: Essays from London*, T. Brighouse and L. Fullick (eds.) Bedford Way Papers, Institute of Education, University of London, 2007, pp. 8-17.

Mackintosh, M., *London – the World in a City*, Greater London Authority Data Management and Analysis Group, London, 2005.

McKenley, J., 'Ethnic diversity in London schools', in *Education in a Global City: Essays from London*, T Brighouse and L Fullick (eds.) Bedford Way Papers, Institute of Education, University of London, 2007, pp. 197-220.

Mokades, J., 'Does every London child matter? The new agenda for children in London', in *Education in a Global City: Essays from London*, T. Brighouse and L. Fullick (eds.), Bedford Way Papers, Institute of Education, University of London, 2007, pp. 122-146.

Olssen, M., J. Codd and A.-M. O'Neill, *Education Policy: Globalization, Citizenship and Democracy*, Sage: London, 2004.

Perec, G., 'Approaches to what?', in *Species of Spaces and Other Pieces*, G. Perec with J. Sturrock (trans. and ed.), Penguin Books, London, 1997, pp. 209-211.

Tight, M., *Researching Higher Education*, Open University Press, Buckingham, 2003.

Trowler, P., *Education Policy*, 2nd ed., Routledge, London, 2003.

United Nations Population Fund [UNFPA], *State of the World Population 2007: Unleashing the Potential of Urban Growth*, [http://www.unfpa.org/swp/2007/english/introduction.html, accessed 5th May, 2008].

Whitty, G., *Making Sense of Education Policy*, Paul Chapman: London, 2002.

Lynn Ang's research specialism is in Early Childhood Studies, pertaining to issues of diversity, professionalism and teacher education in the early education and care of young children 0-8 years. Dr Ang has been successful in securing a number of research grants from funding bodies – including the British Academy and the National College of School Leadership – and has worked internationally in Singapore, Scotland and England.

John Trushell – originally from Yorkshire – studied at the University of Durham before teaching in primary and secondary schools in Durham, Sussex and London. He has lectured and conducted research in and around London – notably King's College London where he completed his PhD – for 25 years.

Teacher Training in an Urban Setting: A Story from East London

Neil Herrington, Caroline Brennan and Kathy Wright

Abstract
This chapter will examine the problem of teacher shortage in East London, and explore initiatives that the secondary initial teacher-training team at the University of East London have implemented – with local boroughs and partner schools - to address this problem with their programme.

Key Words: Secondary teacher training, urban education, social entrepreneurship.

*****

1. The London Context

The introduction of Pevsner's guide to the built environment of East London[1] states that:

> The scale of both the natural and man-made landscape of East London is vast, offering broad vistas and exhilarating horizons unmatched in other parts of London. The Thames is wider here than upstream. East from Canning Town, the empty sheets of water of the Royal Docks stretch for 2 miles to the horizon. In the old 18th Century suburbs, Hawksmoor's proud churches have the grandest Baroque towers in London. Further out at Wanstead, the great 18th Century park rivalled Hampton Court, eating into the fringes of Epping Forest, relics of the ancient Forest of Essex, whose woodland still sweeps south in a broad swathe, from the higher ground on the northern borders where Greater London becomes Essex countryside. From here there is a clear view across some fifteen miles of suburban growth to the City of London and Canary Wharf towers on the site of the West India docks.

Those docks no longer link this area of London to the rest of the world: connectivity is now achieved by the broadband of the businesses that have replaced the cranes and the warehouses. But the world is still represented here. The history of migration into East London is well documented and, indeed, is written in the landscape for those who know how to read it. The Greater London Authority estimated, in 2001, that about one in twenty of the city's resident population - between 350,000 and 400,000 - were refugees and asylum seekers.[2] Moreover, more than two million Londoners were born outside the UK or Republic of Ireland in 175 different countries,[3] confirming the description of London as "the world within a city".[4] Three hundred and sixty home languages are spoken in London schools.[5] The characteristic diversity and cultural capital of the area makes it a rich place, in contrast to the fact that most East London households have incomes lower than the national average with higher rates of poverty and deprivation.[6]

However, often it is not this richness that forms the perception of East London: this is tinted for many people by tales of Jack the Ripper, gangland and television soap operas. These are not particularly positive images, with little made of the descriptions that Pevsner records. This negative perception may be compounded by a "deficit view of the cultural forms associated with specific areas of the city, particularly the inner city, or of cultural forms associated with racial or ethnic groups in the city".[7] The Prime Minister's Strategy Unit [PMSU], in 2004, spelt out the London context:

> London's challenge is to resolve tensions arising from its intensity; great wealth with social inclusion; diversity with tolerance; openness to migration with security and public support; mobility with community; and population and economic growth with quality of place and quality of life.[8]

2. Urban Regeneration

The problems associated with inter-related socio-economic disadvantage and educational under-attainment are long-standing concerns of both national and local policy: urban education has become synonymous with educational disadvantage.[9] The influential 1993 report *Access and Achievement in Urban Education*, by the Office for Standards in Education [OFSTED], stated that underachievement by pupils was apparent from an early stage in primary schooling.[10] The New Labour government, upon election in 1997, determined to tackle disadvantage through education policy.[11] A succession of initiatives were implemented - the creation of Education Action Zones in 1997,[12] the Excellence in Cities programme in 1999[13] and the Schools Facing Challenging Circumstances programme in 2001[14] – ostensibly designed to raise levels of attainment in urban schools. An initiative specific to London – The London Challenge – followed on the appointment of a Commissioner for London Schools and a Minister for London Schools in 2003.[15] But the evidence for a link between school initiatives and area regeneration is tenuous. A study conducted for the Joseph

Rowntree Foundation[16] reported some eclectic if not incoherent practice. The authors identified three basic models of school contribution:

- a community resourcing model in which schools sought to make their facilities, networks and expertise available to otherwise resource poor communities;
- an individual transformation model in which schools focussed exclusively on improving the life chances of individual young people by raising their attainment; and
- a contextual transformation model in which schools sought to raise attainment, but felt that this could only be achieved by involving families and the community and that a wider range of attributes must be developed in pupils.[17]

Schools were engaged in community-oriented activities and could have considerable impact on individual pupils. However, there was neither evidence that schools were able to have large-scale impact on communities as a whole nor evidence that schools were able to achieve transformations of the life chances of large groups of young people.

Within London, direct engagement of schools with communities is made difficult due to the quantity and range of education provision – complemented by access via a good transport infrastructure - which enables a greater choice of schools for those families who possess the economic, cultural, and social capital to negotiate these complexities. Thus, in London, where a secondary school has a mean of 17.19 schools within a ten minute drive (which compares to a figure of 6.74 in other urban areas), pupils are less likely to go to the nearest school: in fact, only 24.09% do so.[18] The Rowntree Foundation study reported that families are encouraged "to choose schools other than their most local one and hence to loosen the ties between particular schools and particular localities".[19]

Even if this were not the case, a national educational policy context which focuses heavily on 'standards' of pupil attainment tends to override desire on the part of schools to engage with their communities.

3. Teacher Supply: National Picture, Local Issue

An annual report of the Chief Inspector of Schools, consciously at risk of stating the obvious, asserted that:

> what makes schools successful, particularly those that seem to have the odds stacked against them… [is] strong leadership, good teaching and excellent communication with parents.[20]

However, OFSTED reported that, in 2000/01, the greatest turnover and wastage of teachers in primary and secondary schools was in the Inner and Outer London boroughs,[21] turnover being defined as a departure from one school for another school and wastage being defined as departure from the school system. Subsequently, teacher vacancies in London were over twice the national average (see Table 1).[22]

Table 1: Teacher Turnover, Wastage & Vacancies in London and England, 2000.

Rates	London	England
Turnover	19.7%	15.3%
Wastage	11.1%	8.9%
Vacancy	2.0%	0.8%

In 2000, a significant proportion of England's teacher shortage was located in East London boroughs, yet there was no provider of secondary teacher-training situated in East London. Two East London boroughs and the University of East London [UEL] approached the Teacher Training Agency [TTA] to point out this untenable situation and to propose that it be rectified at the earliest opportunity. Teacher-supply in England had been managed by the TTA, since 1994,[23] through a system of allocating target numbers of teacher-trainees to particular higher education [HE] institutions, based on a model predicated on national demographics. There are allocations for 'traditional' routes into teaching, for example through the Postgraduate Certificate in Education [PGCE], and through employment-based routes, for example the Graduate Teacher Programme [GTP] and the Overseas Trained Teacher Programme [OTTP]. Notably, the census data for 2001[24] demonstrated that the national demographic was not reflected in the local situation: whereas the population of England had increased by 1.9%, the population of London had increased by 4.1%. This population change was even more marked in certain East London boroughs (see Table 2). Subsequently, in 2001, the TTA agreed to allocate to UEL target numbers of trainees to establish a secondary PGCE.

In East London, teacher-training by employment-based routes - i.e. GTP and OTTP - were supported and structured by the North East London Partnership [NELP] which had been established by the TTA in 2001. NELP initially featured the participation of such HE institutions as Canterbury Christ Church College, the University of Gloucester and UEL but, being the only truly London-based provider in NELP, UEL could respond promptly to the needs of local schools whether these were for the GTP or the OTTP. Thus, UEL became a credible secondary provider in the eyes of many local schools as a direct result of engagement with NELP.

Table 2: Population Change in East London Boroughs, 1991-2001

East London Borough	Population Change, 1991-2001
Barking and Dagenham	12.1%
Hackney	7.9%
Havering	-3.6%
Newham	10.1%
Redbridge	3.2%
Tower Hamlets	16.7%
Waltham Forest	0.3%

Effectively, UEL was engaged in an attempt to create "a labour force recognisably 'local' with personal histories strongly associated" with East London which would counter the effects of "a highly mobile labour force increasingly unattached to particular spaces or locations"[25] in a period when teacher vacancies in secondary schools continued to increase.[26] Nationally, the teacher shortage has persisted (see Table 3) with particular shortages in certain secondary subjects: to the perennial shortage of Mathematics and Science teachers has been added a shortage of Modern Foreign Languages teachers.[27]

Table 3: Teacher Turnover, Wastage & Vacancies in London & England, 2006.[28]

Rates	London	England
Turnover	23%	19%
Wastage	12%	10%
Vacancy	1.2%	0.6%

Teacher shortage has been addressed by financial incentives – e.g. 'golden hellos' to new entrants - and recruitment campaigns conducted by the Teacher Development Agency [TDA], as the TTA was renamed in 2005. These initiatives may be effective at the national and local levels.

4. Social Entrepreneurship

Consistent with the aim of creating a 'local' teacher workforce for East London, the team for secondary initial teacher-training [ITT] at UEL developed an approach within the framework of social entrepreneurship. Entrepreneurship has tended to be regarded in a negative, pejorative way in the public sector. However, a key distinction between entrepreneurship and social entrepreneurship is the value proposition: for the entrepreneur, this is designed to create profit essential for sustainability and personal benefit; for the social entrepreneur, this is designed for transformational social benefit for a target group who may not possess the resources to achieve this benefit otherwise. Social entrepreneurship requires the involvement of different individuals who complement one another, "people with visionary ideas, people with leadership skills and a commitment to make things happen, and people committed to helping others".[29]

The ITT team conducted an analysis of strengths, weaknesses, opportunities and threats – a SWOT analysis (see Figure 1) – and scanned the environment to gather information and learn from other providers, essentially to distil best practice in order to better achieve a sustainable programme.

Scanning the environment, it became apparent that other established teacher-training provision tended to adhere to a conventional model: competitor PGCE programmes were HE-based with the statutory number of weeks on placement in partner schools. Awareness of this restricted provision led to the decision that UEL must offer, from the start, a wider range of routes into teaching, including both conventional PGCE and employment-based routes such as GTP and OTTP. Thus, the secondary team developed a value proposition offering routes to qualified teacher status [QTS] for personnel in local boroughs and in partner schools which comprised tailored packages of situated delivery. This scheme met the needs of schools which were accustomed to providing conventional PGCE placements but which employed adults – e.g. graduate Learning Support Assistants and technicians – who wished to acquire QTS. Schools wished to retain staff who were familiar with the school and who tended to have ties and commitment to working in the locality. Research conducted in London and Manchester indicated a close match between prior life and educational experience of teacher-trainees and the schools in which they sought employment as qualified teachers,[30] thus there was a high probability that the PGCE would provide opportunities for both aspiring teachers and urban schools.

Entrepreneurship has been defined as "the pursuit of opportunity without regard to resources currently controlled"[31] and, correspondingly, the initially inadequate resource situation could not be allowed to limit planning and delivery. School facilities and resources were utilised from the outset for the planning and delivery of subject specialist sessions, and teachers from local schools became involved in the recruitment of prospective trainees. These measures were to pay dividends in the long term insofar as provision became embedded in the local community.

Thus, the secondary team established two categories of clientele: primary clients who were the potential and actual teacher-trainees, and secondary clients who were the potential and actual partner schools. Working with clientele facilitated building capacity within the secondary team, the recruitment of diverse trainees, and building capacity with partnership schools in an urban environment.

Strengths	Weaknesses
• Commitment and support from UEL, some boroughs, some schools and some teachers. • Location, i.e. East London • Experienced lead tutor.	• Limited specialist academic and administrative personnel. • No specialist facilities. • No guaranteed placement schools. • No recent 'history' or reputation. • No trainees recruited. • Many established providers, i.e. competitors.
Opportunities	**Threats**
• To offer wider routes to qualified teacher status than existing provision. • To aid local people to remain within the local employment market. • To build a teaching force that reflects diversity of local community. • To secure sponsorship support.	• Local teacher shortages and turnover may impact on mentoring capacity and support in schools. • Potential shortage of partner schools. • Portfolio of shortage subjects has intrinsic recruitment issues. • Potential under-recruitment and poor quality applicants. • Potential failure to build trust, confidence and credibility.

Figure 1: SWOT Analysis

5. Building Capacity

The number of secondary trainees allocated by the TTA to UEL in 2001 was modest: a target of 55 trainees in four curriculum areas on a programme delivered by a lead tutor managing tutors on temporary contracts. This academic year, however, the target has grown to 280 trainees in nine curriculum areas on a programme delivered by a team of 18 tutors.

Initially, local boroughs and schools had provided access to specialist facilities and resources for delivery of subject specialist lessons. This relationship was consolidated by the formation of a partnership committee with quality assurance and advisory roles. Local boroughs are represented by senior teachers with active involvement in teacher-training in their respective schools. Thus, the ITT program does remain responsive to local needs which shape the provision in terms of curriculum areas offered and numbers of trainees required.

Moreover, ITT tutors have each been embedded, from appointment, in networks comprising boroughs, schools and teachers, connecting tutors with their clientele and enabling tutors to monitor the contribution of the programme to teacher supply in East London. The relationship between tutors and teachers has been systematised since 2006 with the initiation of a Teacher Fellow scheme: Teacher Fellows, recruited from experienced school-based trainers/mentors in partner schools, work together with UEL ITT tutors in a partnership development group, which was praised in a recent report of an OFSTED inspection.[32]

Table 4: UEL Secondary Trainees Employed in Partner, Local & Other Schools

	2003/4	2004/5	2005/6	2006/7
Partner schools	50%	66%	68%	71%
Other local schools	42%	29%	26%	21%
Schools outside the locality	8%	5%	6%	8%

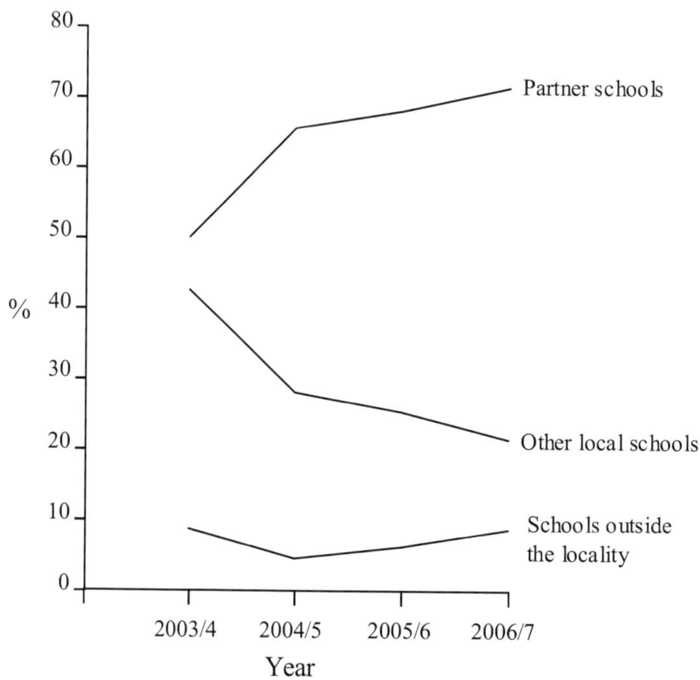

Figure 2: UEL Secondary Trainees' Employment

A gauge of the effectiveness of the initiative to counter teacher shortage in East London is provided by monitoring the destinations of UEL secondary trainees upon achieving QTS. Figures show that, between 2003/4 and 2006/7, the percentage of trainees employed by partner schools in East London has risen from 50% to 71% (see Table 4 and Figure 2). Evidently, the initiative is succeeding in contributing to the creation of a 'local' workforce.

The most recent annual report of the Chief Inspector of Education on children's services and skills commented that "improvements in London schools, especially those in the most challenging circumstances, are outpacing those found nationally".[33] The Chief Inspector asserted that these improvements would be strongly associated with the investment in the London Challenge. The secondary ITT team at UEL believe that, by establishing quality provision of teachers, the UEL partnership has made a modest contribution towards these improvements.

The OFSTED inspection of the secondary ITT provision at UEL for 2007/08 would provide corroboration: the inspectors awarded the team with an overall Grade 1, 'Outstanding'. The report noted, among the key strengths, "strong and effective commitment to inclusion and to schools in east London and the region" and "the exceptionally strong and cohesive partnership". The report also noted that "the vast majority of trainees come from London or its immediate environs" and that "the profile of successive cohorts and their success in gaining jobs in the partnership amply demonstrate the course's commitment to east London and its schools".[34]

Notes

[1] B Cherry, C O'Brien and N Pevsner, *The Buildings of England - London 5: East*, Yale University Press, New Haven and London, 2005, p.1.

[2] Greater London Authority [GLA], *Refugees and Asylum Seekers in London: a GLA Perspective*, GLA Policy Support Unit, London, 2001, p. 1.

[3] M Mackintosh, *London – the World in a City*, Greater London Authority Data Management and Analysis Group, London, 2005.

[4] Ibid., p.6.

[5] P Baker and J Eversley, *Multilingual Capital: The Languages of London's Schoolchildren*, Battlebridge, London, 2000.

[6] R Lupton and A Sullivan, 'The London context', in *Education in a Global City – Essays from London*, T Brighouse and L Fullick (eds) Institute of Education, London, 2007, pp.8-39.

[7] G Grace, 'Urban education: policy science or critical scholarship?' in G Grace (ed) *Education and the City: Theory, History and Contemporary Practice*, Routledge and Kegan Paul, 1984, pp.3-59, p.19.

[8] Prime Minister's Strategy Unit [PMSU], *The London Project*, The Prime Minister's Strategy Unit, London, 2004, p.7.

[9] Hall, A Ash and C Ruffo, *Initial Teacher Training and the Transition to Teaching in Urban Schools*, paper presented at the conference of the British Educational Research Association, Manchester University, 2004, p.2.
[10] Office for Standards in Education [OFSTED] *Access and Achievement in Urban Education*, The Stationery Office, London, 1993.
[11] G Whitty, *The State and the Market in English Education Policy*, paper presented at Beijing Normal University, October 2005, p.4.
[12] Department for Education and Employment [DfEE], *Excellence in Schools*, The Stationery Office, London, 1997.
[13] Department for Education and Employment [DfEE], *Excellence in Cities*, DfEE, London, 1999.
[14] Department for Education and Skills [DfES], *Schools: Achieving Success*, The Stationery Office, London, 2001.
[15] Department for Education and Skills [DfES], *The London Challenge: Transforming London Secondary Schools*, DfES, Nottingham, 2003.
[16] D Crowther, C Cummings, A Dyson and A Millward, *Schools and Area Regeneration*, Policy Press, Bristol, 2003.
[17] Ibid, p.v.
[18] S Burgess, B McConnell, C Propper and D Wilson, 'The impact of school choice on sorting by ability and socioeconomic factors in English secondary education', *Schools and the Equal Opportunity Problem*, L Woessmann and P Peterson (eds),The MIT Press, Cambridge Massachusetts, 2007, pp.273-292, p.280.
[19] Crowther et al, op. cit., p.23.
[20] Office for Standards in Education [OFSTED], *Annual Report of Her Majesty's Chief Inspector of Schools, 2003/04*, The Stationery Office, 2005.
[21] Office for Standards in Education [OFSTED], *Annual Report of Her Majesty's Chief Inspector of Schools, 2001/2*, The Stationery Office, London, 2003, para. 415.
[22] Department for Education and Skills [DfES], *Statistics of Education: School Workforce in England, 2002 Edition*, The Stationery Office, London, 2003.
[23] The Teacher Training Agency was established by the Education Act 1994.
[24] Office for National Statistics, *Census 2001*, The Stationery Office, London, 2001.
[25] Hall et al, op. cit.
[26] S Gorard, B Huat See, E Smith and P White, *Teacher Supply: The Key Issues*, Continuum, London, 2006, p.5.
[27] Ibid., p.4.
[28] Department for Education and Skills [DfES], *Statistics of Education: School Workforce in England, 2006*, Department for Education and Skills, London, 2006.

[29] J Thompson, G Alvey and A Lees, 'Social entrepreneurship – a new look at the people and potential' Management Decision, vol.38-5, 2000, pp. 328-338, p.332.
[30] D Hall, A Ash, C Raffo, S Diamantopoulou and L Jones, *Training Teachers to Work in Urban Schools*, Research and Development Award Report for the Teacher Training Agency, 2005, p.102.
[31] H Stevenson, H Grousbeck, M Roberts and A Bhide, *New Business Ventures and the Entrepreneur*, 5th edition, Irwin/McGraw-Hill, Boston, 1999, p.5.
[32] Office for Standards in Education [OFSTED], *Secondary Initial Teacher Training Partnership Based on University of East London: Inspection Report on Management and Quality Assurance, 2004/05*, Office for Standards in Education, 2005, para.16.
[33] Office for Standards in Education [OFSTED], *Annual Report of Her Majesty's Chief Inspector of Education, Children's Services and Skills: Standards and Quality in Education 2006/07*, The Stationery Office, London, 2007, p.6.
[34] Office for Standards in Education [OFSTED], *University of East London: A Secondary Initial Teacher Training Inspection Report, 2007/08*, Office for Standards in Education, 2008, para.8.

Bibliography

Baker, P. and J. Eversley, *Multilingual Capital: The Languages of London's Schoolchildren*, Battlebridge, London, 2000.

Burgess, S., B. McConnell, C. Propper and D. Wilson, 'The impact of school choice on sorting by ability and socioeconomic factors in English secondary education', *Schools and the Equal Opportunity Problem*, L. Woessmann and P. Peterson (eds),The MIT Press, Cambridge Massachusetts, pp.273-292.

Cherry, B., C. O'Brien and N. Pevsner, *The Buildings of England - London 5: East*, Yale University Press, New Haven and London, 2005.

Crowther, D., C. Cummings, A. Dyson and A. Millward, *Schools and Area Regeneration*, Policy Press, Bristol, 2003

Department for Education and Employment [DfEE], *Excellence in Schools*, The Stationery Office, London, 1997

Department for Education and Employment [DfEE], *Excellence in Cities*, DfEE, London, 1999

Department for Education and Skills [DfES], *Schools: Achieving Success*, The Stationery Office, London, 2001

Department for Education and Skills [DfES], *The London Challenge: Transforming London Secondary Schools*, DfES, Nottingham, 2003.

Department for Education and Skills [DfES], *Statistics of Education: School Workforce in England, 2002 Edition*, The Stationery Office, London, 2003.

Gorard, S., B. Huat See, E. Smith and P. White, *Teacher Supply: The Key Issues*, Continuum, London, 2006.

Grace, G., 'Urban education: policy science or critical scholarship?' in G. Grace (ed) *Education and the City: Theory, History and Contemporary Practice*, Routledge and Kegan Paul, 1984, pp.3-59.

Greater London Authority [GLA], *Refugees and Asylum Seekers in London: a GLA Perspective*, GLA Policy Support Unit, London, 2001

Hall, D., A. Ash and C. Ruffo, *Initial Teacher Training and the Transition to Teaching in Urban Schools*, paper presented at the conference of the British Educational Research Association, Manchester University, 2004.

Hall, D., A. Ash, C. Raffo, S. Diamantopoulou and L. Jones, *Training Teachers to Work in Urban Schools*, Research and Development Award Report for the Teacher Training Agency, 2005.

Lupton, R. and A. Sullivan, 'The London context', in *Education in a Global City – Essays from London*, T. Brighouse and L. Fullick (eds) Institute of Education, London, 2007, pp.8-39.

Mackintosh, M., *London – the World in a City*, Greater London Authority Data Management and Analysis Group, London, 2005.

Office for National Statistics, *Census 2001*, The Stationery Office, London, 2001.

Office for Standards in Education [OFSTED], *Annual Report of Her Majesty's Chief Inspector of Schools: Standards and Quality in Education 2001/2*, The Stationery Office, 2003.

Office for Standards in Education [OFSTED], *Annual Report of Her Majesty's Chief Inspector of Education, Children's Services and Skills: Standards and Quality in Education 2006/07*, The Stationery Office, 2007.

Prime Minister's Strategy Unit [PMSU], *The London Project*, The Prime Minister's Strategy Unit, London, 2004,

Stevenson, H., H. Grousbeck, M. Roberts and A. Bhide, *New Business Ventures and the Entrepreneur*, 5th edition, Irwin/McGraw-Hill, Boston, 1999.

Thompson, J., G. Alvey and A. Lees, 'Social entrepreneurship – a new look at the people and potential' *Management Decision*, vol.38-5, 2000, pp. 328-338.

Whitty, G., *The State and the Market in English Education Policy*, paper presented at Beijing Normal University, October 2005,

Neil Herrington moved from the Black Country to London 18 years ago to take up an appointment at Hainault Forest High School where he became Head of the Science Department and also School Professional Tutor, co-ordinating initial teacher training within the school. His work in school convinced him of the need to address both issues of supply and of quality through initial teacher training and professionakl development, and he moved to the Univeristy of East London where these issues are addressed on a daily basis.

Caroline Brennan, originally from Yorkshire, studied at the University of Sheffield. She taught Modern Foreign Languages in secondary schools in London before moving into initial teacher training: she is currently a Senior Lecturer in the Cass School of Education.

Kathy Wright studied at the University of Lancaster and completed her teacher training at St Martin's College Lancaster. She taught in secondary schools in East London before moving into initial teacher training, first at Angli Polytechnic University and, later, at the University of East London where she started the secondary teacher education programme of which she is Director.

Educating the Outcast? Policy and Practice in the Teaching of Gypsy/Traveller Children

Erika Cudworth and David Cudworth

Abstract
This chapter investigates the challenge posed for teachers in the delivery of a "guaje" education for Gypsy/Traveller children. It considers the cultural interface between Gypsy/Traveller and the dominant settled community, examines the differences in practices, norms and values between Gypsy/Traveller and the mainstream and suggests that these differences raise issues for Gypsy/Traveller, teachers and schools. The chapter asks what particular difficulties might be experienced by Traveller children and those attempting to teach them, in the context of an education system strongly influenced by league tables and parental choice. It is based on an ethnographic study and interviews with primary teachers and other educationalists working in and around East London.

Key Words: Gypsy/Traveller, social inequalities, educational underachievement, marketisation, cultures of learning

*****

1. Introduction: Educational Inequities

The educational under-achievement of Gypsy/Traveller children was first identified in the 1960s. Throughout the 1970s a variety of government initiatives and voluntary agencies attempted to improve educational provision for this most severely deprived group of children. However, despite various initiatives, there has been continuing emphasis in reports of the government and other agencies, throughout the 1980s to the 2000s, on the significant under-achievement of children from these communities. It has been noted both that the curriculum does not recognise Gypsy/Traveller cultures and also that racist hostility towards Gypsy/Traveller children is greater than that experienced by any other minority ethnic population in Britain.

This chapter seeks to further our understanding of the educational under-achievement of Gypsy/Traveller children in the education system by drawing on teachers' stories of educating Gypsy/Traveller children in their classrooms, and on our own ethnographic experiences. We also draw on the tales told by others who work with these children in an educational setting, namely the Traveller Education Support Services (TESS). We attempt to highlight some of the factors that may prevent these children from achieving educational success in the schooling process, and examine the difficulties experienced by those attempting to teach them. Finally, we will suggest ways in which our investigations may be used in order to more adequately meet the needs of children from these communities so that they are able to fulfil their potential, and enjoy their right to an education.

We examine whether limited respect for and understanding of their values, cultures and identities is the main problem surrounding the underachievement of Gypsy/Traveller children. In particular, we consider whether a contrast exists between the particular needs of Gypsy/Traveller children and current school provision that is based on a settled, static, local community. This question is considered in the current context of the 'marketisation' of education, and the arguments made by critics that education is becoming ever more influenced by market forces, a process which erodes equality of opportunity, especially for families from less affluent backgrounds.[1] In particular, this manifests itself in a focus on performance data and parental interests rather than a focus on the needs of children from diverse communities.[2] We make no claims to have 'got it right' in terms of understanding the relationship between Gypsy/Traveller and the schooling process but, by exploring some of the key issues involved in educating children from nomadic communities, we hope to further our understanding of the problems that exist for these children in the current educational system.

2. The Problem of Nomadism

According to the 1996 Race Relations Act, and the subsequent (Amendment) Act 2000, Gypsy/Roma pupils and Travellers of Irish Heritage were legally recognised as racial groups, whilst English-born gypsies have been defined in terms of their living patterns and occupations. Other Traveller groups include New Travellers, who adopt a nomadic lifestyle but are not an ethnic group, and circus and fairground families who do not consider themselves as belonging to any particular ethnic group. Okely considers that a history of cultural isolation from mainstream society combines various travelling communities as a group.[3] Whilst defining these groups as a generic 'whole' may detract from the importance that each group places on certain aspects of their culture and identity, we deploy the collective noun 'Gypsy/Traveller' in order to allude to a commonality across the groups. This commonality, albeit complex, consists of a deep-rooted belief in 'nomadism' and, in particular, a belief in and need for 'mobility'. Furthermore, it is this idea of 'nomadism' which has led to a common pattern of discriminatory treatment, which is often also racist - whether or not the particular group of Gypsy/Traveller is officially afforded an 'ethnicity'. Indeed:

> The majority of these people try to hide their being Gypsy from their neighbours and colleagues, not from any shame of

> their racial origins, but because of the negative image and pejorative connotations the very word 'Gypsy' arouses in the mind of the average British Gauje.[4]

The history of Gypsy/Travellers in Britain, as elsewhere in Europe, has been framed by the struggle bought about by 'modernity' and the creation of the 'nation state' where the integration of commerce, administration and culture is assumed paramount for the survival and prosperity of a national society and economy.[5] The formation of such states, therefore, favoured a sedentarised population where cultural identity linked people to particular geographical space.[6] According to McVeigh, sedentarism became synonymous with the 'modern' - the 'civilising' of society - and, thus, nomadic communities were often seen as 'uncivilised'.[7] Over the course of history, both McVeigh and Okeley contend, such communities have been set up in the minds of the settled community as 'others' in order to justify and legitimate these communities as "criminal, backward, deprived etc" and, therefore, in need of assimilation into the mainstream.[8]

Legislation in the 1960s which increased regulatory power of the local state over caravan sites used by Gypsy/Traveller communities led to the closure of many sites that were not seen as satisfying new government requirements.[9] Despite it being the responsibility of local authorities to provide sufficient sites for communities of Gypsy/Travellers residing in their local area, quite often such provision was limited, inadequate or located on unsuitable, even dangerous land. According to the Department of the Environment in January 1996, 12,620 Gypsies in England and Wales lacked anywhere lawful to camp, a figure that underestimates the scale of this problem as Travellers from other groups were not considered.[10] The close of the century saw some change, with the 1994 Criminal Justice and Public Order Act further criminalizing the encampment of Gypsy/Travellers on unauthorised sites. This Act also removed the obligation of local authorities to provide official sites, thus leaving many travelling families with little choice than to adopt a settled lifestyle.[11]

Despite changes in the occupational practices of many Gypsy/Travellers in England, as well as some families taking up permanent housing, many families continue to value the ideals of 'nomadism' and frequently travel extensively during the summer months, with some groups even travelling periodically all year round.[12] A schooling system based on the presumption of a continuous local education provision for a settled community is, therefore, often at odds with those who adopt a nomadic code of existence. Okely has long suggested that entry into the mainstream is a recipe for cultural assimilation which Gypsy/Traveller parents do not want and which they should resist[13] Stewart also suggests that 'a desire for cultural separation and cultural fears play a crucial role in self-exclusion' by many Gypsy/Traveller children.[14] However, according to Smith "Gypsies and Travellers need mainstream education" in order to realise their equality of opportunity.[15] A recent study of Gypsy/Travellers by Bhopal found that parents had a positive attitude to schooling and saw education beyond basic literacy as important for their children's future.[16] Yet even with the "fortification and promotion of inclusion in the realm of educational policy and practice", it is questionable whether an educational system can ever provide adequate and acceptable educational provision for children from a range of 'nomadic' backgrounds, because that provision is so very much a product of the presumption of a settled mode of existence.[17]

3. Normative Presumptions and the Schooling Process

Educational sociologists have long argued, often critically, that education is a socialising tool that furnishes individuals with appropriate norms and values, and that the education system exists as a means of inculcating all communities in a similar normative framework. However, this normative presumption is predicated on a sedentary code and lifestyle, strongly based on the assumption of a fixed abode and consistent attendance at school. Consequently, for many Gypsy/Traveller children education is often infrequent and usually disrupted.

In the 1960s the Plowden Report considered that Gypsy/Traveller children were "probably the most severely deprived in the country" and that "most of them do not even go to school and the potential abilities of those who do are stunted".[18] The National Gypsy Education Council (NGEC) was founded in 1970 and its offshoot, the Advisory Council for the Education of Romanies and other Travellers (ACERT), in 1973. As a result of pressure from these organisations, government and local authorities began to look more seriously at the problem of underachievement among Gypsy/Travellers. Consequently, a number of different initiatives in the teaching of these children were pursued both within and without the state sector. These included summer schools of volunteers, mobile caravan schools and adult education programmes on site and in mainstream schools.

The Swann Report continued to argue for an urgent need for better educational provision for Gypsy/Traveller children.[19] More recently, the Department of Education and Skills (DfES) estimated that only 15-20 per cent were attending secondary school with 10,000 Gypsy/Traveller children either not receiving an education or receiving education but underachieving.[20] According to a report on 'Ethnicity and Education', this figure has now risen to nearly 12,000 and the actual figure may be higher than this due to many Gypsy/Traveller children concealing their identity for fear of racist bullying.[21] The Commission for Racial Equality consider that the hostility that Gypsy/Traveller children face in British schooling is worse than any other minority ethnic population.[22] This prejudice may be perpetuated by a lack of recognition and representation of these cultures within mainstream schooling. For example, the Office for Standards in Education (OFSTED) and the DfES found that the official UK curriculum of the majority of state schools is still 'failing' to demonstrate appropriate respect for the particular cultures of certain ethnic minority communities, but in particular Gypsy/Traveller communities.[23]

Reports in the early twenty-first century continue to document that the low attendance at school of Gypsy/Traveller children is still acute, a major impediment to their educational success posing an obstacle that needs to be addressed. Therefore the focus of much current intervention has been to enable children to access education during 'travelling time', for example by allowing registration at more than one school.[24] There remains a strong emphasis on attendance targets which are monitored locally by Educational Welfare Officers.[25] Much of the way that school life operates - and the way in which the curriculum is delivered - continues to be at odds with a nomadic existence.[26] Despite a school's legal obligation to secure, allocate and retain a place for Gypsy/Traveller children, many find themselves excluded from state schools, once enrolled, for reasons of non-attendance.[27] As Ivatts notes, the current climate of British education policy is one of promoting 'inclusion', but the emphasis of both central and local government on "paper inclusion" - such as acceptable statistics on attendance and achievement - ignores an "invisible culture of exclusion" whereby Gypsy/Traveller pupils find that they are not genuinely accepted by the schools system because of their 'problematic' background.[28] In the current climate of league tables, test results and standards, a paradoxical situation has been created; whereby schools are required to provide high 'attendance profiles' and good 'test results' at the expense of the responsibility to provide inclusive education.

Since the 1988 Educational Reform Act, some sociologists have powerfully argued that education is increasingly shaped and ordered by market forces.[29] Children are no longer compelled to attend their local school; they and their parents are now consumers and free to select from a range of schools. According to Ball education has become "like any other commodity and the development of the child is a lucrative market opportunity for capital."[30] He goes on to suggest that the market sets up a moral framework that prioritises self-interest and personal motives, at the expense of equity and social justice. Therefore, despite a discourse of inclusive education and the rhetoric around 'Every Child Matters',[31] policy decisions are arguably based on, and dictated by, performance data and initiatives in order for schools to survive in the market.[32]

This marketability of schools has led to a plethora of information about the efficiency of schools and to a preoccupation with performance profiles, which parents see as an extremely important tool when considering to which school they should send their children. Part of the mechanisms in place for highlighting performance data has been the publication of 'league tables' around attendance and children's performance in the governments Standard Attainment Tests (SATs) at Key Stage Two and GSCE results at Key Stage Four. According to Ball, such performance data has resulted in many local authorities becoming obsessed with attainment in tests which, in turn, has led to schools fighting to attract "'motivated' parents and 'able' children" in order to ensure a position at the top of the league tables and therefore the market.[33] Furthermore, resources are increasingly deployed to assist those children likely to perform well in tests rather than those with particular learning difficulties.[34]

This has led many "schools to focus on the symptoms of problems rather than on their causes".[35] For example, many schools are so focused on a high 'attendance profile' that, instead of investigating the reasons behind the low attendance of a particular child in order to support them, they will often simply permanently exclude the child. Therefore, 'the problem' is removed and passed to another school and, as such, the child no longer places a burden on the school's attendance profile or their league table position. For many Gypsy/Traveller children permanent exclusions are often pursued as a result of their poor attendance and underachievement.[36]

In addition, the curriculum of most schools often fails to recognise the particular cultures of Gypsy/Traveller and to incorporate positive images of these communities in terms of what is delivered in classroom teaching and the representations in children's work on display. Many schools find it difficult to deliver the National Curriculum in a flexible way, and fail to use supplementary resources to represent the lives of all cultures, particularly the cultures of Gypsy/Travellers.[37] Although many schools understand the need for a flexible and inclusive approach to the curriculum, government pressures and an emphasis on attendance and achievement targets, mean it is problematic when accommodating low achieving children, especially if these children also fail to attend school regularly. Strategies do shift, and there have been recent attempts to address the needs of underachieving groups in the educational system, such as Gypsy/Travellers, by promoting certain teaching and learning styles which may be more appropriate for these children.[38] Yet such initiatives are framed by a key preoccupation: getting each cohort of children to attend school regularly and reach 'the expected level' of achievement by the end of each year in order to satisfy government targets.

4. Experiences of Teaching Gypsy/Traveller Children

> Member of Traveller Education Support Service (TESS)
> Some of these kids' achievements' are just simply turning up at school. We say that travellers have got different skills

> and knowledge and ways of thinking that are not necessarily what the settled community judges valid.

This section discusses the findings of a study investigating the experiences of those teaching and working with Gypsy/Traveller children. The study attempted to gain an understanding of the difficulties faced by Gypsy/Traveller children within the school system from an educationalists point of view. There were two sources of data: first, semi-structured interviews with educational professionals working with these children; second, a small complementary ethnographic study. Interviews were carried out with members of the Traveller Education Support Services (TESS), and with primary school teachers, primary Head teachers and trainee teachers all with experience of teaching Gypsy/Traveller children. Interviewees collectively possessed a wealth of experiential knowledge and understanding of these children in classrooms and in schools. In order to gain an insight of the specific daily challenges experienced by Gypsy/Traveller children and those teaching them, some ethnographic work was undertaken. One of the authors taught for two days as part of the staff team in a case study school where the majority of children were Gypsy/Travellers. Field notes included comments on achievements, behaviour and engagement.

A. The Importance of Reputation - Attendance and Testing

Due to a fluctuating attendance pattern and a general perception of low attainment, many teachers and schools find it extremely challenging to provide a consistent learning experience for Gypsy/Traveller children, especially in the delivery of a National Curriculum and its associated strategies based on consistent attendance. We found absentee rates were very high for our case study school, especially in the summer term as their families tended to travel either to visit relatives in Ireland or to work in Spain. Children would also travel quite frequently, throughout the year, in order to attend funerals, and celebrate births and marriages, consistent with a Head Teacher's perception that, "Family events are very significant to the Traveller community and family and culture take precedence over education".

All the interviewees in this study felt that the pressures to uphold the requirements of a National Curriculum and the testing regimes in place to check yearly achievement did have implications for the schooling of many Gypsy/Traveller children: one teacher remarked that, "It's all about getting through the yearly plans and making sure all the work is covered for that year and then testing that knowledge". Many teachers become "sucked" into the pressures of "achievement levels" set by the LEA and are reluctant to deviate from the programmes of study as laid down by the National Curriculum and its associated strategies, in the opinion of one member of TESS staff.

This pressure on schools to maintain high attendance profiles is associated with the 'marketisation' of education, and particularly the obsession with the 'image' of a school. Despite their legal obligation to provide a 'base' school place for Gypsy/Traveller children, some schools are reluctant to enrol or support children who are perceived as low achievers, especially when their attendance is poor. For example, a primary school had accepted a Gypsy/Traveller child into their final year but, as one member of TESS staff remarked, this acceptance was at their convenience rather than the child's.

> Member of TESS staff.
> On the very day that I took the mum in for a meeting, they had changed their minds and said actually they have a problem and they wouldn't take him.

Two weeks after the SATs, the school enrolled this child.

Some schools may be ignorant, and/or intolerant towards the lifestyle of many Gypsy/Travellers. One member of the TESS staff noted that the tensions between the culture of school and that of these communities are often exemplified in the 'playing out' of various intercultural encounters:

> Member of TESS staff
> I went to a school and they said that this Romanian family are saying to us, 'We'll curse you because you don't do this,' and the school was getting really uptight about it. But they couldn't understand that this is a family that could speak very little English and have got a very difficult asylum situation. All they needed was a little time to talk things through.

We found a sense of frustration with the efforts to inculcate dominant educational practices in children whose home lives are not conducive to fulfilling the teachers' aspirations for these children:

> Trainee Teacher
> I set a piece of homework one Friday. Children asked if they could borrow a pencil for the weekend, I did not realise at the time that they may not have pens or pencils at home. Only one piece of homework came back completed.

On the whole, we found an overwhelming respect for the liberal tradition of assimilation into the mainstream model in line with much of the literature and in particular a respect for issues around the 'Every Child

Matters' agenda.[39] These children were generally seen, by a head teacher, as 'just kids' like any others who deserve particular support in achieving their 'equality of opportunity'. However, Gypsy/Traveller children were seen by almost all, to have particular needs, and a number of interviewees suggested that the closest comparison would be with refugee children. In both cases, children are often not familiar with school culture and, as a head teacher remarked, "because it is an alien environment the children are very anxious, and need a lot of support to settle in". This was corroborated in an interview with a member of TESS who described the reaction of Gypsy/Traveller families when encountering secondary schools.

> Member of TESS
> We meet families that have been overwhelmed by the hugeness of the school. They have never stepped foot inside such big buildings before. They were frightened walking around clinging on to each other.

B. Cultures of Learning – Lessons in Class

What became apparent for us was a clear subordination of the culture of Gypsy/Travellers within the mainstream schooling process. The tensions bought about by the cultural differences between the school structure, based on a settled mode of existence (despite all its incredible diversity) and the validated knowledge among Gypsy/Travellers is something that we found to be acute. The presumptions of a settled schooling process mean that 'living in and for the moment' presents various kinds of difficulties of which schools need to be aware, and perhaps highlights the problematic interface between a nomadic and a sedentary culture when it comes to education.

> Member of TESS
> A lot of issues come up… like maybe they have to translate for
> their parents on an asylum issue. That kind of needs thing. You got your food and house and all that, education is right at the bottom… if somebody in the family had to go to the dentist then the whole family take the day off to go and that's why you won't be in school and that's the way it goes, because that is the key family issue of the moment… everything is for the day. I think that that is kind of cultural… we're really constrained by everything like mortgage, and getting the car serviced and earn the money to pay this and that… if you are in a caravan, everything you've got is there… your wealth is stored in the things like

> the gold and that's your bank, and everything is cash, you don't owe anybody any money, you haven't got any tax forms to fill out and worrying about all that stuff... it challenges your own morals and values.

Individual teachers are often more aware of the needs of the Gypsy/Traveller children in their classrooms, especially when staff are aware that a 'Traveller' site is part of their locality:

> Teacher
> At the other end of (the) sports pitch was the Traveller site. So it was visible, they could see home from the classroom....all the teachers knew all of the children by name....and families and cousins and parents. So yes, we were very much aware of the needs of the community.

However, most Gypsy/Traveller children are not educated in such environments, and in schools with small numbers of such children, many teachers are often unaware of their backgrounds and/or any particular needs they may have. The head teacher of the case study school observed that, within her wider LEA, few teachers were interested, and "most other Heads are not aware and not interested". A teacher who had two Gypsy/Traveller children enrolled in his classroom just before one Christmas was not informed of their background until some time later. When asked if he was given any background information on the children he replied: "No, you know what it's like, here's a new kid - sort 'em out". Most initial teacher training programmes do not consider the specific situation of these children on their courses. One trainee teacher interviewee, who undertook her teaching practice in a classroom with a high proportion of Gypsy/Traveller children, claimed to have had no "formal training about the culture of Gypsy/Travellers".

For some of the interviewees, it is the demands of the National Curriculum, tests and targets which are major hurdles for these children.

> Teacher
> The SATs, the targets, having to deliver certain kinds of things that are perceived to be the most important things by outside agencies. Teaching to different things other than what the priorities are for those particular children and particular communities at that time, and thus making those communities or those individuals feel excluded from what education should be about.

Particularly problematic are the Primary National Strategies that compel schools to spend an hour on literacy and an hour on numeracy each morning of each day, following a prescribed format. Reconciling the demands of these strategies was the most difficult and frustrating aspect of the work of TESS

> Member of TESS
> The literacy hour is just desperate really. I know it is hard for teachers, (but) I think that when you are on the other side of it you start to realise that there is a little bit more than just delivering the stuff.

Consequently, there are dilemmas for teachers in that they are expected to implement a policy framework that has negative impacts on the possible education of Gypsy/Traveller children. We found a divided response towards the implementation of these strategies. One teacher's view was that these strategies were irrelevant.

> Teacher
> Never taught it, don't believe in it, it is impossible to teach, as a lot of the material would be 'over their heads' or they simply would not relate to it.

A trainee teacher noted that the strategies posed obstacles.

> Trainee Teacher
> I tried to teach from the documentation, but the children were disinterested. They became restless and in one case a boy threw a chair across the room out of frustration with his work. I found a lot of my time was spent on behaviour management and breaking up fights, I have the bruises to prove it!

C. Racism and 'whiteness'

> Member of TESS
> It is not just the children… staff don't see it as a racist issue because she's white and the person bullying her was white. Unfortunately it does go on and is quite common. We hear stories all the time'.[59]

Gypsy/Traveller children face persistent prejudice and racism, a problem that is not always identified by many teachers and schools. Much of the overt prejudice, particularly name calling, seems to become more apparent at secondary school, yet often does not get challenged by staff. In our case study school, staff were very aware of local prejudices and racist behaviour. In this case, there were a small group of parents who were particularly vocal and instrumental in pressurising other parents to withdraw their 'non-traveller' children from the school. The community was very much divided, and we were told that some staff had left the school due to threats that they had received at the school gates.

Elsewhere, some teachers admitted having no knowledge of the existence and role of the TESS. One suggested that, because he had had 'no real problems' with the few Gypsy/Traveller children that he had taught, there would have been no need to contact them. He noted that the children were "just like well-behaved little middle class kids". What is interesting here is the assumption that Gypsy/Traveller children are inevitably a problem and therefore when they are not causing a problem or underachieving, they 'disappear'.

> Member of TESS
> There are probably travellers out there doing very well, achieving brilliantly and we just don't know they exist because they don't come to us.

The normative presumption of much anti-racism in schools has been an issue of white racism against 'non-white' communities, but the issue of 'whiteness' often means that racism against Gypsy/Traveller is not recognised as such. Interestingly, in a number of interviews, the term 'coming out' was used to describe the difficulties for Gypsy/Traveller children acknowledging their identity given the context of persistent prejudice. One member of TESS remarked this reluctance to 'come out' more generally.

> Member of TESS
> Some people are very reticent about coming out as travellers because of the stigma attached to it on a social level; we encounter a lot of that.

D. Towards Good Practice

> Member of TESS
> What works is a topic-based education where every subject is linked to one topic or theme…especially if the topic is something children are already familiar with or know

> something about – this way children draw on what they already know and use this to expand their learning.

Many Gypsy/Traveller children lack self-esteem and confidence in their abilities when faced with an education in the 'mainstream'. In our case study school, children were constantly reassured, provided with opportunities to ask questions about their work and praised and rewarded. The school has also invested in the establishment of positive relationships with parents - employing a community liaison worker to liaise with families on the local site, and having a Gypsy/Traveller parent governor. One teacher reported that parents feel comfortable to visit the school at any time as is necessary, and their support for the school may be enhanced by the unique arrangement of all-age classrooms where children attend the same class with brothers, sisters and cousins. Field notes recorded particular approaches adopted in classrooms.

> Field notes
> Teachers work very hard to keep things practical and focus on basic skills and PSHE (social skills). Practical, visual and creative sessions that include lots of talking, modelling, role play, drama, P.E., art and design technology. Everything is very visual, talking slowly, facial expressions, modelling expected behaviour, doing work alongside them, and going into role. Teachers continually make links with other lessons which involve resources and ideas that relate to the children's own lives and experiences. Children are allowed to ask irrelevant questions and go off task – teachers work hard to think about the learning that is taking place when this occurs and structure a lot of work through play and children's conversations.

All interviewees suggested that Gypsies/Traveller children benefited from a more holistic way of learning knowledge and skills, and this was summated by one teacher in interview.

> Teacher
> They enjoyed inclusion in real life projects… that involved them as part of the community... a little school farm on the plot of land at the back, so digging up the foundations for a base for a chicken shed and mixing up the concrete and making the chicken wire… building all the joints to build a wooden frame… having railway sleepers as raised beds to do vegetable growing, any practical projects like that…

> preparing things for the school fayre on the Saturday and going with the Head to find all the bits that they needed and cart them out and set everything up and get organized.

Many Gypsy/Traveller children often work better outside the classroom as they spend most of their time outside of their caravans and often feel restricted and oppressed within the confines of the classroom walls, one teacher remarked.

> Teacher
> The Traveller girl in that class was forever coming to me hot and flustered saying "can we open the doors and the windows, its really hot in class" and they were used to being outside and doing everything outside and just going to sleep at the end of the day. So we did a lot of taking our work outside and we just worked outside.

The situation of Gypsy/Traveller children is often one of poverty, which impacts on attendance and concentration. This kind of awareness is not reflected in most schools, and simply having the money to send a child to travel to school or ensuring the child gets lunch can raise issues which impact on schooling.

> Member of TESS
> The parent couldn't afford to buy bread to make sandwiches for her child's packed lunch, so it was kind of a school issue but then you get caught up in the story behind that...but if we weren't there to do it then they would not go to school in the first place...I think we see some really poor people.

In the case study school the school meals service sees its responsibility as providing the children with their '5-a-day' fruit and vegetable 'recommended daily allowance'. Food and drink is used to focus and comfort the children, with the school day interspersed with 'snacks', as is the case only in Early Years classrooms in most schools.

5. Conclusion

Since the late 1960s, consecutive government reports have concurred that the underachievement of Gypsy/Traveller children is more pronounced than that of any other social group. By listening to the stories from teachers and others who have worked with these children in schools, we consider that the ongoing situation of underachievement is more problematic than the policy literature would have us believe. From these accounts, three themes have emerged. At one level, there is an ignorance of the cultures of Gypsy/Travellers and the particular educational needs of these children. Alternatively, there is a sense of conflict between addressing these needs in a structure that demands something different. Finally, there are those who have a sophisticated but often also sympathetic understanding of both Gypsy/Traveller communities and the educational requirements of Gypsy/Traveller children, and 'go native' by questioning the demands of the structure altogether.

The difficulties Gypsy/Traveller children experience in their education is exacerbated by an inflexible UK schooling system structured around a centrally controlled statutory curriculum that prescribes what children should be taught and what should be achieved, by a certain age. Of significance in explaining underachievement and disengagement of Gypsy/Traveller children is the tension which exists between the particular learning needs of these children and current provision for a settled, local community. The process of 'marketisation' in education has undermined attempts to secure social equality through schooling. The target setting and agendas of national governments, the rigours of a timetabled and age cohort driven national curriculum and its related strategies remain significantly problematic for the provision of a consistent learning experience for many Gypsy/Traveller children. The pressure on schools to reach government targets often results in the selection of high achieving children in order to secure a prime position in the league tables at the expense of equal opportunities. Gypsy/Traveller children, with the poorest attendance and achievement figures for any social group are therefore undesirable pupils and whatever the rhetoric of 'Every Child Matters', the business of education markets means that some kinds of children matter more.

This said, some real improvements have been made in terms of the participation and successes of Gypsy traveller children within particular mainstream classrooms. Some schools and individual teachers are becoming aware of some of the issues facing these communities, and children are attending school more often. Some are adopting a more flexible and creative approach to delivering the National Curriculum and returning to 'theme' based teaching where everything is taught around a given topic, via real life situations and projects that connect with and make sense to the lives of children. However, it is clear that low attendance, a lack of recognition of their culture in the national curriculum, racism and the pressures of performance data placed on schools, are issues that continue to contribute to the overall educational underachievement of Gypsy/Traveller children. We suggest that a way forward would entail the removal of much of the performance data. A less rigid curriculum and planning regime and a more realistic and flexible attendance policy, would enable schools to be able to adhere fully to an inclusive agenda in order to benefit the majority of all children in the current 'multicultural' educational system.

Notes

[1] S J Ball, *Class Strategies and the Education Market: The middle class and social advantage*, Routledgefalmer, London, 2003; also S J Ball, *Education Policy and Social Class: The Selected Works of Stephen J Ball*, Routledge, London, 2006.
[2] D Gillbourn and D Youdell, *Rationing Education: Policy, Practice, Reform and Equity*, Open University Press, Buckingham, 2000.
[3] J Okely, *The Traveller Gypsies*, Cambridge University Press, Cambridge, 1983, p. 49.
[4] Advisory Council for the Education of Romany and Other Travellers (ACERT), *The Education of Gypsy Traveller Children: Action Research and Coordination*, University of Hertfordshire Press, Hatfield, 1993, pp. 123-4.
[5] J McGovern, 'The emergence of the modern state', in *The Modern State: Theories and Ideologies*, E Cudworth, T Hall and J McGovern (eds), Edinburgh University Press, Edinburgh, 2007, pp. 20-36.
[6] Okely, op. cit.
[7] R McVeigh, 'Theorising sedentarism: the roots of anti-nomadism', in *Gypsy Politics and Traveller Identity*, T Acton (ed), University of Hertfordshire Press, Hatfield, 1997, pp. 7-25.
[8] Okely, op cit.; McVeigh op. cit., p. 28.
[9] L Clements and S Campbell, 'The Criminal Justice and Public Order Act and its implications for Travellers' in *Gypsy Politics and Traveller Identity*, T Acton (ed) op. cit., pp. 61-69.
[10] D Braid, 'The construction of identity through narrative: folklore and the travelling people of Scotland', in *Romani Culture and Gypsy Identity,* T Acton and D Mundy (eds), University of Hertfordshire Press, Hatfield, 1997, pp.40-68, p. 62.
[11] Clements and Campbell, op. cit.; also J Donovan, 'Still Travellers? Housed Travellers in a London borough', in *Traveller Education: Accounts of Good Practice,* C Tyler (ed) Trentham Books, Stoke-on-Trent, 2005, pp. 135-145, p. 136.
[12] Department for Education and Skills (DfES), *Aiming High: Raising the Achievement of Gypsy Traveller Pupils: A Guide to Good Practice*, DfES/0443, Nottingham, 2003.
[13] Okely, op cit.; for an outline of a range of positions see also K Bhopal, 'Gypsy Travellers and Education: Changing Needs and Changing Perceptions', *British Journal of Educational Studies*, vol. 52-1, 2004, pp.47-64, p. 47.

[14] M Stewart, 'The puzzle of Roma persistence: group identity without a nation', in *Romani Culture and Gypsy Identity,* T Acton and D Mundy (eds), University of Hertfordshire Press, Hatfield, 1997, pp.84-98.
[15] D Smith, 'Gypsy aesthetics, identity and creativity' in *Romani Culture and Gypsy Identity,* T Acton and D Mundy (eds), University of Hertfordshire Press, Hatfield, Location, 1997, pp.7-17.
[16] K Bhopal, J Gundara, C Jones and C Owen, *Working Towards Inclusive Education: Aspects of Good Practice for Gypsy/Traveller Pupils*, Research Report No. 238., DfEE, London, 2000.
[17] C Tyler, 'Foreword', in *Traveller Education: Accounts of Good Practice,* C Tyler (ed) Trentham Books, Stoke-on-Trent, 2005, pp.vii-xi.
[18] Lady B Plowden, *Children and their Primary Schools, - Report for the Central Advisory Council for Education*, HMSO, London, 1967, pp. 59-60.
[19] Department for Education and Science (DfES), *Education for All, the Report of the Committee of Enquiry into the Education of Children from Ethnic Minority Groups*, (The Swann Report), HMSO, London, 1985.
[20] Office for Standards in Education (OFSTED), *Provision and Support for Traveller Pupils*, HMI 455, London, 2003, p. 6.
[21] Department for Education and Skills (DfES), *Ethnicity and Education: The Evidence on Minority Ethnic Pupils aged 5-16: A Research Topic Paper 2006 edition,* 2006, p.11; see also I Hancock, 'The struggle for the control of identity', *Transitions,* vol. 4-4, 1997, pp.36-44
[22] Commission for Racial Equality (CRE), *Gypsy and Travellers: A Strategy for the CRE, 2004-2007,* CRE, London, 2003.
[23] Office for Standards in Education (OFSTED), *The Education of Travelling Children - A Report from the Office of Her Majesty's Chief Inspector of Schools*, Reference: HMR/12/96/NS OFSTED, London, 1996; Office for Standards in Education (OFSTED), *Raising the Achievement of Minority Ethnic Pupils – School and LEA Responses*, HMI 170, OFSTED, London, 1999; Office for Standards in Education (OFSTED), *Provision and Support for Traveller Pupils*, HMI 455, London, 2003. Department for Education and Skills (DfES), *Aiming High: Raising the Achievement of Gypsy Traveller Pupils. A Guide to Good Practice*, DfES/0443, Nottingham, 2003.
[24] DfES, 2003, op. cit. p.7.
[25] OFSTED, 2003, op. cit., p. 8.
[26] Tyler, op cit., p. 25.
[27] OFSTED, 1999, op. cit.
[28] A Ivatts, 'Inclusive school – exclusive society: the principles of inclusion', in *Traveller Education: Accounts of Good Practice*, C Tyler (ed), Trentham Books, Stoke on Trent, 2005, pp.1-9, p. 5.
[29] S J Ball, 'Educational reform, market concepts and ethical re-tooling', in *Education Policy and Social Class: The Selected Works of Stephen J Ball*, Routledge, London, 2006, pp. 115-129.

[30] Ball, 2003, op. cit., p. 25.
[31] Department for Education and Skills (DfES), *Every Child Matters: Change for Children*, DFES 1081-2004, DFES, Nottingham, 2004.
[32] Gilborn and Youdell, op. cit., p.1.
[33] Ball, 2003, op. cit., p.8.
[34] S Gewirtz, S J Ball and R Bowe, *Market Choice and Equity in Education*, Open University Press, Buckinghamshire, 2005, p.6.
[35] Ibid., p.160.
[36] OFSTED, 1996, op. cit.; OFSTED, 1999, op. cit.; DfES, 2003, op. cit.
[37] DfES, ibid.
[38] DfES, ibid.; also B Foster and H Horton, 'Traveller education and the strategies' in *Traveller Education: Accounts of Good Practice,* C Tyler (ed) Trentham Books, Stoke-on-Trent, 2005, pp.11-21, p. 21.
[39] See DfES, 2004, op. cit.

Bibliography

Advisory Council for the Education of Romany and Other Travellers (ACERT), *The Education of Gypsy and Traveller Children: Action Research and Coordination*, University of Hertfordshire Press, Hatfield, 1993.

Acton, T. and G. Mundy (eds), *Romani Culture and Gypsy Identity*, University of Hertfordshire Press, Hatfield, 1997.

Ball , S. J., *Class Strategies and the Education Market: The Middle Class and Social Advantage*, Routledgefalmer, London, 2003.

Ball, S. J., 'Educational reform, market concepts and ethical re-tooling' in *Education Policy and Social Class – The selected works of Stephen J. Ball*, Routledge, London, 2006, pp.115-129.

Beckett, L., 'Policy into practice', in *Traveller Education: Accounts of Good Practice,* C. Tyler (ed) Trentham Books, Stoke-on-Trent, 2005, pp.33-43

Bhopal, K., 'Gypsy/Traveller and education: changing needs and changing Perceptions', *British Journal of Educational Studies*, vol. 52-1, 2004, pp.47-64.

Bhopal, K, J. Gundara, C. Jones and C. Owen, *Working Towards Inclusive Education: Aspects of Good Practice for Gypsy/Traveller Pupils*, Research Report No. 238, DfEE, London, 2000.

Braid, D., 'The construction of identity through narrative: folklore and the travelling people of Scotland', in *Romani Culture and Gypsy Identity,* T. Acton and D. Mundy (eds), University of Hertfordshire Press, Hatfield, 1997, pp.40-68

Clay, G. S., 'Opening our eyes: some observations on the attendance of primary aged Traveller pupils registered at schools in a county area of South Wales', in *Romani Culture and Gypsy Identity,* T. Acton and D. Mundy (eds), University of Hertfordshire Press, Hatfield, 1997, pp.152-159

Clements, L. and S. Campbell, 'The Criminal Justice and Public Order Act and its implications for Travellers' in *Gypsy Politics and Traveller Identity*, T. Acton (ed), op. cit., pp. 61-69.

Commission for Racial Equality (CRE), *Gypsy and Travellers: A Strategy for the CRE, 2004-2007*, CRE, London, 2003.

Daymond, L., 'It's all about me – resources at Foundation and Key Stage 1', in *Traveller Education: Accounts of Good Practice,* C. Tyler (ed) Trentham Books, Stoke-on-Trent, 2005, pp.71-80

Department for Education and Science (DfES), *Education for All, the Report of the Committee of Enquiry into the Education of Children from Ethnic Minority Groups* (The Swann Report), HMSO, London, 1985.

Department for Education and Skills (DfES), *Aiming High: Raising the Achievement of Gypsy Traveller Pupils. A Guide to Good Practice*, DfES/0443, Nottingham, 2003.

Department for Education and Skills (DfES), *Ethnicity and Education: The Evidence on Minority Ethnic Pupils Aged 5-16: A Research Topic Paper* 2006 edition, DfES Publications, Nottingham, 2006.

Donovan, J., 'Still Travellers? Housed Travellers in a London borough', in *Traveller Education: Accounts of Good Practice,* C. Tyler (ed) Trentham Books, Stoke-on-Trent, 2005, pp.135-145

Foster, B. and H. Horton, 'Traveller education and the strategies' in *Traveller Education: Accounts of Good Practice,* C. Tyler (ed) Trentham Books, Stoke-on-Trent, 2005, pp.11-21

Gewirtz, S., S J Ball and R Bowe, *Market Choice and Equity in Education*, Open University Press, Buckinghamshire, 2005

Gillbourn, D. and D. Youdell, *Rationalising Education: Policy, Practice, Reform and Equity*, Open University Press, Buckingham, 2000

Ivatts, A., 'Inclusive school - exclusive society: the principles of inclusion', in *Traveller Education: Accounts of Good Practice*, C Tyler (ed), Trentham Books, Stoke on Trent, 2005, pp.1-9

McGovern, J., 'The emergence of the modern state', in *The Modern State: Theories and Ideologies*, E. Cudworth, T. Hall and J. McGovern (eds), Edinburgh University Press, Edinburgh, 2007, pp. 20-36.

McVeigh, R., 'Theorising sedentarism: the roots of anti-nomadism', in *Gypsy Politics and Traveller Identity*, T. Acton (ed), University of Hertfordshire Press, Hatfield, 1997, pp. 7-25.

Okely, J., *The Traveller Gypsies*, Cambridge University Press, Cambridge, 1983.

Office for Standards in Education (OFSTED), *The Education of Travelling Children - A Report from the Office of Her Majesty's Chief Inspector of Schools*, Reference: HMR/12/96/NS OFSTED, London, 1996.

Office for Standards in Education (OFSTED), *Raising the Achievement of Minority Ethnic Pupils – School and LEA Responses*, HMI 170, OFSTED, London, 1999.

Office for Standards in Education (OFSTED), *Provision and Support for Traveller Pupils*, HMI 455, London, 2003.

Plowden, Lady B., *Children and their Primary Schools, - Report for the Central Advisory Council for Education*, HMSO, London, 1967.

Smith, D., 'Gypsy aesthetics, identity and creativity' in *Romani Culture and Gypsy Identity,* T. Acton and D. Mundy (eds), University of Hertfordshire Press, Hatfield 1997, pp.7-17.

Tyler, C., (ed), *Traveller Education: Accounts of Good Practice*, Trentham Books, Stoke on Trent, 2005.

Dave Cudworth taught on the Primary PGCE at UEL from September 2004 – August 2009 before taking up his new post as senior lecturer at DeMontfort

University in Leicester where he teaches on the Education Studies degree programme. Dave is interested in social justice issues and is particularly concerned with the education of Gypsy/Traveller children on which he is reseraching for his PhD. He is also interested in alternative education and environmental education.

Erika Cudworth – very much a Londoner despite the Yorkshire name – studied at the universities of Birmingham, London, Bristol and Leeds before coming to UEL where she is currently Senior Lecturer in International Politics and Sociology. She is author of *Environment and Society*, *Developing Eco-feminist Theory: The Complexity of Difference* and, with Tim Hall and John McGovern, *The Modern State*.

To Have and Have Not: Implications for Teacher-trainees on First School Placements in a Diverse Range of ICT Resource Settings

David Morris and John Trushell

Abstract
This chapter reports a small-scale study concerning the experiences with ICT of teacher-trainees on placements in 51 Infant and Primary schools. Consistent with research studies and government reports, disparities were found in terms of ICT provision, support for ICT resources and access to ICT. Notably, Infant schools in the study were more likely to be in 'double jeopardy': no networked computers and no support for ICT. The implications of these findings for the primary sector and for teacher-training are discussed.

Key Words: Information and communication technology, infant schools, primary schools, teacher-training.

*****

1. Introduction

While maintaining that the level of Information and Communications Technology [ICT] resources in the United Kingdom [UK] compares favourably with those of other countries, government agencies concede that these figures conceal wide variations in the level and quality of ICT provision in the UK.[1] These variations have immediate implications for 'the ability of practising teachers to use ICT effectively with their pupils'[2] and for the in-school experiences of teacher-trainees in their use of ICT with pupils, and further implications for their effective use of ICT as practising teachers.

Recent figures indicate an improvement in the computer-to-pupil ratio - from 8:1 in 2003 to 6.1:1 in 2005[3] - and an increase in the proportion of primary schools with networked computers, from 91% in 2004 to 97% in 2005.[4] However, a survey in 2004 noted that only 63% of primary schools achieved a computer-to-pupil ratio of 8:1, and that only 82% of the smallest primary schools had a network.[5] Such variations were attributed to differentials in expenditure, insofar as:

> Primary schools judged as having 'Very Good' ICT resources had spent approximately five times as much on computer equipment in the previous year than schools with 'Poor' ICT resources.[6]

There are correspondingly wide variations in levels of technical support for ICT:[7] only 10% of primary schools had dedicated in-house technical support while 28% of primary schools depended on local education authority services and, in many primary schools, teachers undertook the day-to-day administration, maintenance and support tasks.[8] Government agencies view technical support as 'a central plank' of any whole-school strategy, but concede that support is an ongoing problem.[9]

Good ICT resources and technical support depend upon the commitment of primary school leaders who have 'strong vision' for ICT.[10] However, primary school leaders can have an alternative vision if persuaded - by such bodies as the Alliance for Childhood[11] - that computers are potentially 'detrimental to health and learning'.[12] These leaders would perpetuate existing modes of teaching whilst, at best, accommodating ICT, but would prioritise neither the acquisition of ICT resources nor the provision of technical support. Moreover, practising teachers - and teacher-trainees - may manifest principled 'technology refusal',[13] if convinced by Healy that computer use 'not only subtracts from important developmental tasks but may also entrench bad learning habits'. [14]

Clearly, advocates of ICT must vigorously refute criticisms that ICT jeopardises children's health and development and reassure practising teachers and teacher-trainees that ICT is, at the very least, a 'benign addition',[15] and that ICT can contribute to children's social and intellectual development. Provision for practising teachers' continuing professional development [CPD] could provide reassurance and opportunities for reflecting and transforming existing modes of teaching, although previous attempts by the government have failed to achieve this. The main aim of a later strategy, the New Opportunities Fund (NOF) training, was 'to raise the standard of pupils' achievements by increasing the expertise of serving teachers in the use of ICT in subject teaching'.[16] However, government agencies admitted that NOF training had only been effective in a third of primary schools, and that, in around 50% of primaries, the scheme had failed to build on teachers' ICT skills or to enable them to address pedagogical issues adequately.[17] The situation regarding CPD would appear unchanged when considering a General Teaching Council survey which found that ICT was the most commonly perceived need for CPD:[18] 56 per cent of teachers considered that CPD on using ICT in their teaching was required over the coming year.[19]

Initial training for teacher-trainees [ITT] should provide opportunities for teacher-trainees 'to make effective use of information technology in the classroom',[20] but variations in ICT resources, support for ICT and teachers' attitudes towards ICT could adversely affect these opportunities. ITT places stress on ensuring that teacher-trainees see ICT being modelled by teacher-educators and teachers in their work.[21].

Rationally, 'trainees need systematic preparation in... practical classroom knowledge' - and 'by definition that aspect of training... can only be provided by teachers working in their own classrooms and schools'[22] - but impoverished ICT resources, poor support for ICT and restricted use of ICT by teachers during school placement may jeopardise the benefits of any modelling of ICT provided by teacher-educators during an ITT course.[23]

The quality of teacher-trainees' experience of ICT in classrooms can be determined by three crucial factors: ICT resources, classroom teachers' ICT skills and classroom teachers' attitudes to ICT. These factors can be further categorised: 'have and have nots', related to ICT resources (and support); 'can and cannots', related to the necessary skills; and 'do and do nots', related to perceived relevance.[24]

Notably, previous research has reported that teacher-trainees' observation of restricted ICT use by teachers-mentors on the earliest school placement corresponded with restricted use of ICT applications by those teacher-trainees on subsequent and final placement,[25] and accordingly, 'classroom teachers who do not themselves use computers will not encourage teacher education students to use computers with students'.[26]

The small-scale study, reported below, investigated the implications of problematic ICT resources and support for ICT for teacher-trainees undertaking their formative first school placement during which the trainees were required to undertake an ICT-related task.

2. Methodology

Data for the study were collected by questionnaires returned by primary teacher-trainees on completion of their ICT-related task undertaken as an element of their first school placement.

The Primary PGCE programme required trainees to undertake a series of classroom-based tasks on school placement in the university's partnership boroughs, which receive diverse amounts of funding from the DfES.[27] Before their teaching practice, trainees were cautioned that ICT resource settings could vary between schools and were given examples of what poor or good classroom practice might look like.

The ICT task involved the use of a painting package/program by a teacher-trainee with a group of children. The task required that trainees engaged children in a process of drafting whereby successive versions of pupils' work were saved and printed. Trainees were required to note children's responses, annotate print outs and evaluate the exercise. Evidence required included lesson plans, print outs of work and a reflective commentary.

Trainees were requested, on a purely voluntary basis, to complete a separate questionnaire with a view to informing this piece of research. Both teacher-trainees and the classrooms/schools in which the task was undertaken were guaranteed anonymity. Teacher-trainees provided 51 questionnaires.

The questionnaire required information on the institution in which the placement was undertaken - location, type of school (nursery, infants, junior, junior mixed infants), pupils on roll, and the year group - and the ICT resources and support for ICT available. ICT resources were audited in terms of the number of computers available in the classroom and the number of networked computers available in the school. Support for ICT was also audited, e.g. in terms of the services of an ICT technician and/or the provision of support service by a helpline. Responses to these items were verified by reference to independent sources, e.g. school web-sites and OFSTED reports.[28]

The questionnaire required information on the task undertaken: the painting package or program used, the number of children who participated in the task, the number of computers used, and the number of children to each computer.

Each trainee was required to rate ease of access to ICT resources, whether her/his ICT skills and subject knowledge were adequate to teach the children, to rate the extent to which the trainee was supported by the classroom teacher, and to rate the ease of completing the task with the children. Ratings were provided by four-point Likert scales, which featured validity indicators for each point. Further opportunities for amplificatory comments were provided by the questionnaire, e.g. 'Please provide a brief explanation to qualify your answer'.

Thus, the data collected concerning the ICT-related task were amenable to descriptive statistical analysis by background variables with further details from the comments provided by teacher-trainees.

3. Findings

Data were collected from 51 trainees on placement in 51 institutions, comprising 12 Infants and 39 Primaries. Data were collected from 6 Foundation classes, 20 Key Stage 1 classes and 25 Key Stage 2 classes. The institutions, and the respective classes, were situated in 11 education authorities in Greater London/ Thames Gateway: thus, the data collected were not embedded in any particular authority. The data, presented below, concerns the institutions' ICT resources, the institutions' support for ICT and the trainees' experience of undertaking the ICT-related task in those institutions.

A. Resourcing

Analysis of all institutions disclosed that the mean number of computers in class was 1.608 (sd 0.696) and the mean number of networked computers in school was 14.353 (sd 7.104). The ratio of networked computer to pupils was 1:33.135 (sd 39.926).

Data concerning computers in classrooms were first analysed by sector, i.e. Infant and Primary, disclosing that Infant schools had a greater number of computers in classrooms than Primary schools, although this was not significant (see Table 1). A two-sample t-test disclosed no significant differences between these means ($t = 1.364$, $p = 0.1893$, 18 df).

Table 1: Computers in Class by Institution

	Mean Computers in Class	Standard Deviation
Infants	1.917	0.900
Primary	1.513	0.885

Data were then analysed by Foundation and Key stages across sectors. The data indicated that the mean numbers of computers in classrooms declined from Foundation to Key Stage 2 (see Table 2). However, a series of two-sample t-tests disclosed no significant differences between the means of computers in classes in the Foundation and Key stages.

Table 2: Computers in Foundation, Key Stage 1 & Key Stage 2 Classes

	Mean Computers in Class	Standard Deviation
Foundation	2.0	1.095
Key Stage 1	1.65	0.875
Key Stage 2	1.48	0.872

Data concerning networked computers were analysed by sector, i.e. Infant and Primary, disclosing that Primary schools had greater numbers of networked computers than Infant schools (see Table 3). A two-sample t-test disclosed that the mean of Primary schools was significantly greater [<.01] than the mean of Infant schools ($t = 2.976$, $p = 0.0089$, 16 df): thus, Primary schools were better equipped in terms of networked computers.

Table 3: Networked Computers in School by Institution

	Mean Networked Computers	Standard Deviation
Infants	9.083	7.217
Primary	15.974	6.314

Data were then analysed by Foundation and Key stages across sectors. The data indicated that the mean number of networked computers from Foundation to Key Stage 2 were consistent (see Table 4).

Table 4: Networked Computers in Foundation, Key Stage 1 & Key Stage 2 Classes

	Mean Networked Computers	Standard Deviation
Foundation	14.167	7.494
Key Stage 1	14.050	7.763
Key Stage 2	14.640	6.751

An implication of Tables 3 and 4 was that Foundation and Key Stage 1 pupils in Infant schools were less well resourced with networked computers than such pupils in Primary schools, although this finding must be tentative due to small sample size.

Comparison, by a two-sample t-test, of networked computers available to Foundation and Key Stage 1 pupils in Infant schools and in Primary schools disclosed a significant difference [<.01] (see Table 5): Foundation and Key Stage 1 pupils in Primary schools are potentially better resourced than their peers in Infant schools.

Table 5: Networked Computers at Foundation & Key Stage 1 in Infants & Primaries

	Infants [n = 12]		Primaries [n = 14]		t	p	df
	Mean	sd	Mean	sd			
Networked Computers	9.083	7.217	18.357	4.781	3.794	0.0013	18

The networked computer to pupils ratio for Primary schools was 1:23.247 (sd 8.69) while the ratio for Infant schools was 1:15.274 (sd 12.607): these ratios were not significantly different, but the sample of Infant schools included four schools with no networked computers for which networked computer resources in the remaining eight Infant schools compensated, an artefact which contributed to the large standard deviation. The presence of four infant schools with no networked computers is consistent with the figures reported by BECTA, i.e. only 97% of primary schools had networked computers,[29] and those previously reported by survey in 2004, i.e. only 82% of the smallest primary schools had a network (ibid.: 3).[30]

B. Support

Analysis of data from all institutions disclosed the following orders of support:

- both technician and helpline support were available to 20 institutions (0.392);
- technician support alone was available to 10 institutions (0.196);
- helpline support alone was available to 9 institutions (0.176); and
- 12 (0.235) institutions had neither technician or helpline support

Further analysis by sector disclosed the orders of support for both sectors (see Table 6).

Table 6: Support Available to Institutions

	Technician & Helpline	Technician Only	Helpline Only	No Support
Infant	0.333 [n = 4]	0.25 [n = 3]	0.083 [n = 1]	0.333 [n = 4]
Primary	0.410 [n = 16]	0.179 [n = 7]	0.205 [n = 8]	0.205 [n = 8]

The figures demonstrate that similar proportions of Infant and Primary schools had technician support (Infants - 0.583; Primaries – 0.590). However, the proportion of Infant schools with access to helplines (0.416) was considerably less than the proportion of Primary schools with access to helplines (0.615). The proportion of Infant schools with no support (0.333) was greater than the proportion of Primary schools with no support (0.205).

Further analysis by Foundation, Key Stage 1 and Key Stage 2 disclosed the orders of support for these sectors (see Table 7).

Table 7: Support Available by Sector

	Technician & Helpline	Technician Only	Helpline Only	No Support
Foundation	0.333 [n = 2]	0.333 [n = 2]	0.167 [n = 1]	0.167 [n = 1]
Key Stage 1	0.250 [n = 5]	0.250 [n = 5]	0.200 [n = 4]	0.300 [n = 6]
Key Stage 2	0.520 [n = 13]	0.120 [n = 3]	0.160 [n = 4]	0.200 [n = 5]

The figures demonstrate that, irrespective of sector, more than half of classrooms had technician support (Foundation - 0.667; Key Stage 1 - 0.500; Key Stage 2 – 0.640). Similarly, access to helplines was approached or achieved in half of the classrooms (Foundation - 0.5; Key Stage 1 – 0.45; Key Stage 2 – 0.68). Notably, Key Stage 1 pupils were more likely to have no support than Key Stage 2 and Foundation pupils.

The implications of Tables 6 and 7 are that Foundation pupils in Infant schools are more likely to have no support (0.333) than such pupils in Primary schools (0.167), and that Key Stage 1 pupils, whether in Infant and Primary schools, are most likely to have no support, although these finding must be tentative due to small sample size.

C. Task

51 trainees undertook the ICT teaching task. These trainees had previously self-audited their ICT on entry to the PGCE programme and, on a four-point Likert scale of proficiency, achieved the mean rating of 2.87 (sd 0.575), indicating above moderate proficiency. The mean ratings for proficiency for trainees on placements in Infant and Primary schools and for trainees on placements in Foundation, Key Stage 1 and Key Stage 2 classes were not significantly different when subjected to two-sample t-tests.[31]

Trainees on placement rated ease of access to ICT resources for the task on a four-point Likert scale: mean ease of access was 2.92 (sd 1.03). Trainees whose responses indicated that ICT resources were not easy to access provided additional information such as "Printer not working", "Printer didn't function properly and some computers not functioning" and "Computers are very old, and crash easily".

Trainees rated ease of completion of the ICT task with pupils on a four-point Likert scale. The mean rating for ease of task completion was 2.471 (sd 0.946). Eight trainees indicated that the task was not easy to complete, and six trainees provided additional pertinent comments.

Three trainees reported technical difficulties: a trainee on a nursery placement in an Infant school — who had previously reported "Computers are very old, and crash easily" — reiterated "Technical problems (and time constraints)"; two trainees on Primary (Later Years) placements reported, respectively, "Both printers were 'out of order'... floppy disc faulty" and "Too many things went wrong... The children are supposed to have their own login, but these were not working... the computers crashed... so teaching time was cut short".

Trainees reported use of an extensive variety of painting programs and packages. Two trainees remarked the unsuitability of programs for particular ages of pupils, e.g. a trainee on nursery placement in an Infant school noted of a painting program that it was "not suitable for young children" while a trainee on a Primary (Later Years) placement noted that a painting program was "not very challenging" for Year 6 children.

One trainee on a Primary (Later Years) placement alleged that the task was difficult due to scarce ICT resources:

> Getting time in the ICT suite proved very difficult indeed. School was a 2 form entry with 2 ICT suites to share.

Trainees' perceptions of the adequacy of their ICT skills and of their subject knowledge were estimated by four-point Likert scales. The means of trainees' perceived adequacies were, respectively:

- ICT skills 3.47 (sd 0.542); and
- Subject knowledge 3.29 (sd 0.502).

Trainees were asked whether the task had required the assistance of their classroom mentor: eight trainees indicated that they had required no assistance from the mentor. The remaining forty-three trainees rated the amount of assistance required by the classroom mentor on a four-point Likert scale: the mean of assistance [n = 43] required was 1.930 (sd 1.078).

Data concerning trainees' perceptions were analysed by sector of placement (see Table 8), i.e. Infant (n = 12) and Primary (n = 39), disclosing that only two trainees on Infant placements indicated that they had required no assistance from the mentor while six trainees on Primary placements indicated that they had required no assistance from the mentor.

Table 8: Infant and Primary Placement Trainees' Perceptions of ICT Task

	Trainees' ICT Skills	Trainees' Subject Knowledge	Ease of Access	Ease of Completion	Mentor Support
Infant	3.750 (sd 0.452)	3.417 (sd 0.515)	2.583 (sd 1.084)	2.417 (sd 0.900)	2.300 (sd 1.059)[1]
Primary	3.385 (sd 0.544)	3.256 (sd 0.498)	3.026 (sd 1.103)	2.487 (sd 0.970)	1.818 (sd 1.074)[2]

[1] n = 10 [2] n = 33

However, a series of two-sample t-tests disclosed one difference of significance: the mean of trainees' adequacy of ICT skills on Infant placements was significantly greater [<.05] than that of trainees on Primary placements ($t = 2.328$, $p = 0.0300$, 21 df). The inference may be drawn that the perceived adequacy of ICT skills to complete the ICT task on Primary placements was restricted compared with that on Infant placements, and this may correspond with relative difficulty of programs encountered in Primary classrooms.

Data concerning trainees' perceptions were analysed by Foundation and Key stages across sectors (see Table 9), i.e. trainees on Foundation placements (n = 6), trainees on Key Stage 1 placements (n = 20) and trainees on Key Stage 2 placements (n = 25). Data disclosed that:

- the two trainees on Infant placements who had indicated that they had required no assistance from their mentor were in Foundation classrooms; and
- the six trainees on Primary placements who had indicated that they had required no assistance from their mentor were equally divided between Key Stage 1 and Key Stage 2 classrooms.

Table 9: Foundation, Key Stage 1 & Key Stage 2 Trainees' Perceptions of ICT Task

	Trainees' ICT Skills	Trainees' Subject Knowledge	Ease of Access	Ease of Completion	Mentor Support
Foundation	3.500 (sd 0.548)	3.167 (sd 0.408)	3.000 (sd 1.549)	2.167 (sd 1.169)	2.000 (sd 1.414)[1]
Key Stage 1	3.600 (sd 0.503)	3.350 (sd 0.489)	2.800 (sd 0.894)	2.450 (sd 0.759)	2.176 (sd 0.728)[2]
Key Stage 2	3.360 (sd 0.569)	3.280 (sd 0.542)	3.000 (sd 1.041)	2.560 (sd 1.044)	1.727 (sd 1.241)[3]

[1] n = 4 [2] n = 17 [3] n = 22

A series of two-sample t-tests disclosed no significant differences. However, these results by Foundation, Key Stage 1 and Key Stage 2 (see Table 8) - and for Infant and Primary Placements (see Table 7) - are remarkably consistent insofar as:

- the mean for Trainees' ICT Skills is consistently the highest, implying that all trainees were most confident with their ICT skills to accomplish the task;
- the mean for Trainees' Subject Knowledge is consistently the second highest mean, implying that Subject Knowledge was perceived as less adequate than ICT skills (although none of the sub-groups' means were significantly different); and
- the mean for Ease of Access is consistently the third highest mean, implying that access was perceived as less adequate than either ICT Skills and Subject Knowledge.

Thereafter, the mean for Ease of Completion is the fourth highest mean: this mean would represent the outcome of the interaction of the three factors of ICT Skills, Subject Knowledge and Ease of Access. Finally, the least of the means is for Mentor Support, although the magnitude of the standard deviations relative to the means - especially that of Key Stage 2 trainees (Table 9) and, correspondingly, Primary trainees (Table 8) - indicates that there was great variation in levels of mentor support required by individual trainees.

5. Interpretation and Discussion

The data collected and analysed raises concerns for ICT resources and support for ICT in the primary sector and has particular implications for the Primary PGCE and prospective teachers at UEL.

The data of this small-scale is consistent with those data of contemporary large-scale surveys[32] insofar as these studies discerned diversity in levels of resourcing and support in the institutions. However, the trend for Infant schools to emerge as "have nots" has not been discerned by large scale studies.

When institutions were disaggregated into Infant and Primary schools, Infant schools were found to have significantly fewer [<.01] networked computers than Primary schools. Thus, Foundation and Key Stage 1 pupils in Infant schools had significantly less access [<.01] to networked computers than their peers in Primary schools. A contributory factor was that four Infant schools were 'have nots' in terms of networked computers, i.e. these schools had no network computer resources.

A compounding factor for Infant schools was the relative lack of support for ICT: a third of Infant schools had no support for ICT compared with a fifth of Primary schools. This lack of support - which must impose upon classroom teachers day-to-day administration, maintenance and support tasks[33] - is worrying when considering the incidence of computers (and peripherals) reported as not working by teacher-trainees while undertaking their ICT-related task during placements. Research has reported trainees facing the "usual problems" of equipment not working[34] - a scenario which acts as a barrier to increasing the use of technology in the classroom.[35]

The data collected concerning teacher-trainees' ICT task indicated that there were three factors which contributed to the ease of completion of the ICT related task: trainees' ICT skills, trainees' subject knowledge and ease of access. The consistently lowest rated factor, i.e. the most problematic, whether in Infant or Primary schools, or in Foundation, Key Stage 1 or Key Stage 2 classes, was ease of access to ICT resources.

The teacher-trainees' mean ratings for subject knowledge pertinent to the task were no different for Infant or Primary schools. Intriguingly, those trainees on placements in Infant schools had mean ratings for ICT skills pertinent to the task which were significantly greater [<.05] than their peers in Primary schools (see Table 8), although there was no significant difference between their ICT skills on entry to the PGCE programme. Yet these trainees' mean rating for assistance by teacher-mentors was greater (although not significantly) when demand for assistance by teacher-mentors might have been reasonably anticipated to be less. Notably, this relatively greater need for assistance occurred in Infant schools which were 'have nots' in terms of networked computers and were less likely to have technical support for ICT.

Evidently, a small number of the teacher-trainees in this study experienced placements in Infant schools where pupils were in double jeopardy: no networked computers and no support for ICT. This constitutes an impoverishment of their experience as teacher-trainees and their prospects of becoming practising teachers who use ICT effectively with their pupils. The challenge for ITT providers is to minimise the adverse effects of such 'have not' placements by arranging compensatory 'have' placements. Trainees who are 'cans', i.e. possessing the necessary skills, who complete placements in 'have not' institutions may be at greater risk of becoming 'do nots' with restricted perception of the relevance of ICT.

To address issues raised by this study, the ICT element of the programme for teacher-trainees at the UEL currently affords every trainee the opportunity to observe and teach for one day in an infant school which participated in the ICT Test Bed Project[36] co-ordinated by BECTA, 2002-2006. This allows trainees to observe good practice in an environment where levels of technical support are high and where pupils' ICT skills and capability are well above the national average. Trainees also have the opportunity to plan and deliver lessons which enhance learning and teaching using a wide spectrum of ICT tools.

Although teacher-trainees may be able to benefit from these arrangements, the same provision does not hold for pupils being taught in 'have not' schools. Concern for such inequality is shared by some educationalists who fear that those children who are not gaining access to ICT and developing their ICT skills will be excluded from employment opportunities and participating fully in society,[37] a vocational rationale echoed by Higgins who emphasises that it is the responsibility of schools to equip pupils with the skills that will enable them to engage with technologies in the workplace when they leave school.[38] If variations in levels of resourcing, technical support and teacher proficiency exist, then clearly pupils' access to ICT will be prone to the same diversity.

Certainly, in 2003, the Department of Education's evaluation of ICT in primary schools presented a sector where opportunities for children to access ICT were far from equal. Children in many schools had few opportunities to learn how to use spreadsheets, to create and manipulate graphical images or to use the communication facilities offered by ICT. Children in less than half of schools were provided with a sufficiently broad and challenging range of ICT skills.[39] OFSTED also reported that it was only in a minority of schools where children were making effective use of databases, digital cameras and presentation software to enhance work across the curriculum.[40]

Disparities in ICT provision and access have been addressed by successive government initiatives. Curriculum Online (funded at £100m a year, 2003-2006) provided schools with the opportunity to acquire a range of

ICT resources. The Building for Schools programme (funded at over £2 billion, 2005-2008) encouraged designs that embraced ICT. The Computers for Pupils programme (funded at £60m, 2006-2008) aimed to putting computers into the homes of disadvantaged pupils. Eligibility for Computers for Pupils is confined to Key Stages 3 and 4, excluding Key Stage 1 and 2 pupils. However, there is an argument for starting with the primary sector: if disadvantaged pupils in primary schools are equipped with a computer at home (as is the case in some primary Test Bed Schools) then, surely, they will possess the requisite skills when they enter secondary school.

A good number of the boroughs that work in partnership with UEL receive less than average DfES funding per pupil, so finding ways of further monitoring ICT provision in partnership schools, and providing teacher-trainees with a balanced experience of facilitating teaching and learning using ICT, clearly warrants further monitoring and study.

It will be interesting to see to what extent the digital divide matters: will it be one of the biggest civil rights issues of the millennium, or will it be more of a matter of choice in contemporary society?

Notes

[1] Office for Standards in Education (OFSTED), *ICT in Schools: The Impact of Government Initiatives Five Years On* [HMI 2050], OFSTED, London, 2004, p.4; British Educational Communications and Technology Agency (BECTA), *Becta Review 2006: Evidence on the Progress of ICT in Education*, BECTA , Coventry, 2006, p.5.

[2] L Taylor, 'How student teachers develop their understanding of teaching using ICT' *Journal of Education for Teaching*, vol.30-1, 2004, pp.43-56, p.43.

[3] BECTA, op. cit., p.9.

[4] Ibid., p.12.

[5] G Prior and L Hall, *ICT in Schools Survey 2004* [ICT in Schools Research and Evaluation Series – No.22], BECTA/DfES, Coventry/London, 2004, p.3.

[6] OFSTED, op. cit., p.23.

[7] Ibid., p.5.

[8] BECTA,op. cit., p.14.

[9] OFSTED, op. cit., p.12.

[10] BECTA, op. cit., p.5

[11] see C Cordes and E Miller (eds) *Fool's Gold: A Critical Look at Computers and Childhood*, Alliance for Childhood, 1999, accessed 23rd January, 2008 <http://www.allianceforchildhood.net/projects/downloads/frontmatter.pdf>.

[12] L Plowman and C Stephen, 'A "benign addition"? Research on ICT and pre-school children', *Journal of Computer Assisted Learning*, Vol.19-2, 2003, pp.149-164, p.151.

[13] see M Wild, 'Technology refusal: Rationalising the failure of student and beginning teachers to use computers' *British Journal of Educational Technology*, Vol. 27-2, 1996, pp. 134–143.

[14] J Healy, *Failure to Connect: How Computers Affect Our Children's Minds - For Better or Worse*, Simon and Schuster, New York, 1998, p.205.

[15] L Cuban, *Oversold and Underused: Computers in the Classroom*, Harvard University Press, Cambridge, Mass, 2001, p.67.

[16] M Kirkwood, T van der Kuyl, N Parton and R Grant, *The New Opportunities Fund ICT Training for Teachers Programme: Designing a Powerful On-line Learning Environment*, a paper presented at the European Conference on Educational Research, Edinburgh, 20th-23rd September, 2000.

[17] Office for Standards in Education [OFSTED], *ICT in schools: Effect of government initiatives - Pupils achievement - Progress Report* [HMI 423] London: The Stationery Office, 2002, p.22.

[18] L Sturman, K Lewis, J Morrison, E Scott, P Smith, B Styles, G Taggart and A Woodthorpe, *General Teaching Council Survey of Teachers 2005*, General Teaching Council for England [GTCE], London, 2005, p.6.

[19] Ibid., p. 45.

[20] M Bell, 'The missing majority' *Times Educational Supplement: Computers Update*, 18th October 1996, p.6.

[21] Taylor, op. cit., p.43.

[22] T Maynard, and J Furlong, 'Learning to teach and models of mentoring' in *Mentoring*, D McIntyre, H Haggar and M Wilkin (eds), Kogan Page, London, 1993, pp. 69-85, p.71.

[23] G De Landsheere, 'The information society and education' in *Education and the Information Society*, M Eraut (ed), Cassell, London, 1991, pp.115-163.

[24] N McLean, 'Foreword and introduction' in *Digital Divide: A Collection of Papers from the Toshiba/BECTA digital divide seminar*, Coventry: BECTA, 19th February 2002, p2.

[25] J Trushell, A Slater, R Sneddon and H Mitchell, 'Insights into IT capability on a teacher-mentored primary PGCE course', *Computers and Education*, Vol.31-3 1998, pp. 329-347.

[26] A Jones, 'Refusing or ignoring? An investigation of student teachers' perceptions and use of computers' in *Untangling the Web: Establishing Learning Links*, S McNamara and E Stacey (eds), Proceedings Australian Society for Educational Technology Conference, 7th-10th July 2002. Melbourne, accessed 19th February, 2008 <http://www.ascilite.org.au/aset-archives/confs/2002/jones.html>.

[27] The DfES funding reform for 2003-4 shows educational spending per primary school pupil for each of the London boroughs. Five out of eight of

the univerity's partnership boroughs fall in to the bottom half of the league table for spending.

[28] The authors acknowledge the assistance of Anton Beackon and Asif Ali in the validation of the data in these items.

[29] BECTA, op. cit., p.12.

[30] Prior and Hall, op. cit., p.3.

[31] Trainees on placement in Infant schools [n = 12] achieved a mean of 2.806 (sd 0.577) and trainees on placement in Primary schools [n = 39] achieved a mean of 3.091 (sd 0.539): differences between these means were not statistically different.

Trainees on placement in Foundation classes (n = 6) achieved a mean of 3.00 (sd 0.0), trainees on placement in Key Stage 1 classes (n = 20) achieved a mean of 2.842 (sd 0.602), and trainees on placement in Key Stage 2 classes (n = 25) achieved a mean of 2.909 (sd 0.610): differences between these means were not statistically different.

[32] OFSTED, op. cit., and BECTA, op. cit.

[33] BECTA, op. cit., p.5.

[34] A Pritchard, 'Meeting the requirements of the initial teacher training National Curriculum for the use of Information and Communications Technology in subject teaching, with one year's cohort of postgraduate primary trainees' *Journal of Information Technology for Teacher Education* , Vol.10-3, pp.293-309, p.302.

[35] S Higgins, *Does ICT Improve Learning and Teaching in Schools?*, British Educational Research Association: Nottingham, 2003, p.18.

[36] Twenty-eight schools and three Further Education colleges, located within 'test beds' of social disadvantage, participated in the ICT Test Bed Project which was funded at £34 million, 2002-2006.

[37] J Powney, K Lowden and S Hall, *Young People's Life-Skills and the Future*, Research Report No.98, Scottish Council for Research in Education [SCRE], Glasgow, 2000, p.9.

[38] Higgins, op. cit., p.4.

[39] Department of Education [DOE], *An Evaluation by the Education and Training Inspectorate of Information and Communication Technology in Primary Schools 2001-2002*, DoE, London, 2003, p.15.

[40] OFSTED, op. cit., p.14.

Bibliography

Bell, M., 'The missing majority' *Times Educational Supplement: Computers Update*, 18th October 1996, p.6

British Educational Communications and Technology Agency (BECTA), *Becta Review 2006: Evidence on the Progress of ICT in Education*, BECTA , Coventry, 2006

Cordes, C. and E. Miller (eds) *Fool's Gold: A Critical Look at Computers and Childhood*, Alliance for Childhood, 1999, accessed 23rd January, 2008 <http://www.allianceforchildhood.net/projects/downloads/frontmatter.pdf>.

Cuban, L. *Oversold and Underused: Computers in the Classroom*, Harvard University Press, Cambridge, Mass, 2001.

De Landsheere, G., 'The information society and education' in *Education and the Information Society*, M Eraut (ed), Cassell, London, 1991, pp.115-163.

Department of Education [DOE], *An Evaluation by the Education and Training Inspectorate of Information and Communication Technology in Primary Schools 2001-2002*, DoE, London, 2003.

Healy, J., *Failure to Connect: How Computers Affect Our Children's Minds - For Better or Worse*, Simon and Schuster, New York, 1998.

Higgins, S., *Does ICT Improve Learning and Teaching in Schools?*, British Educational Research Association: Nottingham, 2003.

Jones, A., 'Refusing or ignoring? An investigation of student teachers' perceptions and use of computers' in *Untangling the Web: Establishing Learning Links*, S McNamara and E Stacey (eds), Proceedings Australian Society for Educational Technology Conference, 7th-10th July 2002. Melbourne, accessed 23rd January, 2008 <http://www.ascilite.org.au/aset-archives/confs/2002/jones.html>.

Kirkwood, M., T. van der Kuyl, N. Parton and R. Grant, *The New Opportunities Fund ICT Training for Teachers Programme: Designing a Powerful On-line Learning Environment*, a paper presented at the European Conference on Educational Research, Edinburgh, 20th-23rd September, 2000.

McLean, N. 'Foreword and introduction' in *Digital Divide: A Collection of Papers from the Toshiba/BECTA digital divide seminar*, Coventry: BECTA, 19th February 2002, p.2.

Maynard, T. and J. Furlong, 'Learning to teach and models of mentoring' in *Mentoring*, D. McIntyre, H. Haggar and M. Wilkin (eds), Kogan Page, London, 1993, pp. 69-85.

Office for Standards in Education [OFSTED], *ICT in schools: Effect of government initiatives - Pupils achievement - Progress Report* [HMI 423] London: The Stationery Office, 2002

Office for Standards in Education (OFSTED), *ICT in Schools: The Impact of Government Initiatives Five Years On* [HMI 2050], OFSTED, London, 2004.

Plowman, L. and C. Stephen, (2003) 'A "benign addition"? Research on ICT and pre-school children', *Journal of Computer Assisted Learning*, Vol.19-2, 2003, pp.149-164.

Powney, J., K. Lowden and S. Hall, *Young People's Life-Skills and the Future*, Research Report No.98, Scottish Council for Research in Education [SCRE], Glasgow, 2000

Prior, G. and L. Hall, *ICT in Schools Survey 2004* [ICT in Schools Research and Evaluation Series – No.22], BECTA/DfES, Coventry/London, 2004.

Pritchard, A., 'Meeting the requirements of the initial teacher training National Curriculum for the use of Information and Communications Technology in subject teaching, with one year's cohort of postgraduate trimary trainees' *Journal of Information Technology for Teacher Education* , Vol.10-3, pp.293-309.

Sturman, L., K. Lewis, J. Morrison, E. Scott, P. Smith, B. Styles, G. Taggart and A. Woodthorpe, *General Teaching Council Survey of Teachers 2005*, General Teaching Council for England [GTCE], London, 2005.

Taylor, L., 'How student teachers develop their understanding of teaching using ICT' *Journal of Education for Teaching*, vol.30-1, 2004, pp.43-56.

Trushell, J., A. Slater, R. Sneddon and H. Mitchell, 'Insights into IT capability on a teacher-mentored primary PGCE course', *Computers and Education*, Vol.31-3 1998, pp. 329-347.

Wild, M., 'Technology refusal: Rationalising the failure of student and beginning teachers to use computers' *British Journal of Educational Technology*, Vol.27-2, 1996, pp.134–143.

David Morris taught in inner city primary schools – including as ICT co-ordinator and Senior Manager in a Beacon school – before joining the Primary Initial Teacher Training team. He has been seconded to the British Educational Communications and Technology Agency [BECTA] to research ICT competencies in the teaching workforce.

John Trushell – originally from Yorkshire – studied at the University of Durham before teaching in primary and secondary schools in Durham, Sussex and London. He has lectured and conducted research in and around London – notably King's College London where he completed his PhD – for 25 years.

The Men in White Coats: Teacher Trainees' Perceptions of Scientists

Hazel Dorrington and John Trushell

Abstract
This chapter reports a small-scale study of 89 primary teacher-trainees' perceptions of scientists as disclosed by their drawings of two scientists. Analysis of the trainees' drawings demonstrated that certain artefacts – laboratory coats, laboratory equipment and laboratories – frequently featured in these drawings. Analysis indicated that while there was a strong likelihood for the scientists in the drawings to be female and male, the likelihood of both scientists being female was less than being male. The implications for teacher-training are considered.

Key Words: Scientists, primary teacher-trainees, gender, primary pupils.

*****

1. Introduction

Public perceptions of scientists are marked by ambivalence: the scientist tends to be perceived either as saviour-hero or as mad villain.[1] The archetypal mad scientist was established by the aspiring natural philosopher in Mary Shelley's *Frankenstein* in 1818,[2] "when science was still the province of the gentlemanly scholar".[3] These gentlemanly amateurs were displaced by the professional scientists during the 1830s[4] – the term 'scientist' was coined by William Whewell in 1833[5] – and the saviour-scientist became established:

> Figures such as Pasteur, Semmelweis, Curie and Faraday swirl before us in images of bearded dedication, white coats, retort stands and glass flasks. Service to humanity shines in their eyes. Stiff poses frozen in the moment of greatness for posterity to revere.[6]

While these images of the saviour-scientist and the mad scientist have proved resilient, so has the explicit masculinity of the scientist, from the gentlemanly scholar to the bearded dedication of the professional scientist. This perceived masculinity of the scientist is of concern in contemporary cultures that are striving for gender equality and in which, it is believed, gendered perceptions of scientists have prevented girls and women from full participation in science.

2. Researching Perceptions of the Scientist

Research into public perceptions of scientists has been documented as long ago as the 1950s,[7] the dawning of an 'Age of Anxiety'[8] which witnessed a decline in "public confidence that scientists fully understood and controlled the consequences of their experiments".[9] However, the contemporary concern with gendered perceptions was marked by a study in 1983 which asked 4807 children in primary schools, between kindergarten and grade 5, to draw a picture of a scientist.[10] The study found that children held a stereotyped image of a scientist as a man – who was balding and bearded and who wore a laboratory-coat - and that the prevalence of this stereotype amongst the children increased with age. A smaller study of 76 primary school pupils, in 1988, noted that the stereotypical male image of the scientist was gendered: when asked to draw a scientist, not one male pupil drew a female scientist while only 23 out of 45 female students drew a female scientist.[11] These stereotypical images have persisted: a 1997 study of 117 fifth grade pupils found that 80% of pupils depicted scientists as males, and 93% depicted scientists as white.[12] A recent study of 9 year-olds and 14 year-olds in six European countries – Czech Republic, France, Italy, Poland, Portugal and Romania – produced 1,102 drawings: only 272 drawings depicted women scientists and, of these 272 drawings, a mere 60 were drawn by boys.[13]

One agency by which these stereotypes may be transmitted is the teacher: as a 1997 study of 49 students enrolled on a teacher certification course found, the students' drawings resembled, in terms of stereotypical content, those produced by children: for example, 84% of the students drew male scientists, 58% drew the scientists wearing laboratory coats.[14] Thus, teachers become implicated in the perpetuation of these stereotypes, as one researcher observed in 2001:

> teachers' stereotypes are the same as their students' on most significant characteristics… Are teachers unwittingly communicating a biased viewpoint and prompting children to create a distorted image of scientists?[15]

If a teacher holds a stereotypical view of scientists, this may be consciously or unconsciously passed on to their pupils. Buldu remarked that:

> Teachers at the early childhood level and at elementary grades – perhaps more than at any other instructional level – play a vital role in creating children's perceptions about science and scientists.[16]

A teacher who believes that scientists are white, middle-aged men is in peril of preventing their pupils from perceiving themselves as prospective scientists. Before we can challenge the stereotypical perceptions of scientists held by children, we need to determine whether these perceptions are held by their teachers. Once teachers' perceptions are known, these may be challenged, if necessary, to prevent stereotypical perceptions being perpetuated.

3. Methodology

Trainee teachers on a one year Primary PGCE Programme at the University of East London [UEL] were each provided with a piece of plain paper and given the following instructions:

> 'Draw two scientists working. You can label your drawing if you wish. You can colour your drawing in if you wish. You will not be given any further instructions.'

Trainees were asked to draw two scientists as it was felt that this would not compel trainees to choose between drawing a male or female scientist. O'Maoldomhnaigh and Hunt found that, when participants were given the opportunity to complete two drawings, the frequency of drawings of female scientists increased.[17] Trainees were given the option of labelling their drawings as this would enable them to make their ideas more explicit, especially if they felt that they had poor drawing skills.

The trainees were asked to work individually without discussing their drawings with each other, as it was felt that they might influence one another in what they drew. No time limit was set, but most trainees finished their drawings in around ten minutes.

Drawings were collected from 89 trainees, and these drawings were coded against a checklist of features – comprising 14 items – which was developed from a checklist devised by Chambers for his study in 1983,[18] supplemented with features drawn from checklists from studies conducted by Finson et al in 1995,[19] and Barman et al in 1997.[20] Each drawing was coded by three independent coders, who were asked to indicate their level of agreement that a particular feature was present or absent on a scale of 1-5. The criteria applied were:

- award of a rating of 5 indicated that the feature should be definitely present in a drawing, e.g. feature corroborated by a label;
- award of a rating of 4 indicated that the feature was discernibly present;

- award of a rating of 3 indicated that the feature was neither discernibly present or absent, e.g. gender of a stick person drawing;
- award of a rating of 2 indicated that the feature was discernibly absent; and
- award of a rating of 1 indicated that a feature was definitely absent.

A sub-sample of drawings were coded and then discussed by the coders to ensure consistency. The remaining drawings were then coded by each coder in turn. The coders' ratings were collated and the means calculated for each trainee.

4. Findings

Data are presented for the entire sample and by sub-samples of gender, age and first degree discipline. Trainees were divided into categories of first degree disciplines derived from Becher who proposed the following disciplinary groupings:

- Pure sciences (e.g. physics) - 'hard-pure';
- Humanities (e.g. history) and pure social sciences (e.g. anthropology) - 'soft-pure';
- Technologies (e.g. engineering) - 'hard-applied'; and
- Applied social sciences (e.g. education) - 'soft-applied'.[21]

Data are presented below for the entire sample, 89 participants, and by sub-categories of gender, age and first degree discipline.

A. All Respondents

The inter-coder reliability that was calculated for the 14 items was moderately strong, i.e. 0.640. However, inter-coder reliability was adversely affected by two items with lower reliability: 'Caucasian(s) only' had an inter-coder reliability of 0.348 and 'Middle-aged/elderly' had an inter-coder reliability of 0.359. These features were difficult to discern in many drawings. When these items were excluded, inter-coder reliability achieved 0.687.

The means and standard deviations of all of the trainees were calculated for the fourteen variables (see Table 1), and consideration of these means disclosed the following positive tendencies:

- a marked tendency for scientists to be depicted with symbols of their research (e.g. instruments and laboratory equipment);
- a marked tendency for scientists to be depicted in a laboratory; and
- a tendency for scientists to be depicted wearing a lab coat.

Negative tendencies were also disclosed:

- a marked tendency for there to be no secrecy indicators;
- a marked tendency for there to be no invocation of mythic stereotypes (e.g. Frankenstein);
- a tendency for two scientists to be not depicted as females only;
- a tendency for there to be no depiction of technology; and
- a tendency for the scientists not to have facial hair.

Table 1: Means and Standard Deviations for Fourteen Variables

Variable	Mean	Standard deviation
Wearing a lab' coat	3.73	1.37
Wearing eye glasses	3.18	1.68
Facial hair	1.63	1.25
Symbols of research	4.54	1.07
Symbols of knowledge	2.33	1.54
Technology	1.45	1.02
Relevant captions	2.30	1.31
Male gender only	2.28	1.55
Female gender only	1.38	0.76
Caucasian(s) only	3.46	0.54
Middle-aged/elderly	2.76	0.70
Mythic stereotypes	1.11	0.40
Secrecy indicators	1.07	0.41
Working in lab'	4.37	0.94

Thus, while these scientists have retained their 'white coats, retort stands and glass flasks',[22] they have lost their beards. Nevertheless, a paired t-test of the means for scientists to be male gender only and female gender only disclosed that the mean for male gender only was significantly greater than that for female gender only ($t = 4.996$, $p = <.0001$, 88df).

B. Sample by Gender

The 89 participants comprised 72 female and 17 male trainees. The means and standard deviations were calculated for the variables of the sub-samples of gender.

The positive and negative tendencies apparent for the entire sample (see Table 1) were largely consistent for the sub-samples of gender (see Table 2). However, further analysis by a series of two-sample t-tests disclosed significant differences for the following variables:

- Relevant captions - male mean significantly greater than female mean [$t = 3.358$, $p = 0.0027$, 23 df];

- Male gender only - male mean significantly greater than female mean [t = 3.204, p = 0.0041, 22 df];
- Caucasian only - male mean significantly greater than female mean [t = 2.858, p = 0.0089, 23df]; and
- Middle-aged/elderly - male mean significantly greater than female mean [t = 3.709, p = 0.0010, 26 df].

Table 2: Means and Standard Deviations for Fourteen Variables by Gender

Variable	Female		Male	
	Mean	sd	Mean	sd
Wearing a lab' coat	3.74	1.40	3.69	1.31
Wearing eye glasses	3.17	1.71	3.24	1.56
Facial hair	1.62	1.26	1.71	1.25
Symbols of research	4.61	0.99	4.25	1.36
Symbols of knowledge	2.31	1.51	2.43	1.70
Technology	1.47	1.10	1.39	0.64
Relevant captions	2.08	1.22	3.24	1.28
Male gender only	2.03	1.43	3.37	1.59
Female gender only	1.41	0.82	1.23	0.39
Caucasian(s) only	3.38	0.52	3.78	0.53
Middle-aged/elderly	2.64	0.67	3.25	0.60
Mythic stereotypes	1.05	0.23	1.37	0.74
Secrecy indicators	1.03	0.15	1.27	0.89
Working in lab'	4.40	0.94	4.25	0.94

These results would indicate that female ITT students were less likely to include relevant captions and less likely to draw both scientists as male. While the results also show that female ITT students were less likely to draw the scientists as Caucasian and much less likely to draw the scientists as middle-aged or elderly, these items had a low inter-coder reliability and should be interpreted with caution.

However, these tendencies are apparent in the drawing by a female trainee, 24 years old with a 'soft-pure' degree (see Figure 1). While the trainee uses captions, features of the drawing are consistent with the female tendency.

Figure 1 shows a drawing of two primary pupils (aged 8 and 9 respectively) engaged in scientific activity. The caption explains that the children are 'two scientists carrying out an experiment/investigation to explore friction'. The trainee has drawn one boy and one girl. A notable feature is that the girl is shown in a very active role, 'measuring the distance travelled by the car'. The drawing and the captions would indicate that the trainee has drawn one white and one black child.

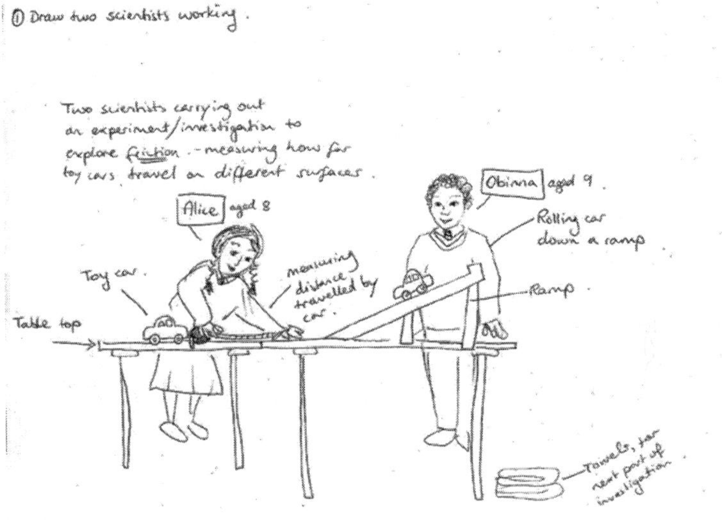

Figure 1: Two Scientists – Alice and Obima

C. Sample by Age

The 89 participants comprised 18 aged 20-24 years, 41 aged 25-39 years, 13 aged 30-34 years, 9 aged 35-39 years and 8 aged 40 years and over. The means and standard deviations were calculated for the variables of the sub-samples of age.

The positive and negative tendencies apparent for the entire sample (see Table 1) and for the sub-samples of gender (see Table 2) were largely consistent for the sub-samples of age. Further analysis by a series of two-sample t-tests disclosed only significant differences for wearing eye glasses:

- participants aged 20-24 were significantly less likely to depict scientists wearing glasses than participants aged 24-29 [t = 2.769, p = 0.0092, 33 df] and 30-34 [t= 2.525, p = 0.0175, 28 df]; and
- participants aged 40 and over were significantly less likely to depict scientists wearing glasses than participants aged 24-29 [t = 3.831, p = 0.0028, 11 df] and 30-34 [t = 3.588, p[= 0.0033, 13 df].

Table 3: Means and Standard Deviations for Fourteen Variables by Age

Variables	20-24	25-29	30-34	35-39	40->40
Wearing a lab' coat	3.39 (sd 1.59)	3.89 (sd 1.35)	3.82 (1.16)	3.81 (sd 0.91)	3.38 (sd 1.81)
Wearing eye glasses	2.50 (sd 1.56)	3.73 (sd 1.60)	3.77 (sd 1.24)	2.59 (sd 1.76)	1.63 (sd 1.39)
Facial hair	1.48 (sd 1.18)	1.81 (sd 1.39)	1.59 (sd 1.38)	1.30 (sd 0.56)	1.50 (sd 1.17)
Symbols of research	4.39 (sd 1.23)	4.67 (sd 0.91)	4.33 (sd 1.36)	4.63 (sd 1.11)	4.46 (sd 1.10)
Symbols of knowledge	2.72 (sd 1.70)	2.12 (sd 1.45)	2.00 (sd 1.52)	2.63 (sd 1.61)	2.71 (sd 1.68)
Technology	1.43 (sd 1.01)	1.33 (sd 0.83)	1.74 (sd 1.47)	1.93 (sd 1.40)	1.13 (sd 0.35)
Relevant captions	2.09 (sd 1.08)	2.32 (sd 1.40)	1.95 (sd 1.33)	3.04 (sd 1.21)	2.46 (sd 1.28)
Male gender only	1.81 (sd 1.50)	2.27 (sd 1.50)	2.28 (sd 1.34)	2.48 (sd 1.94)	3.21 (sd 1.64)
Female gender only	1.22 (sd 0.79)	1.41 (sd 0.64)	1.67 (sd 1.18)	1.19 (sd 0.44)	1.33 (sd 0.71)
Caucasian(s) only	3.48 (sd 0.47)	3.44 (sd 0.58)	3.33 (sd 0.47)	3.67 (sd 0.44)	3.46 (sd 0.71)
Middle-aged/elderly	2.48 (sd 0.66)	2.79 (sd 0.68)	2.87 (sd 0.63)	2.78 (sd 0.71)	3.04 (sd 0.95)
Mythic stereotypes	1.00 (sd 0.00)	1.17 (sd 0.55)	1.10 (sd 0.28)	1.15 (sd 0.24)	1.00 (sd 0.00)
Secrecy indicators	1.00 (sd 0.00)	1.11 (sd 0.58)	1.13 (sd 0.32)	1.04 (sd 0.11)	1.04 (sd 0.12)
Working in lab'	4.39 (sd 0.86)	4.37 (sd 0.97)	4.41 (sd 1.10)	4.41 (sd 0.81)	4.25 (sd 1.02)

D. Sample by First Degree Disciplines

Categorised by first degree disciplines, the 89 participants comprised 3 hard-pure students, 8 hard-applied students, 36 soft-pure students and 42 soft-applied students. The hard-pure and hard-applied categories were conflated, for analysis, to provide a hard category, and the means and standard deviations were calculated for the variables of the sub-samples of first degree discipline.

Table 4: Means and Standard Deviations for Fourteen Variables by First Degree Discipline

Variables	Hard		Soft-Pure		Soft-Applied	
	Mean	Sd	Mean	Sd	Mean	Sd
Wearing a lab' coat	3.79	1.19	3.60	1.51	3.82	1.31
Wearing eye glasses	3.42	1.38	2.83	1.78	3.42	1.65
Facial hair	2.06	1.60	1.34	0.97	1.77	1.34
Symbols of research	4.91	0.30	4.40	1.25	4.56	1.02
Symbols of knowledge	2.61	1.74	2.37	1.54	2.22	1.52
Technology	1.27	0.42	1.61	1.19	1.37	0.97
Relevant captions	2.76	1.45	2.32	1.23	2.17	1.34
Male gender only	2.18	1.66	2.30	1.53	2.30	1.57
Female gender only	1.21	0.43	1.38	0.76	1.42	0.83
Caucasian(s) only	3.64	0.41	3.14	0.60	3.45	0.52
Middle-aged/elderly	2.79	0.79	2.69	0.74	3.45	0.52
Mythic stereotypes	1.24	0.54	1.16	0.53	1.03	0.15
Secrecy indicators	1.06	0.20	1.16	0.63	1.01	0.05
Working in lab'	4.52	0.67	4.35	1.04	4.35	0.92

The positive and negative tendencies apparent for the entire sample (see Table 1), the sub-samples of gender (see Table 2) and the sub-samples of age (see Table 3) were largely consistent with the tendencies apparent in the sub-samples by degree discipline. Further analysis by a series of two-sample t-tests disclosed only a significant difference for 'Symbols of research': the mean for the hard category was significantly greater than that for the soft-pure category [$t = 2.241$, $p = 0.0302$, 43 df].

Drawings by two trainees may be contrasted: one drawing by a hard-pure graduate, a male 29 year-old (see Figure 2) and another by a soft-applied graduate, a female 26 year-old (Figure 3).

The names, clothing and hairstyles would indicate that the hard-pure graduate has drawn a male and a female scientist. Notably, Bob the male scientist is bald, bespectacled, wearing a laboratory coat and holding a test tube – a further instance of a white coat and a glass flask. Bob is complemented by a female scientist, Gertrude, who wears safety goggles, rather than spectacles, and a laboratory coat. The pose and expressions of these two scientists – broad (demented?) grin, open laboratory coat and hand in pocket – may imply that the female scientist is little more than an analogue of the male scientist. Both are implicated in the explosion (blue flames) from the test tube.

Figure 2: Two Scientists – Bob and Gertrude

Figure 3: Two Scientists in a Laboratory

The soft-applied graduate's drawing (see Figure 3) depicts a male and a female scientist, as indicated by hairstyles. Both scientists are wearing laboratory coats – pockets filled with pens - and the male scientist may be wearing safety goggles or spectacles. The drawing features an array of instruments: Bunsen burner, tripod, glass flask, test tube and thermometer. Notably, the male scientist is positioned behind the bench, directly engaged in an experiment, while the female scientist is positioned away from the bench holding a folder or a clipboard. The female scientist does not perform the same role as the male scientist: he is engaged in research while she appears responsible for recording results, a more supportive or subordinate role.

5. Discussion

Analyses of the data – whether by entire sample or sub-samples by gender, age or first degree discipline – demonstrate, by the presence of particular features, the persistence of the stereotypical image of the scientist wearing a laboratory coat, in a laboratory with laboratory equipment and scientific instruments: the "white coats, retort stands and glass flasks"[23] of yesteryear's saviour scientists. The feature of facial hair was, however, absent.

The absence from most trainees' drawings of such features as secrecy indicators and mythic stereotypes might suggest the demise of the stereotypical mad scientist. Intriguingly, the data indicate that trainees did not include technology such as computers in their drawings: such technology may have invoked the contemporary stereotype of the scientist as geek or nerd.[24]

The discernible gender of the two scientists drawn by all teacher-trainees indicated that the two scientists were definitely unlikely to be both female, and unlikely to be both male: the inference to be drawn is that the two scientists tended to be depicted as female and male. However, the depictions of female scientists were not necessarily positive: as Figure 2 shows, the female scientist may be depicted as an analogue of the male scientist; and, as Figure 3 show, the female scientist may be depicted as subordinate to the male scientist. Further research should be designed with consideration of these possibilities.

When the drawings are considered by the sub-samples of gender, male trainees were considerably likelier to draw two male scientists than were female trainees. Moreover, male trainees were likelier to draw two Caucasian scientists. The male teacher-trainees were apparently in greater peril of perpetuating the stereotypical perception of scientists as white and male. And this despite contemporary women scientists having been feted in the media, from Baroness Susan Greenfield, Fullerian Professor of Physiology at the University of Oxford and Director of the Royal Institution of Great Britain, to Dr Laura Grant, co-presenter of the television series 'The Big Experiment'.

This media coverage could be utilised by teachers – and teacher-trainers - consistent with the recommendation of Buldu that, in order to dispel stereotypical perceptions of scientists, teachers should "provide exposure to a variety of role models, including female scientists, scientists representing a larger array of cultures and scientists conducting research in both field and lab settings".[25] But, before engaging in such consciousness-raising for pupils and trainees, it is essential that teachers and teacher-trainers reflect whether they are, in thoughts and deeds, perpetuating the stereotypes of yesteryear.

Notes

[1] S Locke, 'Fantastically reasonable: ambivalence in the representation of science and technology in super-hero comics', *Public Understanding of Science*, vol.14-1, 2005, pp.25-46, p.42.
[2] J Uglow, 'Introduction: "Possibility"', in *Cultural Babbage: Technology, Time and Invention*, F Spufford and J Uglow (eds), Faber and Faber, London, 1996, pp.1-23, p.11.
[3] J Turney, *Frankenstein's Footsteps: Science, Genetics and Popular Culture*, Yale University Press, New Haven and London, 1998, p. 45.
[4] K Malik, *Man, Beast and Zombie: What Science Can and Cannot Tell Us about Human Nature*, Weidenfeld and Nicolson, London, 2000, p.91.
[5] D Swade, '"It will not slice a pineapple": Babbage, miracles and machines', in *Cultural Babbage: Technology, Time and Invention*, F Spufford and J Uglow (eds), Faber and Faber, London, 1996, pp.34-52, p.41.
[6] Ibid., p.34.
[7] M Mead and R Metraux, 'Image of scientists among high school students' *Science*, vol. 126, issue 3270, 1957, pp. 384-390.
[8] A Schlesinger deemed the period to be 'an age of anxiety' in *The Vital Center*, Houghton Mifflin, Boston, 1949, p.1, after W H Auden's poem *The Age of Anxiety*, Random House, New York, 1947, for which Auden was awarded the Pulitzer Prize in 1948, and Leonard Bernstein's Second Symphony, in 1949, *The Age of Anxiety*.
[9] D Longhurst, 'Science fiction: the dreams of men', *Gender, Genre and Narrative Pleasure*, D Longhurst (ed), Unwin Hyman, London, 1989, pp.192-212, p.196.
[10] D W Chambers, 'Stereotypic images of the scientist: Draw-A-Scientist Test', *Science Education*, vol.67-2, 1983, pp. 255-265.
[11] M O'Maoldomhnaigh and A Hunt, 'Some factors affecting the image of the scientist drawn by older primary school pupils', *Research in Science and Technological Education*, vol.6-2, 1988, pp.159-166.

C R Barman, K L Ostlund, C C Gatto and M Halferty, *Fifth grade students' perceptions about scientists and how they study and use science.* Paper presented at the Association for the Education of Science Teachers Conference, 1997.
[13] P Rodari, 'Science and scientists in the drawings of European children', *Journal of Science Communication*, vol.6-3, pp.1-12.
[14] I Rahm and P Charbonneau, 'Probing stereotypes through students' drawings of scientists', *American Journal of Physics*, vol. 65-8, 1997, pp.774-778.
[15] T E McDuffie, 'Scientists – geeks and nerds? Dispelling teachers' stereotypes of scientists', *Science and Children*, no. 39, 2001, pp. 16-19.
[16] M Buldu, 'Young children's perceptions of scientists: a preliminary study', Educational Researcher vol.48-1, 2006, pp.127-138, p. 130.
[17] O'Maoldomhnaigh and Hunt, op. cit.
[18] Chambers, op. cit.
[19] K D Finson, J B Beaver, and B L Cramond, 'Development and field test of a checklist for the Draw-A-Scientist Test', *School Science and Mathematics*, no. 95, 1995, pp.199-205.
[20] Barman et al, op. cit
[21] T Becher, 'The significance of disciplinary differences', *Studies in Higher Education*, vol. 19-2, 1994, pp.151-161, p.154.
[22] Swade, op. cit.
[23] Ibid.
[24] McDuffie, op. cit., p.16.
[25] Buldu, op. cit.

Bibliography

Barman, C.R., K.L. Ostlund, C.C. Gatto, and M. Halferty, *Fifth grade students' perceptions about scientists and how they study and use science.* Paper presented at the Association for the Education of Science Teachers Conference, 1997.

Becher, T., 'The significance of disciplinary differences', *Studies in Higher Education*, vol. 19-2, 1994, pp.151-161.

Buldu, M., 'Young children's perceptions of scientists: a preliminary study', Educational Researcher vol.48-1, 2006, pp.127-138.

Chambers, D.W., 'Stereotypic images of the scientist: Draw-A-Scientist Test', *Science Education*, vol.67-2, 1983, pp. 255-265.

Finson, K.D., J.B. Beaver, and B.L. Cramond, 'Development and field test of a checklist for the Draw-A-Scientist Test', *School Science and Mathematics*, no. 95, 1995, pp.199-205.

Locke, S., 'Fantastically reasonable: ambivalence in the representation of science and technology in super-hero comics', *Public Understanding of Science*, vol.14-1, 2005, pp.25-46.

Longhurst, D., 'Science fiction: the dreams of men', *Gender, Genre and Narrative Pleasure*, D. Longhurst (ed), Unwin Hyman, London, 1989, pp.192-212.

McDuffie, T. E., 'Scientists – geeks and nerds? Dispelling teachers' stereotypes of scientists', *Science and Children*, no. 39, 2001, pp. 16-19.

Malik, K., *Man, Beast and Zombie: What Science Can and Cannot Tell Us about Human Nature*, Weidenfeld and Nicolson, London, 2000.

Mead, M. and Metraux, R., 'Image of scientists among high school students' *Science*, vol. 126, issue 3270, 1957, pp. 384-390.

O'Maoldomhnaigh, M. and A. Hunt, 'Some factors affecting the image of the scientist drawn by older primary school pupils', *Research in Science and Technological Education*, vol.6-2, 1988, pp.159-166.

Rahm, I. and P. Charbonneau, 'Probing stereotypes through students' drawings of scientists', *American Journal of Physics*, vol. 65-8, 1997, pp.774-778.

Rodari, P., 'Science and scientists in the drawings of European children', *Journal of Science Communication*, vol.6-3, pp.1-12.

Swade, D., '"It will not slice a pineapple": Babbage, miracles and machines', in *Cultural Babbage: Technology, Time and Invention*, F. Spufford and J Uglow (eds) Faber and Faber, London, pp.34-52.

Turney, J., *Frankenstein's Footsteps: Science, Genetics and Popular Culture*, Yale University Press, New Haven and London, 1998.

Hazel Dorrington was born in Custom House, East London, and has lived and worked in the area ever since, barring a period when she attended the University of Sheffield. A primary school teacher for almost 15 years, she is currently the programme leader for the Primary Initial Teacher Training and also contributes to the Foundation Degree for Teaching Assistants.

John Trushell – originally from Yorkshire – studied at the University of Durham before teaching in primary and secondary schools in Durham, Sussex and London. He has lectured and conducted research in and around London – notably King's College London where he completed his PhD – for 25 years.

Constructing and Deconstructing Newly-qualified Teachers' Values in an Urban Context

Gerry Czerniawski

Abstract
This chapter is concerned with some of value positions and perspectives that London-based newly qualified teachers have identified as central to their professional identity. Interviews were carried out between 2001 and 2003 with nine London-based teachers from the end of their training into the first two years of their employment. The data is part of wider cross-national research carried out for a PhD thesis that was based on a grounded analysis of interview data with teachers working in cities in Norway, Germany and England as they moved through the process of becoming teachers from the end of their teacher training courses into the first two years as qualified teachers. The chapter shows how the professional values of newly qualified teachers are mediated in different ways through the situatedness of key values surrounding becoming a teacher in London. After clarifying what is meant by 'values' the chapter briefly describes the London context in which teachers and pupils are socialised. It then examines what Veenman[1] has termed the 'transition shock' experienced by teachers as they move from training to employment. Extracts from the interview data are presented and discussed highlighting the role that critical incidents[2] play in the authoritarianism that many believe is an essential (yet in some cases regrettable) aspect of becoming a teacher in London.

Key Words: Values; identity; professional socialisation; teachers

*****

1. Introduction

The term 'teachers' values' refers to what teachers regard as worthwhile. These values are constructed over time, through social interaction in the home, school, community and wider social setting. Values, in this broad sense, can include particular 'goals' (e.g. happiness and welfare), types of behaviour (e.g. keeping promises and treating people with respect) or certain qualities of character (e.g. generosity and loyalty).[3] Some of these values may be more stable and less resistant to change, while others will be more susceptible to influence. Before any decision is made to teach, some values (e.g. those concerning justice, fairness, respect for different people etc) will have already been established before embarking on teacher training programmes and may well influence this occupational choice. Values are carried by people but they can change, be extended and elaborated on through life experience. Values are also not of a piece but can come into tension and conflict with the values that circulate within the institutions in which people work. This in turn can create dissonance for teachers if these values differ from some of their own.

While I do not wish to exaggerate the difference between the urban and metropolitan setting of London with other cities in the UK, the city provides a dramatic socialising experience for both pupils and teachers alike. Children in London are more likely to live in households where no one is working than their counterparts in other cities in Britain.[4] London encompasses inner-city areas with marked socio-economic disadvantage accompanied by higher concentrations of social housing, higher relative population densities and greater ethnic diversity than other cities within the UK.[5] 28 per cent of pupils across London are known to be eligible for free school meals with this figure rising to 39 per cent in inner-London.[6] London's 2600 plus primary, secondary and special schools are host to over three hundred and sixty languages.[7] Children from minority ethnic families in London comprise 41 per cent of all London's children, accounting for 52 per cent of all those living in poverty.[8] It is these conditions that confront a workforce in London that, compared to the rest of the country, is relatively under-experienced. 20 per cent of pupils in London are taught by somebody with less than three years experience.[9] 3.8 per cent of teachers in England and Wales are unqualified and this figure rises to 10.2 per cent in London as a whole and up to 17 per cent in some London boroughs.[10] And yet, despite many of the socio-economic challenges that face many teachers and pupils in London, the average performance of sixteen-year-old students in this city at schools and colleges is now higher than the national average.[11] Equally surprising is the fact that the new professional standards for qualified teacher status make no reference to teachers who are being trained within urban and metropolitan locations such as London.[12] These points combine to create a dramatic arena for the newly qualified teacher to deconstruct the values they have on leaving their training institutions.

Teachers have reported experiencing 'transition shock'[13] when moving from teacher training into their first period of employment as a teacher. This period is one in which the values that they have constructed, by the time they have left university, are held up to scrutiny once they are working as a member of the teaching occupation.

Research suggests that the first few years of teaching are significant in relation to influencing teachers' values and, for many, the decision whether or not to remain within the profession. Writing about the Australian context, Ginns et al note that "the school and classroom experiences of beginning teachers may either catalyze or inhibit a lasting commitment to effective teaching".[14] The first few months have been described as a period of 'sink or swim',[15] a term used by Hatch to describe the isolated conditions of teachers' work. Referring to this initial period as one of 'survival', Shindler et al[16] argue that this time can involve feelings of inadequacy, stress, confusion and disillusionment. In the UK, Tickle is similarly pessimistic about many aspects of the transitions from teacher training to classroom teaching, arguing that many classrooms are sites where "the crucifixion of teachers' learning occurs".[17] However, not all accounts of the transition are painted in this negative light. Researching the views of beginning teachers in New South Wales on their induction into teaching, Carter[18] has suggested that the processes of becoming a teacher involve varying degrees of personal and professional growth. Many of his respondents' views of their futures in teaching[19] were optimistic as indeed were their perspectives on their induction. Nearly all of the beginning teachers involved in the study indicated that their values concerning teaching had changed over the course of their first year as a teacher to accommodate a broader social agenda. For many of the respondents in Carter's study, teaching was no longer simply about the delivery of a formal curriculum. Coping with, and learning from, the variety of challenges they had faced when learning to teach, had changed the way they viewed their work as teachers. Serving as carer, role model, guide and teacher of life skills had become key aspects of their work which they valued. Furthermore, Carter also found that an ethos of support and collegiality was associated with more optimistic experiences of beginning teachers and the effectiveness of school based induction. The transition from university to full-time work can therefore broaden the stock of values for some teachers as they encounter new roles, new professional contacts and different institutional expectations.

That said, the sociability (or lack of sociability) in teaching means that, in some settings, teachers, new to the profession are more likely to display a conservative tendency to "accept things as they are".[20] The acceptance of existing dominant values arguably takes place when the institutional setting that the new teacher joins is made up of a culture centred around a politically dominant group of experienced colleagues.[21] A desire to 'survive' and fit into the new culture they have entered can result in a reluctance to challenge the voiced 'wisdoms' of the dominant group and may also contribute to a reluctance to reflect upon the practice, theories and values inculcated during teacher training. The importance of the availability of other colleagues to talk to during this period has also been highlighted by Jones.[22] In her research with ten newly qualified secondary teachers in England, she explored the ways in which teachers reconciled their personal values with other, more experienced teachers with whom they worked during a process characterised by Tickle as full of 'turbulence' and 'discontinuities'.[23] With large class sizes, high contact hours, much paper-work and the quantity of meetings, it comes as a shock for many emerging teachers in London how little one-to-one time they actually have to 'care' for their students.[24] Jones argues that many teachers experience crises, conflicts and dilemmas and consequently feel a strong need to discuss the 'discrepancies arising from the mismatch of their original expectations [of being a teacher] and the reality encountered in the classroom'.[25]

Flores and Day[26] have also drawn attention to these shifts and mismatches in values that newly qualified teachers report. Their study looked at the professional identities of fourteen teachers in Portugal in their first two years on the job. They point to the value-shifts that some emerging teachers experience when juggling between the pedagogic values in their training that celebrated social constructivism and the individual child and the different values they encountered in the complex and demanding reality of the classroom:

> The teachers themselves recognised there was a shift in their teaching from a more inductive and student-centred approach towards a more 'traditional' and teacher-centred one (even if their beliefs pointed in the opposite direction) owing to problems associated with classroom management and student control.[27]

Their interviews with teachers flagged up accounts that highlighted gaps between 'ideals' (as student and student teachers) and the 'real world' of schools and classrooms (as teachers). Their data revealed a mismatch between emerging teachers' initial beliefs and images about teaching and the roles they were expected to perform as first year teachers. There was also a mismatch between what they think ought to happen and what they could actually do. These mismatches in values tended to affect those teachers who had failed to establish good working relationships with other colleagues which, in turn, led to reported feelings on behalf of the respondents of inadequacy, stress and a desire to leave the profession.

Teachers can sometimes experience dilemmas[28] or tensions between the competing priorities of communication of subject content, interest/concern for students and some of the priorities of the schools in which they work. For example, a teacher might be employed by a school that, in valuing its position within the English league tables, chooses to adopt policies that exclude some pupils from entering certain exams for fear of losing their competitive position. This can cause a dilemma for a teacher who holds more egalitarian values about education. Dilemmas can affect the values of teachers in different ways. Some time ago, Lacey[29] demonstrated, for example, how many teachers 'strategically comply' with the values of their place of work as they become socialised into the school culture, even though these values might not match their own deep-seated values and beliefs surrounding teaching. There is a difference between these more deep-seated values and the more procedural/organisational values that some teachers find themselves up against. In practice this means that, while they hold on to their own values, they give the impression[30] of adopting the values of the school. For example, a teacher who places little value on dress codes or adherence to particular school ceremonies might nevertheless conform to those values despite private reservations. Similarly, student behaviour (e.g. the chewing of gum, 'inappropriate' language etc) that contravenes the institutional values of the school but not those held by the teacher nevertheless might have to be dealt with despite reservations on the part of the teacher concerned. Lacey[31] has been highly influential in generating a model that captures the range of ways teachers adapt their own values to the new conditions in which they find themselves. He proposed three types of coping strategies: *strategic compliance* (referred to above), in which an individual complies with an authority figure's definition of the situation but retains private reservations; *internalized adjustment*, whereby an individual complies with a situation in both action and belief; and *strategic definition*, in which the individual brings about change within the formal power while retaining their own value systems. This latter strategy is one more suited to teachers employed in positions of power in which change can be brought about via the position of responsibility they hold. However, it can also be applied to teachers who, for a variety of reasons, might be in positions to influence the behaviour and practices of teachers with whom they work. For example Stephens et al[32] have noted that one of the many advantages of engaging trainee teachers at schools is access to new sources of ideas, resources and practices these schools can inherit.

'Critical incidents'[33] can also be experienced by the emerging teacher where tensions exist between their own and institutional values. For example, the teacher who is faced with a student taking drugs or one who has become pregnant is caught between values centred around her/his responsibility to the child, the parents, the school and the values enshrined within a legal institutional framework. Sometimes, with little opportunity to discuss the source of these dilemmas with other members of staff, these tensions can go unresolved. This can lead to crises for newly qualified teachers as they struggle, very often alone, to find a solution. These 'critical incidents' require the teacher to possess:

> physical, mental and emotional stamina in order to cope with the often painful process of reappraising their personal and professional beliefs and values and modifying their idealistic assumptions that contradicted the reality experienced in schools.[34]

The complex experience of being a newly qualified teacher is frequently subject to chance: placement in employment; institutional conditions of service; the views of senior teachers about their own roles as professional tutors and mentors; along with assessors, and managers and their conceptions of newly qualified teachers. Tickle not only recognises the complexities and ambiguities these emergent teachers may experience but also the futility of attempts to standardise such experiences:

> We should not, I believe, simply assume that continuity is achievable in some smooth, transitional sense, regulated by so-called standards of a career-entry profile. Rather we might be prepared for discontinuities; for new radically different experiences; for turbulence both between and within the pre-service, induction and in-service periods of professional education. We might even acknowledge and learn from the fact that in some aspects of social life in some communities initiation processes - rites of passage - are intended to disrupt, disturb and radically change the outlooks, commitments and even the identities of initiates.[35]

We can therefore see how turbulence may exist for many newly qualified teachers when the values that drive them are at odds with the values of the schools in which they gain first employment. We can also see how schools, for many new teachers, may well be sites of value conflict. This period of 'painful beginnings'[36] has been described as a:

> two-way struggle in which teachers try to create their own social reality by attempting to make their work match their personal vision of how it should be, whilst at the same time being subjected to powerful socialising forces of the school culture.[37]

This 'personal vision' can be made up of values that teachers have brought with them, both altruistic and pragmatic, prior to stepping into full-time employment. Values within the schools in which these teachers first work may come into conflict with the altruistic values these teachers initially possessed and many of the values they encountered within the universities in which they trained. For many trainees this period involves a transition from some of the idealism and the theoretical input they have received during their training to the relative isolation of being a full-time teacher. This transition can provide a variety of value tensions that emerging teachers encounter once into the 'reality shock' of the classroom.

2. Methodology

All teachers participating in this study were interviewed three times over a period of two years from 2001 to 2003. The teachers volunteered to take part and were chosen from a cohort of PGCE students at a teaching college in London. As secondary PGCE student teachers they would be expected to teach pupils aged between eleven and eighteen. The catchment area of this particular teaching college implied that all of the beginning teachers interviewed would be going on to work in a variety of different types of secondary school within the inner city area. The nine teachers were made up of three men and six women. Two of the women were 'African-Caribbean' with the remaining participants being white. These teachers ranged in age from their early twenties through to their early forties with some having worked in other fields before entering teaching. These teachers had been trained for employment in a variety of different types of secondary school and, indeed as pupils themselves, they came from a variety of secondary schools.

In the interviews that provide the data for this study, teachers identify some of the critical incidents that they had experienced in the London classroom. They also talk about the authoritarian stance which they feel they have to adopt as part of their professional identity. Both factors contribute to the particular cocktail mix of values that construct being a teacher in London.

3. Findings

Teachers' interpretations of 'critical incidents' have been important in understanding teacher values and practice.[38] A critical incident refers to an experience which, as defined by the respondent, results in a change of professional behavior.[39] Critical incidents are going to be experienced by many trainees early on in their professional lives at a time when they are probably less secure in terms of their professional values and their experience of managing children.

In her second interview, Carmen talked about how her maternal and subject specialist roles can merge, albeit uncomfortably, when there are 'critical incidents'.

> Carmen (second interview).
> Just recently we had a boy who had been off school for several days. A good boy from a caring family and he hasn't been into school now for long time and he always attends. I was worried and called home and was told that he had witnessed his older brother being attacked at the door by a gang of youths with a baseball bat. He was beaten in front of his family and what do you do. I have spent so much

> time worrying and trying to get a councillor and police and his family are afraid for him. And this worries me and when I see his friends in class it's difficult not to think of him and try to get them to get him to come back.

Such critical incidents, as experienced by emerging teachers like Carmen, can lead to crises for some newly qualified teachers as they struggle, very often alone, to find a solution. Such incidents require the teacher to possess physical, mental and emotional stamina in order to cope with the often painful process of reappraising their personal and professional values in light of the real experience of being a teacher. Often these vivid experiences seem remote from the ideas of training that they have only so recently left behind them. The emotional involvement that Carmen has with her pupils was not uncommon amongst the other teachers that I interviewed. For example, Liz was enjoying her job as a teacher but described a particular incident with one of her pupils being forced into an arranged marriage.

> Liz (second interview).
> She had said 'no' she did not want to and they had also told her that if she even talked to a boy she would get pregnant so that is why she would not sit next to or talk to any boy at school. And we were trying to make her fit in by asking everyone to talk to her and wondering why she would not talk back. We had to draw pictures of a penis because she did not know what one was and she was really scared about getting married. So I had to report it to the social services and went through their social services at school and I sat with her and drew pictures with her and she went home and came back the next day and said 'yes' she did want to leave home and is now in a women's refuge… I get angry because surely this is not my job. I mean, a part may be but this continually happens.

Liz, at the time of this incident, was relatively inexperienced as a teacher and this situation involved a variety of cultural values that collided with her own emerging professional values as a teacher. Incidents like these drain the physical, mental and emotional reserves of energy that are so essential to these emerging teachers. While anger is the emotion that Liz expresses as the outcome of her situation, it is a sense of frustration that Edward (below) experienced in a situation that called for immense emotional intelligence[40] on his part as one of his pupils was pulled out of school weeks before she was about to complete her courses:

> Edward (third interview).
> It does get to you and sometimes it's so hard to remain 'pc'. My school has a multi-cultural mix and I had one girl come up to me and tell me that her friend was no longer at college because she was being married off. I had taught this girl and she had been in my tutor group. She told me that perhaps I could talk to the family as I knew them. I spoke to the tutor and eventually went around there… They were of course sweet and offered me tea and said all the right things and agreed that she would come back to school and I felt good, felt I had really achieved something by doing the visit. She of course never came back into college. I felt gutted by that.

Emotional intelligence is the ability to identify, understand, experience, and express human emotions.[41] Regardless of whether or not it was 'right' for Edward to take the action that he did, his immediate emotional response was to get involved and - by feeling 'good' - confirmed his belief that this was part of his professional role.[42] Sadly, however, he was not rewarded with the outcome for which he had hoped.

Critical incidents are more likely to be experienced by teachers in London than in other metropolitan areas.[43] We see, in these extracts, examples of teachers who care immensely about the work that they do and the young people with whom they are engaged. We also see teachers who are working within a context where, very early on in their careers, they may well be dealing with acute dilemmas as part of their daily job as teachers. As such, the role that is being constructed for these teachers (e.g. through their university training, policy documents, textbooks etc) is being powerfully deconstructed by the realities of the London classroom.

The complexities of classrooms in many London schools is such that many of these teachers are trying, emotionally, to deal with their early experiences of being a teacher and are feeling coerced into being repressive because they are facing children who, in many cases, are not very pro-school. There is, for example, an almost wistful sense as Roby (below) conveys this desire for an authoritarianism which he feels that he lacks.

> Roby (second interview).
> Once they've got to the age where they are questioning whether they really want to learn RE [Religious Education] or are not interested in learning Religious Studies, that's when I have problems controlling them. Then, obviously, they are at that age where they tend to be a bit more rebellious anyway. So that's probably a job that I find very difficult to do. I think I am awful at it but, you know, I

> don't have that 'don't-fuck-with-me' aura that some teachers seem to be able to cultivate. So, you know, teaching year ten boys I really don't look forward to.

The desire for and value placed on the 'don't-fuck-with-me' aura is a feature of the contrived distance that makes up the professional identities of many teachers in England.[44] Roby is not alone in his desire to be able to 'turn-on' this form of 'authoritarianism'. Eleanor, in her second interview, talks almost with relish of her ability to be 'evil and strict'.

> Eleanor (second interview):
> I am not that friendly with any of my classes now, and they used to come to me with all sorts of problems… like if I shouted at them or really mad at them they could tell and they would do the work straight away... with my younger classes I am really really evil and strict. Last year I was little bit more smiley and it got to me with some of my classes. I really had to hammer down to make them do some work… you have to be a complete cow bag.

There are clear ambiguities in this short quote as Eleanor deconstructs her teaching role. What 'got to' her is her inability to cope with curriculum delivery with a more humanitarian approach to teaching that she, on one level, believes should be part of her role as a teacher. Her inability to juggle these roles results in her valuing the formation of the contrived distance and authoritarianism that some of these teachers believe to be a part of their role. In contrast to Roby and Eleanor, Sylvia's approach to students (below) seems relatively unthreatening, despite her use of the word 'scary' and her acknowledgment that this is desirable at times.

> Sylvia (second interview).
> I think some aspects of classroom management are authoritarian… If I am talking and trying to make a point I don't like it if people are talking or talking at the back of the class. I think it is rude and they will miss out on something quite important… It might be that I just look at the person or I may walk over very quietly and ask them very quietly. I have found that the quieter I use my voice the more scary it can come over. They know I mean business and if I have to keep them back they know that the systems in place to deal with them will be used by me.

Finally, Edward brings the issue of gender to the fore when comparing differences in how he believes males and females deal with behavioural issues. He talks of a particular difficult year nine class he covered because of an absent teacher.

> Edward (third interview).
> I do not have to do anything… I think as a man you can appear more threatening when you need to and the voice can be used to command fear in a way a woman cannot do. That's a huge generalisation and there are some scary women teachers here but in general I think that's the case.

Many of the sample interviewed in this study are working in schools in often complex and challenging circumstances and where they feel torn between wanting to deliver their subject and maintain caring relationships with their students. There is, however, also a sense in these interview extracts that, within the culture of teaching, it is acceptable to cultivate an authoritarian stance. More importantly, it is seen by some as a desirable and perhaps necessary element to the professional 'tool kit' that a London-based teacher can deploy.

5. Discussion

Although all nine teachers interviewed in this study were teaching in London, their schooling backgrounds varied from comprehensive, to grammar school, to private, constructing a rich and varied set of values relating to what 'being a teacher' might conceivably mean. This means that, during their training, these teachers will have encountered (directly or through seminar discussions) a variety of approaches to teaching and learning in very different contexts. The English PGCE school-based requirement (24 weeks secondary) is significantly higher, in terms of time spent in school, than any other European country.[45] These factors mean that trainee teachers in London are likely to have greater experience of a wider variety of schooling than their European counterparts teaching in other European cities. However, while these London teachers' values range from the subject-centred and authoritarian to more broadly humanitarian and child-centred, the relentless pace of teaching in London combined with a variety of critical incidents often encourages these teachers to become more authoritarian as they emerge as teachers.

Many of these emerging London-based teachers also contest and de-construct their own values during their first teaching posts. Their values are thrown into disarray once they leave the cocoon of their training institutions and enter their first full-time period of employment. Values implicit within learner-centred classroom approaches to teaching, frequently advocated by teacher training colleges may place the new teacher in a difficult position when those same values are not shared by those in their school.[46] This can be a source of tension and ambiguity[47] for the newly qualified teacher. There were for example, in this sample, teachers who were caught between conflicting values of the kind of teachers who they would like to be, the kinds of teachers who they thought they were, what their training and the institution in which they worked told them about the role of the professional teacher and the form of assessment teachers needed to deploy with their students. Cultural differences in different locations play an important role in determining what is considered acceptable pedagogic practice. Teaching cultures in many schools in London actively encourage the authoritarianism and 'contrived distance'[48] that some of the teachers in this study have highlighted.

The frequency of 'critical incidents'[49] that many teachers reported influenced their notion of teaching as a form of social work. This caring aspect of the work that they do was not something relished by the majority of trainees interviewed. Care as a value, for these teachers, clustered around both the pastoral and academic roles for which they are employed. The tutorial responsibilities that some English schools place on these teachers endorse both these functions. Teachers in this sample recognised care as being of significant value in their professional repertoire. However, for some, a sense of caring was also a means of gaining better academic results and, therefore, a response to the particular form of accountability associated with being a professional teacher in England. In other words, a 'good'[50] teacher is more likely to be one that has high retention and achievement rates rather than necessarily being a greater 'carer'. This last point is a source of concern for this author and something that politicians and policy-makers in England should take on board in light of the current 'crisis of childhood'.[51]

Notes

[1] S Veenman, 'Perceived Problems of Beginning Teachers', *Review of Educational Research*, vol. 54-2, 1984, pp.143-178

[2] See 1) G Ketchtermans, 'Teachers and their career story: a biographical perspective', in *Research on Teacher Thinking: Understanding Professional Development.* 2) C Day, J Calderhead and P Denicolo, (eds), Falmer Press, London, 1993, pp.198-220. 2) P Woods, *Critical Events in Teaching and Learning*, Falmer Press, London, 1993. 3) M Jones, 'Reconciling personal and professional values and beliefs with the reality of teaching: findings from an evaluative case study of 10 newly qualified teachers during their induction', *Teacher Development*, vol. 7-3, 2003, pp.385-401.

[3] A Cribb and N Barber, *Developing Pharmacy Values: Stimulating the Debate - A Discussion Paper*, Kings' College, London, and School of Pharmacy, London, May 2000, Kings College London

[4] R Lupton and A Sullivan, 'The London context', in *Education in a Global City – Essays from London*, T Brighouse and L Fullick (eds) Institute of Education, London, 2007, pp.8-39.

[5] D Hall, A Ash and C Raffo, *Initial Teacher Training and the Transition to Teaching in Urban Schools*, paper presented at the British Educational Research Association Conference, School of Education, University of Manchester, Manchester, 16th – 18th September 2004.

[6] S Bubb and P Earley, 'The school workforce in London', in *Education in a Global City – Essays from London*, T Brighouse and L Fullick (eds) Institute of Education, London, 2007, pp.147-169.

[7] P Baker and J Eversley, *Multilingual Capital*, Battlebridge Publications, London, 2000.

[8] Lupton and Sullivan, op. cit., p.11.

[9] Bubb and Earley, op. cit., p.151.

[10] Ibid., p.152.

[11] T Brighouse T, 'The London challenge – a personal view', in *Education in a Global City – Essays from London*, T Brighouse and L Fullick (eds) Institute of Education, London, 2007, pp. 71-95.

[12] Training and Development Agency, *The Professional Standards for Teachers – Qualified Teacher Status*, TOA313/06.07/COL, The Training and Development Agency for Schools, London, 2007.

[13] Veenman op. cit.

[14] I Ginns, A Heirdsfield, B Atweh and J Watters, 'Beginning teachers becoming professional through action research', *Educational Action Research*, vol. 9-1, 2001, pp. 111-133, at p.111.

[15] JA Hatch, 'What preservice teachers can learn from studies of teachers work', *Teaching and Teacher Education*, vol. 15-2, 1999, pp.229-242.

[16] J Shindler, A Jones, C Taylor and H Cadenas, *Don't Smile till Christmas: Examining the Immersion of new Teachers into Existing Urban School Climates*, Charter College of Education, Los Angeles, 2004.

[17] L Tickle, *Opening Windows, Closing Doors: Ethical dilemmas in educational action research.* Blackwell, Oxford, 2002 p. 2.

[18] M Carter, *Beginning Teachers and Workplace Learning: An exploration of the process of becoming a teacher*, paper presented at the 13th Annual International Congress for School Effectiveness and Improvement (ICSEI), 2000, New South Wales Department of Education and Training.

[19] Six schools were used as case studies to investigate working conditions and practices, to provide more detailed insight into the range of factors affecting the process of becoming a teacher, and to examine the nature of the learning arising from teachers' induction experiences. Beginning teachers and their

mentors and supervisors at each of these schools were interviewed on four occasions during the course of the 1998 school year.
[20] K Bleach, 'Off to a flying start? Induction procedures for newly qualified teachers in secondary schools in the Republic of Ireland', *Mentoring and Tutoring*, no. 6, 1998, pp. 55-65, at p.57.
[21] A Hargreaves, 'The emotional practice of teaching', *Teaching and Teacher Education*, vol. 14-8, 1999, pp. 835-854.
[22] M Jones, 'Reconciling personal and professional values and beliefs with the reality of teaching: findings from an evaluative case study of 10 newly qualified teachers during their induction', *Teacher Development*, vol. 7-3, 2003, pp.385-401.
[23] Tickle, op. cit.
[24] G Czerniawski, *Self, Setting and Context – A Study of the Professional Socialisation of Beginning and Newly Qualified Teachers*, a dissertation submitted in partial fulfilment of the requirements for the award of MA Sociology of Education, Department of Policy Studies, London University Institute of Education, 1999.
[25] Jones, op. cit., p.394.
[26] MA Flores and C Day, 'Contexts which shape and reshape new teachers' identities: a multi-perspective study', *Teaching and Teacher Education*, no. 22, 2006, pp. 219-232.
[27] Ibid., p.227.
[28] CP Lewis-Shaw, 'Measuring values in classroom teaching and learning', *Perspectives on Practice and Meaning in Mathematics and Science Classrooms*, D Clarke (ed.), Springer, New York 2001, pp.155-196.
[29] C Lacey, *The Socialisation of Teachers*, Methuen, London, 1977.
[30] E Goffman, *The Presentation of Self in Everyday Life*, Doubleday Anchor, New York, 1959.
[31] Lacey, op. cit.
[32] P Stephens, F Egil Tonnessen and C Kyriacou, 'Teacher training and teacher education in England and Norway: a comparative study of policy goals', *Comparative Education*, vol.40-1, 2004, pp.109-130
[33] Jones, op. cit.
[34] Ibid., p. 398.
[35] Tickle, op. cit., p.11.
[36] M Huberman, *The Lives of Teachers*, Teachers College Press, New York, 1993.
[37] C Day, *Developing Teachers: The Challenges of Lifelong Learning*, Falmer Press, London, 1999, p.59.
[38] Ketchterman, op. cit., Woods, op. cit. and Jones, op. cit.
[39] Jones, op. cit.
[40] D Goleman, *Emotional Intelligence*, Bantam Books, New York, 1995.
[41] Ibid.

[42] J Arthur, J Davison and M Lewis, *Professional Values and Practice – achieving the Standards for QTS*, Routledge-Falmer, Oxford, 2005.
[43] Stephens, et al. op. cit.
[44] Ibid.
[45] M Maguire and J Dillon, 'Developing as a student teacher', in *Becoming a Teacher – Issues in Secondary Teaching*, J Dillon and M Maguire (eds), Open University Press, Buckingham, 2001, pp3-10.
[46] Shindler et al, op. cit.
[47] Tickle, op cit.
[48] Stephens et al, op. cit.
[49] Jones, op. cit.
[50] Arthur et al, op. cit.
[51] D Haydon, 'Crisis in the classroom', in *Childhood in Crisis*, P Scraton (ed), Routledge, London, 2004, pp.31-42. and P Scraton (ed), *Childhood in Crisis*, Routledge, London, 2004.

Bibliography

Arthur, J., J. Davison and M. Lewis, *Professional Values and Practice – achieving the Standards for QTS*, Routledge-Falmer, Oxford, 2005.

Baker, P. and J. Eversley, *Multilingual Capital*, Battlebridge Publications, London, 2000.

Bleach, K., 'Off to a flying start? Induction procedures for newly qualified teachers in secondary schools in the Republic of Ireland', *Mentoring and Tutoring* No.6, 1998, pp.55-65.

Brighouse T., 'The London challenge – a personal view', in *Education in a Global City – Essays from London*, T. Brighouse and L. Fullick (eds), Institute of Education, London, 2007, pp. 71-95.

Bubb S. and P. Earley P., 'The school workforce in London' *Education in a Global City – Essays from London*, T. Brighouse and L. Fullick (eds), Institute of Education, London, 2007, pp.147-169.

Carter, M., *Beginning Teachers and Workplace Learning: An exploration of the process of becoming a teacher*, paper presented at the 13th Annual International Congress for School Effectiveness and Improvement (ICSEI), 2000, New South Wales Department of Education and Training.

Cribb, A. and N Barber, *Developing Pharmacy Values: Stimulating the Debate - A Discussion Paper*, Kings' College, London, and School of Pharmacy, London, May 2000 Kings College London

Czerniawski, G. *Self, Setting and Context – A Study of the Professional Socialisation of Beginning and Newly Qualified Teachers*, a dissertation submitted in partial fulfilment of the requirements for the award of MA Sociology of Education, Department of Policy Studies, London University Institute of Education, 1999.

Day C., *Developing Teachers: The Challenges of Lifelong Learning*, Falmer Press, London, 1999.

Flores, M.A. and Day, C., 'Contexts which shape and reshape new teachers' identities: a multi-perspective study', *Teaching and Teacher Education*, No. 22, 2006, pp. 219-232.

Ginns, I., A. Heirdsfield, B. Atweh and J. Watters, 'Beginning teachers becoming professional through action research', *Educational Action Research*, Vol 9-1, 2001 pp. 111-133.

Goffman E., *The Presentation of Self in Everyday Life*, (Doubleday Anchor) New York, 1959.

Goleman D., *Emotional Intelligence*, Bantam Books, New York, 1995.

Hall, D. A. Ash and A. Raffo, *Initial Teacher Training and the Transition to Teaching in Urban Schools*, paper presented at the British Educational Research Association Conference, School of Education, University of Manchester, Manchester, 16th – 18th September 2004.

Hargreaves, A., 'The emotional practice of teaching', *Teaching and Teacher Education*, Vol 14-8, 1999, pp. 835-854.

Hatch, J.A., 'What preservice teachers can learn from studies of teachers work', *Teaching and Teacher Education*, vol. 15-2, 1999, pp.229-242.

Haydon, D., 'Crisis in the classroom', in *Childhood in Crisis*, P. Scraton (ed), Routledge, London, 2004, pp.31-42.

Huberman, M., *The Lives of Teachers*, Teachers College Press, New York, 1993.

Jones, M., 'Reconciling personal and professional values and beliefs with the reality of teaching: findings from an evaluative case study of 10 newly qualified teachers during their induction', *Teacher Development*, vol. 7-3, 2003, pp.385-401.

Ketchtermans, G., 'Teachers and their career story: a biographical perspective', in *Research on Teacher Thinking: Understanding Professional Development*, C. Day, J. Calderhead and P. Denicolo, (eds), Falmer Press, London, 1993, pp.198-220.

Lacey. C., *The Socialisation of Teachers*, Methuen, London, 1997.

Lewis-Shaw, C.P., 'Measuring values in classroom teaching and learning', *Perspectives on Practice and Meaning in Mathematics and Science Classrooms*, D. Clarke (ed.), Springer, New York, 2001, pp.155-196.

Lupton, R. and A. Sullivan, 'The London context', in *Education in a Global City – Essays from London*, T. Brighhouse and L. Fullick (eds) Institute of Education, London, 2007, pp.8-39.

Maguire, M. and J. Dillon, 'Developing as a student teacher', in *Becoming a Teacher – Issues in Secondary Teaching*, J. Dillon and M. Maguire (eds), Open University Press, Buckingham, 2001, pp.3-10.

Scraton P., *Childhood in Crisis*, Routledge, London, 2004.

Shindler J., A. Jones, C. Taylor and H. Cadenas, *Don't Smile till Christmas: Examining the Immersion of new Teachers into Existing Urban School Climates*, Charter College of Education, Los Angeles, 2004.

Stephens, P., F. Egil Tonnessen and C. Kyriacou, 'Teacher training and teacher education in England and Norway: a comparative study of policy goals', *Comparative Education*, Vol.40-1, 2004, pp.109-130

Tickle, L., *Opening windows, closing doors: Ethical dilemmas in educational action research.* Blackwell, Oxford, 2002

Training and Development Agency, *The Professional Standards for Teachers – Qualified Teacher Status*, TOA313/06.07/COL, The Training and Development Agency for Schools, London, 2007.

Veenman, S., 'Perceived Problems of Beginning Teachers', *Review of Educational Research*, vol. 54-2, 1984, pp.143-178.

Woods, P., *Critical Events in Teaching and Learning*, Falmer Press, London, 1993.

Gerry Czerniawski worked for ten years in the multicultural environment of the London Borough of Newham - teaching Socila Sciences and Humanities at secondary and post-sixteen levels – before gradually moving into teaching political sciences and education within higher education (The Open University, University of Northampton, London Metropolitan University and Institute of Education, London). Gerry's PhD (King's College, London) focuses on the formation of values and teacher identities.

"If You Could Wave a Magic Wand…" - Special Educational Needs in London: Diversity, Complexity and Context

Suzanne Mackenzie

Abstract
This chapter presents an analysis of data collected - by interviews and focus groups - from staff working in special educational needs in London. The analysis highlighted challenges to respondents' professionalism such as lack of time, paperwork and behaviour. The frustrations of the demands of policy - and how this impacted on working with outside agencies, parents, teaching assistants and others - were common and powerful themes within the respondents' experiences. The most significant challenge for respondents in the study was working with colleagues: all participants - teachers, special educational needs co-ordinators and teaching assistants - identified communication problems, mutual misunderstandings and a mismatch of expectations as major barriers to carrying out their roles. The daily demands of working in complex local authority and school environments impacted upon their ability to carry out their roles effectively. The conclusion of the chapter identifies the significance of the study for the implementation of policies such as Every Child Matters and the Children's Plan: crucial to the success of such policies are staffing to support special educational needs, internal communication and effective external liaison. This study demonstrates the impact of demands upon staff on a daily basis and how working in special educational needs in London brings its own particular challenges.

Key Words: Special educational needs, special educational needs coordinators, teachers, teaching assistants.

*****

1. Introduction

The role of the special educational needs co-ordinator [SENCO] has been given greater attention recently in Government announcements on special educational needs [SEN], partly due to the SENCO's ostensibly pivotal role in SEN policy and strategy.[1] There also has been much discussion of the role of other staff in the provision of support for children with SEN and disabilities as a result of reforms such as Every Child Matters[2] and the Children's Plan.[3]

Previous research has indicated variations in the manner in which those staff who work in SEN carry out their diverse roles, and this diversity - combined with time constraints - has meant that the working in SEN is enormously demanding.

Research findings have highlighted paperwork and the time involved in paperwork as major burdens on those working in SEN.[4] Of more significance to SENCOs, however, was the attitudes of other staff: relationships with other colleagues were problematic for special education teachers in their workplace settings. General education teachers did not understand the role and responsibilities of a special education teacher.[5] The attitudes of other colleagues made a difference as to whether staff would remain working in special needs education. In particular, the decision to stay within special needs education corresponded strongly with support from effective headteachers.[6] In previous research,[7] special needs teachers frequently reported feeling only 'tolerated' by their colleagues and headteachers, and felt that many of their colleagues did not understand their roles or practice. Further, some SEN staff reported facing outright hostility from their colleagues, particularly from those who resented the accommodations that special educators were asked to make for special needs students.[8] This hostility and toleration could be compounded by issues relating to the gender of staff who work in SEN.[9] Moreover, the challenging behaviour of special needs students has been reported to be burdensome to those staff who work in SEN.[10]

The following research aims to complement existing research by examining the daily experiences of working in SEN in diverse and challenging settings within London. The study will examine the effects of:

- paperwork, time, meeting parents' needs and behaviour issues in challenging schools and local authorities in the context of limited budgets and increased pupil need; and
- supporting pupils with SEN for staff working in diverse contexts.

The study will also consider the challenges of working in a 'gendered' area of school services and the implications this has for the self-conception of those working in SEN.

2. Methodology

Evidence of increasing diversity and complexity of contexts was investigated by the use of three focus groups, comprising one group of teachers, one group of students, and one mixed group of teaching assistants [TAs] and SENCOs. The total sample size of the London-based study was thirty-three. The study used an opportunity sample based on responses to an advert placed in two major special needs magazines, the magazine of a teacher union, a personal letter to all SENCOs in an inner London borough, and an electronic request that went to all students in the university in which the author was working.

Subsequently, eight SENCOs, a specialist sensory support teacher and three TAs were interviewed, and six respondents were interviewed by e-mail. The students were undergraduates attending a London university studying modules on special educational needs and inclusion. Many were also working as TAs. The transcripts of the focus groups and interviews produced the data for analysis via NVivo and were informed by Huberman's 1983 study, *The Lives of Teachers.*[11]

The use of qualitative techniques provided interviewees with the opportunity of telling their diverse stories in their own ways. The diversity of each story illustrated clearly the complexity of working in SEN within London. This helped in the reconstruction and interpretation of meaningful features and incidents in respondents' lives.[12] Within qualitative educational research, there is a developing body of thought concerning the connection between teachers' private lives, the personal and biographical aspects of their careers, and how these interact and shape professional reflections and actions.[13] The literature on teachers' work and professional lives makes it clear that expertise, capability, personal and professional biography, situational, emotional and psychological factors, as well as the complexity of the pupils whom they teach, and changes over time and circumstance, influence their effectiveness of teachers.[14] The longer project from which this chapter is drawn focused on many of the above challenges faced by those working in SEN, but this present chapter focuses more on the practical and everyday issues around time, paperwork and behaviour management, and moves on to look and school and local authority contextual issues.

All participants were asked to complete a consent form and were issued with an information sheet for the project. Respondents were informed that they had the right to withdraw from the project at any point. Due to the nature of the responses, some participants were concerned that they might be identified by their school or their local authority. Therefore, all identifying information has been changed, including names of participants, schools and local authorities. This perhaps has led to a degree of artificiality in the names substituted in the chapter, but this was felt to be necessary in order to render the participants completely anonymous.

3. Day-to-day challenges of working in SEN

The section that follows will discuss key issues that emerged from the data. Paperwork and time, parents and pupil behaviour were particularly demanding in the context of working in London, in schools with pupils (and parents) with complex and diverse needs.

A. Paperwork and Time

Time and paperwork were mentioned by only seven of the respondents as significant issues, which is surprising given that previous research findings have highlighted these factors as major burdens on those working in SEN.[15] The respondents who perceived paperwork as a significant issue were SENCOs, which is less surprising, as paperwork is often perceived to be the most arduous aspect of the role.[16]

One SENCO, Colin, discussed the importance of having time out of the classroom to carry out his duties as SENCO whilst also maintaining some teaching.

> Colin (Primary SENCO).
> I think you cannot do the role of the SENCO in your own class. It needs to be a non-class based job - or if you get enough time out of class - to do the job to the best of your ability. Like I said before, some days are very quiet but some days can be very very busy and they demand things, they put demands on the job like deadlines, you can't do that… In saying that I do believe that SENCOs should have a role in the classroom in a sense of maybe booster classes or small group teaching. I think that's important, to have a role in raising attainment across the whole school…
> I've met a lot of SENCOs who don't teach and I find that hard to believe really, but they say, "It's all the paperwork and everything." Yeah, it's true, but you're still a teacher at the end of the day.

The significance of paperwork was noted, although some staff appeared to be moving towards having an assistant to carry out some aspects of the tasks.

> Colin (Primary SENCO).
> I think [that the role of the SENCO] can be too demanding. I think it's important. I think we should have assistants to SENCOs that deal that with the paperwork. I mean, I have an assistant for an hour a week and I wanted an assistant to help with the paperwork in a sense of, "Here's the paperwork, this is where it goes in the folder, and can you please ensure it goes in the folder."'

The frustration related to the paperwork needed for statutory assessment was remarked, and how much time it took to access any resources that might be made available in inner London local authorities, as demonstrated by this interview with Colin (Primary SENCO).

> *What kind of things do you like least about working in special needs?*
>
> The process, the amount of time it takes, frustration that you have to fill in a long application for exceptional resource funding when it's blatantly clear there is a problem, and also the fact that you get - if you do get accepted for it - that you have to wait a whole term for it.
>
> *If you were to change the process what kind of things would you change?*
>
> The application and the length of time it takes to actually get to the professionals in that are required.

Paperwork was seen as particularly important due to the increasing number of children identified as having SEN in London schools:

> Colin (Primary SENCO).
> …the person on the other end of the line or in your meeting expects you to know what the children are like, especially if you are on the transition and they're going to year 7. Depending on the size of your school they've got about 500 pupils and they want to know probably about 150 that are on the special needs register, school action, whatever, IEP, and they expect you to know what the difficulties are and everything.

Three SENCOs commented that the paperwork was a deterrent to those considering a SENCO role. As articulated by one of them:

> Colin, (Primary SENCO).
> I think [teachers] will be put off by the amount of paperwork and what it requires.

Perception of lots of paperwork put off one particular teacher in wanting to move into the SENCO role:

> Penelope (Secondary classroom teacher).

> To be blunt, [what I like the least is] all the paperwork and having to struggle with reticent colleagues who don't want to teach students with SEN. I'm not too keen on [the SENCO role] anymore.

Although paperwork was seen as somewhat burdensome, its importance was recognized:

> Jane (Primary TA).
> While some of [the SENCO role] is paper-pushing it's important paper: pushing it's getting the resources in, getting the money there to pay for the support.

One SENCO noted that what she liked least about working in SEN was that it was 'Bureaucratic, too much paperwork'.

> Linda (Secondary SENCO).
> I wouldn't encourage anyone to be a teacher these days but if they were seriously thinking about it I'd explain a typical day's/week's work as being a SENCO and the demands put upon you, the difficulties in trying to juggle things in the workplace but emphasise the rewards when you see something "click" in a child. I like what I do despite the frustrations!

Another SENCO, when asked about what could be changed, noted the constraints of time and paperwork.

> Caroline (Primary SENCO).
> I think as well - because there are always so many things that teachers are asked to do - that is difficult. So I think giving people more time in a less crowded day - so that they could, you know, think of a bit more about the SEN children in the class. And I suppose you would reduce the amount of paperwork because that is kind of changing slowly - some of it is beginning to disappear. Yeah, more time.

Overall, paperwork was recognised as an important (although burdensome) aspect of working in SEN, due to the increasing numbers of children with SEN in London schools, and the consequent complexity of liaison with external agencies.

B. Parents

The challenges of working with parents in Inner London schools was addressed by two respondents, particularly in the context of increasing pupil mobility and diversity.

> Colin (Primary SENCO).
> What I find very difficult is explaining to parents of different cultures, the… especially the Asian culture. And you have the language barrier problem but, fortunately, I've been lucky in that we've got translators within our school that can do that… I think that's going to be an ongoing problem in Eastborough because they're so many cultures. [Pupil mobility] makes it worse in the sense that you want to make the referral but before the actual referral gets back to you they've gone and it's a shame because it's a long process. It takes about four weeks to get a reply back and, when you get a reply, you think, 'Yeah, things can get moving.' That's if they moved to another school within the borough. Okay, you're in the same borough but you have to transfer all that information to that person child then have to start building new relationships and it just goes round in a circle.

The respondent went on to discuss a recent difficulty with a parent and the frustrations this could bring.

> You're so frustrated and you think to yourself, "Is it actually worth all the time for?" I mean, an example was there was [a] meeting arranged, a lot of people gave their time and the parent didn't turn, wasn't going to turn up, so I actually had to persuade him to. So I rang up and said, "Come down here now because there's a massive meeting." And that was harsh but, at the end of the day, it's for the child.

Two respondents, however, did point out that working with parents could be a rewarding part of the job.

> Siobhan (Primary SENCO).
> The parents do still email me now and ring me and my mobile number. You have a relationship with the parents, properly. It's not just a job, you know. They know [that] you love their children and you want… and you know my other colleagues. That's why I work in the field.

> Lorna (Secondary SENCO).
> Back to what [I] was saying about the SENCO role, a lot of it is awareness-raising, information-giving, being an advocate for students and perhaps the parents who don't always access the usual channels.

C. Behaviour

Only one SENCO and one focus group touched on behaviour as a significant challenge, perhaps partly because staff who work in SEN perceive it as part of their role to deal with challenging behaviour and, therefore, not as burdensome as other studies have found.[17] One SENCO, however, did see it as the most challenging aspect of her job.

> Caroline (Primary SENCO).
> I think the most difficult thing probably is behaviour, because it can just be very wearing if you've got a child who is finding it very difficult to behave in the classroom. It's just challenging, finding ways round it, to keep on working at it.

The gendered nature of behaviour was discussed by one SENCO, and whether gender was a significant factor in managing challenging behaviour.

> Colin (Primary SENCO).
> The strategy [in my school] was to get good teachers regardless of whether you're male or female. In the last school it was interesting that the upper school we had predominantly male [teachers] and in the lower school is predominantly female, and that that is deliberately done due to behaviour […] I don't think it's the gender you are [that makes you deal more effectively with behaviour] I think it depends on your personality and character. I mean that in my present school there are some men who don't need to shout, they speak softly all the time and saying that, there are some women teachers that have a strong personality and it comes out, so I don't believe I really think that a people that think oh that's because you're a man you can deal with behavior better but then again I believe that females can deal that behaviour because they've got that that maternal instinct.

Responses from TAs focused more on the impact of behaviour, perhaps due to their role in dealing with individual pupils on a day-to-day basis. Surprisingly, behaviour was not such a negative issue for individual TAs in interview, despite the previous literature on the challenges of behaviour management, but this may be because they are expected to deal with it as part of their role of working in SEN and often take on a more sociological/environmental discourse in explaining the causes of behaviour. However, there was greater focus on behaviour by the TA focus group, but this could be an artifact of the focus group method during which an initial mention of behaviour issues sparked off wider discussion, with respondents sharing many anecdotes in the focus group setting. The fact that this focus group was comprised mainly of TAs means that there was a commonality of experience, and participants felt relaxed with one another, leading to a greater focus on this particular issue. Respondents recognized that, although behaviour was an issue, especially in London schools, a wider perspective on the causes of behaviour problems was needed.

> Una (Primary TA).
> I've been at my school for 9 years so I when went in there I couldn't believe the children. In Easttown, the school I'm in, there's quite a lot of children with behaviour issues. I couldn't believe it. I know when I was in school years ago there didn't seem to be anything like that: you didn't run out the class, you didn't answer the teacher back, you didn't throw a chair. But now it all seems, all the children seem to have so many issues, and then it comes out in behaviour or… and then the children will play up [or] perhaps, somehow, they know how to play the system, how to play the teachers, how to get out of class.

> Angela (Primary TA).
> I think a lot of that, though, is because children now are more aware of what their rights are, and I think a lot of teachers do, or have done in the past, they do see it as just naughty, just naughty children, you know. A lot of teachers never looked beyond the being naughty. I know with the experiences with my son - he goes to a school for… a special school for children with emotional and behavioural difficulties - and he went to a mainstream primary and, at one point, it was a split placement but, you know, my experiences with him was very much when he was younger, 'He's just being naughty, it's just for attention.' And you know, they didn't look for any environmental factors, it was just a naughty child, and sometimes, if you look beyond that, it's a very different picture.

Some TAs perceived working with children with behaviour problems positively, and discussed behaviour in its wider social context.

> Angela (Primary TA).
> With behaviour you, kind of, you've got a starting point and then you can see a progression and then you've got a different - often a different - finishing point and you can actually feel like you've done something and you've improved something and you've helped that child to progress.
>
> Una (Primary TA).
> I think I've a lot of patience with the children with behaviour problems and, I mean, I don't want to say that they are a challenge, but I like something that makes me think or try to use strategies to keep them… calm them down. I get on with the children very well, those with difficulties. And thinking about my own childhood, when there wasn't anything like that… and also my daughter is quite privileged… a lot of these children have issues. Where we live, in Easttown, it's not the most affluent area and I just sometimes feel that I just want to take all the children home, you do, you know what I mean? You get that sense that you just want to look after them. Maybe that's the wrong attitude to have, I don't know, but I do like the naughty children.

4. Attitudes of staff

Colleagues posed challenges for all respondents in the study: whether special educational needs co-ordinators, teachers or teaching assistants, participants identified obstacles posed by colleagues - communication problems, mutual misunderstandings and a mismatch of expectations - when performing out their roles.

A. Teaching Assistants

TAs often pointed to negative attitudes of colleagues towards inclusion, especially when they observed non-inclusive pedagogy. Attitudes towards TAs as staff were often perceived to be gendered (see below). Five participants noted negative or stereotypical staff attitudes to children with SEN, whilst themselves displaying a discourse of 'care' in their own descriptions of their work.[18] TAs considered some practice in schools to be a form of internal segregation.

Femi (Primary TA).
Some of them *[children with SEN]* are excluded within the class, they [have] arranged a class in such a way that the child sits by the corner and doesn't participate in the learning with the peers so that, again, I think affects the child.

Keisha (Primary TA).
There is a lot of unfairness. The experience I had before I started uni' with a child with Downs Syndrome… Most of the time, they are being ignored, and its seeking more attention and I don't have it, I have other children to attend to, and you find out that… that the child needs a one-to-one *[sic]* all the time because that is the only way you can, you know, make him or her to understand a bit. But, you see… but some of them need extra more care and these Downs Syndrome *[sic]*.

Jill (Primary TA).
I think sometimes they set unrealistic expectations as well. I mean, the specific child I was talking about before, their LSA had been told that they are not allowed to hold her hand and I'm thinking, "Why, why?" Because they have a policy of not holding the other children's hands unless they are hurt, or walking down the street or whatever. But she's not of that ability. Her natural reaction is, if we're going somewhere, you're going with me, and I'm holding my hand out. And I just think it's a bit, you know. They're not allowed to sit her on their lap, and it think it's a bit sad because she is not of the maturity yet to understand. It's not expected of other children, and I just think, you know, they are still little. I mean, they're only 4 years old anyway, and I don't think that should be expected of any of them, especially someone with a special need.

Tensions within TA groups sometimes caused problems within schools, and one TA reflected on the gendered nature of relationships between teachers.

Jane (Primary TA).
I don't like the dynamics of working in a school. I don't like the all-female environment and the cattiness that goes along with it, and all the hierarchy - 'We should be doing this, we

should be doing that' - and you should do that and you should bow to this one because she's been there fifteen years and they've got so much experience.

Some SENCOs saw TAs as 'caring', sometimes to the detriment of the academic aspects of their work.

Caroline (Primary SENCO).
I make it very clear to the point of saying in meetings, you know what you are doing is good, but they've really got to develop some independence. And I'd try and keep an eye on what sort of happening in the rooms as well, and it has got better and it's kind of a natural instinct of people to want obviously …a mothering instinct.

The increased complexity brought about by changes to staff roles was remarked, and how these changes affected mainstream staff's attitudes towards SEN.

Kay (Primary SENCO).
One teacher, her face fell, and I was like, 'What? What's wrong?' And she said, 'I'm really sorry but, whenever I see you, I just think of another job that you're gonna give me to do.' And I just think often, you know, that's how it's perceived by teachers. But certainly, with support staff, I just remember a few years ago, there was all this business about contracts in Eastborough, about the changes. And, often in many places that I've worked in, it's Learning Support Assistants who are working with, like, autistic children and things like that, and then they were the teaching assistants who were, like, working in the classroom. Now there seems to be this hierarchy.

B. Headteacher attitudes

One respondent who was working in support for pupils with sensory difficulties remarked the negative influence of her headteacher, particularly the perception that work in SEN was valued. This was often reflected in the attitudes of other staff (see previous section).

Maria (Secondary, sensory support teacher).
I'm quite unfulfilled. I have a really easy day with the kids but I don't feel in that rigour towards what I do: I don't really think anybody cares about it. The headmaster doesn't involve himself in any areas to do with inclusion.

And he doesn't come and see the unit. OFSTED didn't even bother to come in and see us as all while they were there, which I found rather surprising and disturbing. And there doesn't seem to be any sense of urgency or importance. I… we all get the same impression, actually, that mainstream look at us and think, 'Well, we don't have to bother with John or Anne because they've got the support teachers, there they'll differentiate.' But we can't differentiate, we don't know what the teacher is going to do from one minute to the next, so they won't come up and see us and we don't go down and see them: because of this there isn't any joint planning.

The SENCOs in this study felt that their role was misconstrued, or that there was a general lack of understanding of SEN issues. In a time of increasing demands on all teachers, and an increasingly diverse working context, it was felt that teachers did not have an understanding of SEN issues, either due to lack of interest or, in some cases, a lack of time, as mainstream teachers find themselves overwhelmed by the challenges of working in an urban context.

Caroline (Primary SENCO).
[The hardest aspect is] I suppose, being that person that liaises with everybody, so you are trying to liaise with parents and other professionals and, then, teachers - class teachers and support teachers - and sometimes you, sort of, you try and pass things on. They don't always get done, at one end or the other, and that can be a bit frustrating. And sometimes it can be a bit difficult working with parents who don't who aren't terribly supportive, but equally staff sometimes.

Additionally, the increased demands of working in London were reported to be contributing to increasing resentment on the part of the mainstream classroom teachers.

Siobhan (Primary SENCO).
[The SENCO role is] a hard job to do, and it's a very hard job to do well… It probably depends on the school: one, because of the funding issues; two, because of the number of children with special needs and the complexity of need. And you've got children coming in, now, from all over the world as well, particularly with children coming from

> eastern Europe … And then it's very difficult for teachers because they haven't got any support in their class because, in my last school, they used to… all the support was tied up with statements and so, then, teachers become resentful, even if they're good teachers. They're, like, 'Well, last year we all had our own teaching assistants and now all our teaching assistants are being taken up by statemented pupils.' And you think, 'Oh god, how am I going to manage because we've got all these kids in our classes, we just aren't getting any input and support'. Most SENCOs aren't qualified for the job, have no training. A lot of authorities are running down their advisory services and, even then, the advisory teachers are not… I'm not sure how qualified they are in special needs, even if they… that's their area. So it's a pretty dire situation at the coal face.

SENCOs, teachers and TAs all pointed to what they perceived as generally negative views towards children with SEN that were held by other classroom teachers. Carol, an existing primary teacher and aspiring SENCO, expressed what, for her, was the most frustrating thing about working in SEN.

> Carol (Primary teacher).
> [The hardest aspect is] Being unable to change people's attitudes to SEN. I strongly believe children with SEN must be included in activities at school, but others believe that nothing much can be done to 'help' the child.

The teacher/aspiring SENCO focus group also noted this frustration.

> Lisa (Secondary teacher).
> And I think, maybe, in our thinking, we're light years ahead of the class teacher, if you like, in that we are working in a different model in the school that we've been placed in. It's how we move people on from one stage to the next stage. You're dealing with prejudice, aren't you, and a reluctance to accept that the children are correctly placed, all those sorts of things. It's a very complex operation to be able to explain to people.

> Tracy (Secondary teacher).
> And you're isolated.

Lisa (Secondary teacher).
Yeah, no-one shows you how to do these things!

In some schools, staff working in SEN felt undervalued and, again, the association of SEN work with supposedly female qualities of 'caring' and 'nurturing' were brought out.

Maria (Secondary sensory support teacher).
So, you know, I've got a lot of expertise, but I'm treated by mainstream in a very patronising way and I think they think I'm some sort of Mum who's doing this job for a bit of pin money and I'm not. I've got probably more experience than they have.

TAs in particular felt that they were often seen as 'nurses', rather than as education staff, as demonstrated by this focus group exchange.

Angela (Primary TA).
Working in SEN generally, I don't think people see it as an intellectual job. I think, a lot of the time, you are just classed as an extra pair of hands even if you work…

Elaine (Primary TA).
… a nurse.

Angela (Primary TA).
Yeah.

Elaine (Primary TA).
… a nurse, because we work with children who had really bad medical needs, who were seen as more a nurse rather than a…

Angela (Primary TA).
… a carer.

Elaine (Primary TA).
Yes.

Angela (Primary TA).
… more than a [teacher].

Elaine (Primary TA).

> Yeah, because they didn't, at the school - I don't know if its changed 'cos I haven't been there for a few months, but when I worked at the school - it was more needs rather than the curriculum. I think I must have seen children, like, being read a story to about 5 times and painting and things like that. It was more, 'Right, we need to do catheters. We need to do the tubes. We change their nappies. It was more...
>
> Una (Primary TA).
> Did they have nurses in?
>
> Angela (Primary TA).
> Yes.
>
> Elaine (Primary TA).
> They had nurses in, but I was trained to do diazepam for epilepsy, I was trained to do catheters, other needs, things like that. So I was more of a nurse.

When asked about the biggest barrier when working in SEN, one SENCO remarked those 'barriers and constraints caused by a lack of understanding of real SEN issues by line management/local authority etc, the fact that interventions for SEN pupils are primarily influenced by budgetary issues, and the stigma attached to SEN' (Shanelle, Secondary SENCO). Another SENCO noted that some colleagues defaulted to integration rather than inclusion for pupils with SEN.

> Julie (Secondary Pupil Referral Unit Co-ordinator).
> Personally speaking, what I have found that has not changed is the reaction of some teachers and support staff. While schools are rushing to self-identify as 'inclusive' schools, the comments of some staff show that they still have notions of forcing integration into the school's regime for children with special needs. I still am having to remind staff about what inclusive practice means and trying to get them to make the necessary adjustments in planning and resourcing to meet the needs of children with SEN.

Liaison with external agencies was seen to be important, although it could be problematic. External liaison, given recent policy changes, has become a much more demanding aspect for those working in SEN. The problems of working with local authorities (LAs) in London were touched on by several respondents, although most were sympathetic to the demands being placed on LAs.

Colin (Primary SENCO).

> I understand it's not always… is not their fault, it's just the way things are. It's just that I get a bit frustrated when a child comes to your school and [it] is very clear that they are working well below the national average and nothing's being done about it. At the moment, we have a child in year 5 who has missed school in a huge style. That's not on, and I know it's harsh words to use for someone to have slipped through the net. I wish other schools could actually say, you know, be honest about it instead of trying to justify that they have done their best. We are not here to blame each other, we just need to be honest with each other and say we need to do something fast, but there's no fast response to those sort of the problems. The educational psychology input is very good. The service that I have a problem [with] is the NHS who seems to have dumped all their problems on us without training and expect us to follow programs. It's just not on really, I mean, and we haven't got the manpower to actually deliver any of the program.

Liaison was perceived as the most difficult part of the job by Caroline, and liaising on a whole-school basis has become increasingly demanding, given the greater diversity of need in mainstream schools.

> Caroline (Primary SENCO).
> I suppose one of the most frustrating things is the length of time it can take if you make a referral to an outside agency and that is not anybody's fault, they've got lots of children to see. That, sometimes that can be a bit frustrating.

For Caroline, the problems of working in SEN in London were partly attributable to problems with liaison with external agencies.

> Caroline (Primary SENCO).
> If you could wave a magic wand you'd obviously reduce the time you wait for referrals, by magically creating speech and language therapists and things like that. And, I don't know really, I suppose sometimes there's a sort of resistance around things and I think you would want to try and change

> people and give people more time to be able to take these things on.

For one outer London Primary SENCO, the stresses associated with the role were exacerbated by a lack of local authority support.

> Siobhan (Primary SENCO).
> Somebody said to me the other day that SENCOs only do the job now for the maximum three years and, when I look around, present SENCOs, the stress… [Teacher's name] in my school, he's been off with stress. In our authority we've got no special needs advisers, they have just gone and they're not saying how they're replacing them, and so it's all very well saying 'inclusion'- how are we get to do it?

A secondary school SENCO concluded that the consequences of the pressures of working in London were that SEN staff were becoming 'plate jugglers'.

> Lorna (Secondary SENCO).
> [You have to be a] very good plate juggler. I do feel that you do have to have a multi-track mind. I do find, in the day, I do have to switch very quickly from all kinds of things: from working with individuals to talking to parents… Today, I saw a student about aspirational grades, and I'm going to have to talk to the Deputy Head on that… and you know I've got a parent, I've got somebody from the LEA ring me up… So it is a lot, you do need to hold to a lot of different kinds of roles in place and be prepared not to say, 'I'm gonna do that and then I'm going to do this.' You have to kind of have it… all the plates spinning, I should say rather, plate juggling.

5. Conclusion

This study has shown that those working in SEN in London are faced with complex and diverse problems, arising partly from the particular challenges of multi-agency working within London local authorities. The diverse populations, and particular challenges of working in London, give rise to frustrations around paperwork, behaviour, relationships with parents, and the attitudes of colleagues.

Respondents notably discussed their own work within a 'caring' and 'nurturing' discourse which appeared to be very meaningful to them, and they believed themselves to be 'caring' and 'nurturing' and, therefore, more suited to working in SEN. However, female respondents also contended that other, non-SEN staff made presumptions about them regarding their 'natural' appropriateness of working in SEN due to their being female: they felt that their work was devalued and gendered insofar as they were viewed as carers and nurturers rather than academic support workers. Discourses of 'caring' were quite strong within the student group, with students in particular describing work in SEN within a 'caring' discourse. This, perhaps, reflected qualities of the respondents: nearly all were female, older, and had children themselves, and were working in a TA role that is often presumed, perhaps incorrectly, to have a 'caring' dimension which predominates.

Although no respondents in this study referred to leaving the profession, it is possible that the increased demands of policy initiatives such as Every Child Matters[19] and the Children's Plan[20] may lead to an increase in those leaving special needs work. This would replicate the trend in America, where policy changes have lead to a shortage of special educationalists.[21] The tensions and frustrations referred to in the study could threaten the successful delivery of policy, as effective multi-agency working and strong intra-school relationships are vital to the delivery of policy on a day-to-day basis. Recognition of the particular challenges of working in London schools is needed within SEN policy if the currently committed but overstretched workforce is to be retained.

Author's note: I would like to thank the TAs, teachers, SENCOs and students who gave up their valuable time to participate in this research project. I would also like to thank Dr. Lynn Ang and Dr. John Trushell for their invaluable comments, constructive criticism and encouragement throughout the writing of this chapter. My thanks also go to Dr. Tom Burt for discussion around the initial ideas.

Notes

[1] For a summary of recent research, see S Mackenzie, 'A review of recent developments in the role of the SENCo in the UK', *British Journal of Special Education,* vol.34-4, 2007, pp.212-218.
[2] Department for Education and Skills, [DfES], *The Children Act 2004 - Guidance*, 2004, accessed 9th October, 2006 <http://www.everychildmatters.gov.uk/strategy/guidance>.
[3] Department for Children, Schools and Families [DCSF], *The Children's Plan*, 2007, accessed 2oth December, 2007 <http://www.dfes.gov.uk/publications/childrensplan>.
[4] See 1) D Crowther, A Dyson and A Millward, 'Supporting pupils with special educational needs: issues and dilemmas for special needs coordinators in English primary schools,' *European Journal of Special Needs Education*,

vol.16-2, 2001, pp. 85-97. 2) T Lingard, 'Does the *Code of Practice* help secondary school SENCOs to improve learning?' *British Journal of Special Education*, vol. 28-4, 2001, pp.187-190. 3) E Cowne, 'What do special educational needs coordinators think they do?', *Support for Learning*, vol.20-2, 2002, pp.61-68. 4) C Czwed, 'Reconsidering the role of the primary special educational needs coordinator: policy, practice and future priorities', *British Journal of Special Education*, vol.34-2, 2007, pp.96-104. 5) Mackenzie, op. cit.

[5] R S Gehrke and K McCoy, 'Sustaining and retaining beginning special educators: It takes a village', *Teaching and Teacher Education,*,vol. 23-4, 2007, pp. 490-500.

[6] See 1) B S Billingsley, *Cultivating and Keeping Special Education Teachers: What Principals and District Leaders Can Do,* Thousand Oaks, Corwin Press, 2005. 2) K Singh, and B S Billingsley, 'Intent to Stay in Teaching: Teachers of Students with Emotional Disorders Versus Other Special Educators,' *Remedial and Special Education,* vol. 17-1, 1996, pp.37-48.

[7] Mackenzie, op cit.

[8] P Jones, '"They are not like us and neither should they be": issues of teacher identity for teachers of pupils with profound and multiple learning difficulties,' *Disability and Society,* vol. 19-2, 2004, pp. 159-169.

[9] J Eichinger, 'Job Stress and Satisfaction Among Special Education Teachers: effects of gender and social role orientation', *International Journal of Disability, Development and Education,* vol. 47-4, 2000, pp. 397-412.

[10] J MacBeath, M Galton, S Steward, A MacBeath, and C Page, *The Costs of Inclusion: A study of inclusion policy and practice in English primary, secondary and special schools,* Victoire Press, Cambridge, 2006.

[11] M Huberman, *The Lives of Teachers*, Cassell, London, 1983.

[12] G Hitchcock and D Hughes, *Research and the Teacher*, Routledge, London, 1989.

[13] C Day, P Sammons, G Stobart, A Kington and Q Gu, *Teachers Matter: Connecting Lives, Work and Effectiveness*, Open University Press, Maidenhead, 2007.

[14] See A Hargreaves, *Changing Teachers, Changing Times - Teachers' Work and Culture in the Postmodern Age*, Cassell, London, 1994, and P Woods and B Jeffrey, "The reconstruction of primary teachers' identities", *British Journal of Sociology of Education* Vol. 23-1, 2002, pp. 89-106.

[15] Crowther et al, op. cit.; and see also Lingard, op. cit., Cowne, op. cit., Czwed, op. cit.

[16] Mackenzie, op. cit.

[17] MacBeath et al., op. cit.

[18] J Corbett, *Bad-mouthing: the Language of Special Needs,* London, Routledge, 1996.

[19] Department for Education and Skills, op. cit.
[20] Department for Children, Schools and Families, op. cit.
[21] Billingsley op. cit.

Bibliography

Billingsley, B. S., *Cultivating and Keeping Special Education Teachers: What Principals and District Leaders Can Do,* Thousand Oaks, Corwin Press, 2005.

Cowne, E., 'What do special educational needs coordinators think they do?', *Support for Learning*, vol.20-2, 2002, pp. 61-68.

Corbett, J., *Bad-mouthing: the Language of Special Needs,* London, Routledge, 1996.

Crowther, D., A. Dyson and A. Millward, 'Supporting pupils with special educational needs: issues and dilemmas for special needs coordinators in English primary schools,' *European Journal of Special Needs Education*, vol. 16-2, 2001, pp. 85-97.

Czwed, C., 'Reconsidering the role of the primary special educational needs coordinator: policy, practice and future priorities', *British Journal of Special Education*, vol. 34-2, 2007, pp. 96-104.

Day, C., P. Sammons, G. Stobart, A. Kington and Q. Gu, *Teachers Matter: Connecting Lives, Work and Effectiveness*, Open University Press, Maidenhead, 2007.

Department for Children, Schools and Families [DCSF], *The Children's Plan*, 2007.

Department for Education and Skills, [DfES], *The Children Act 2004 - Guidance*, 2004.

Eichinger, J., 'Job Stress and Satisfaction Among Special Education Teachers: effects of gender and social role orientation', *International Journal of Disability, Development and Education,* vol. 47-4, 2000, pp. 397-412.

Gehrke, R. S., and K. McCoy, 'Sustaining and retaining beginning special educators: It takes a village', *Teaching and Teacher Education,*,vol. 23-4, 2007, pp. 490-500.

Hargreaves, A., *Changing Teachers, Changing Times - Teachers' Work and Culture in the Postmodern Age*, Cassell, London, 1994.

Hitchcock, G. and D. Hughes, *Research and the Teacher*, Routledge, London, 1989.

Huberman, M., *The Lives of Teachers*, Cassell, London, 1983.

Jones, P., '"They are not like us and neither should they be": issues of teacher identity for teachers of pupils with profound and multiple learning difficulties,' *Disability and Society,* vol. 19-2, 2004, pp. 159-169.

Lingard, T., 'Does the *Code of Practice* help secondary school SENCOs to improve learning?' *British Journal of Special Education*, vol. 28-4, 2001, pp. 187-190.

MacBeath, J., M. Galton, S. Steward, A. MacBeath, and C. Page, *The Costs of Inclusion: A study of inclusion policy and practice in English primary, secondary and special schools,* Victoire Press, Cambridge, 2006.

Mackenzie, S., 'A review of recent developments in the role of the SENCo in the UK', *British Journal of Special Education,* vol. 34-4, 2007, pp. 212-218.

Singh, K. and B. S. Billingsley, 'Intent to Stay in Teaching: Teachers of Students with Emotional Disorders Versus Other Special Educators,' *Remedial and Special Education,* vol. 17-1, 1996, pp. 37-48.

Woods, P. and B. Jeffrey, 'The reconstruction of primary teachers' identities', *British Journal of Sociology of Education* Vol. 23-1, 2002, pp. 89-106.

Suzanne Mackenzie studied Sociology - with a particular emphasis on Sociology of Education - at Leeds University and, having qualified as a teacher in 1992, worked in London as a teacher and manager in schools and post-sixteen institutions and with voluntary organisations in the disability sector where she was responsible for education policy and training in SEN and disability equality. She has completed a Post-graduate Diploma in Social Policy and an MA in Education and she is currently completing her PhD.

Drumming up Enthusiasm: Using Steel Pans with Adults and Children with Special Educational Needs

Lionel McCalman

Abstract
The potential of one culture to be integrated or absorbed into another's experience - especially when the two cultures co-exist - is well understood in multicultural societies. Adopting the music/musical instruments of one country is an example of cross-cultural communication or cultural porosity – and this has been part of the human character for generations. Within this paradigm, large sections of these transcultural products are likely to suit the musical taste of diverse groups and individuals globally. Steel pan music has historically been regarded as traditionally Caribbean and as 'ethnic' music but, increasingly, has come to be seen as a world musical genre in its own right, one which can make a useful contribution to the musical curriculum in schools and other settings. This chapter explores how steel pan workshops have been used with adults and primary school pupils with special educational needs and considers the extent to which social inclusion may be achieved through steel pan tuition and participation in steel bands.

Key Words: Steel pans, music teaching, special educational needs, inclusion.

*****

1. Introduction

Many attributes make London a distinctive city, not least that, in the 2001 census, over 40% of Londoners were not white British.[1] This sector of the population is set to increase, confirming London as having perhaps the most exotic population composition of any city on the planet.[2] Because of this diversity, the London 2012 Olympic Games are expected to be celebrated by a cultural extravaganza, with London displaying civic pride in its cosmopolitanism and multiculturalism. Steel pans will undoubtedly play their part as these are an established feature of multiculturalism: in fact, steel pans became emblematic of multiculturalism, as immortalised in the satirical definition, in the 1980s, of multicultural education as the 3Ss, steel bands, saris and samosas.[3]

An aim of the London 2012 Olympic Games – and a responsibility of the Olympic Delivery Authority - is "the creation of a platform for regeneration" to "ensure economic and social benefits for one of the most impoverished areas of London", the East End.[4] This Olympic initiative is only the most recent of a host of initiatives intended to regenerate East

London, an area notorious for poverty and deprivation.[5] The New Labour government, upon election in 1997, prioritised the issues of urban deprivation and social exclusion.[6] Social exclusion has been defined as "a process of long-term non-participation in the economic, civic and social norms that integrate and govern the society in which an individual resides" and which is differentiated from poverty and deprivation by a focus on disengagement.[7] Debates on social exclusion have drawn inspiration from two main sources: first, from debates concerning diverse communities that existed on the margins of society in France and, second, debates concerning the underclass in the United States of America.[8]

The New Labour government established, in 1997, a Social Exclusion Unit, a cross-departmental think-tank, which identified key risk factors of social exclusion:

> low income; family conflict; being in care; school problems; being an ex-prisoner; being from an ethnic minority; living in a deprived neighbourhood in urban and rural areas; mental health problems, age and disability.[9]

The government resolved to tackle social exclusion by reducing these risk factors – and acting with those already at risk – and re-integrating those who become excluded into society.[10] Government action to tackle social exclusion focussed on:

> better co-ordination between Departments, more strategic approaches, better use of evidence, more partnership working and a bottom-up approach that empowers individuals and communities to help themselves.[11]

The case studies, reported below, concerning steel pans and adults and children with special educational needs should be viewed in this social exclusion context insofar as individuals and communities are being encouraged to help themselves. Recent government research has reported that the provision of instrumental music services has "extended opportunities to children with [special educational needs]" and "increasing opportunities for social inclusion through involvement with music".[12]

2. The Caribbean Connection

While historians record that - although hidden and underplayed - there has been a black presence in Britain since the sixteenth century,[13] the migration that impacted on the popular imagination was the arrival of the *SS Empire Windrush* which docked at Tilbury on the 22nd June 1948. Four hundred and ninety-two West Indians disembarked, responding to a state-sponsored initiative to bring Caribbean ex-servicemen to Britain to fill labour posts. However, most notably, the first steel band ever to leave the Caribbean - The Trinidad All-Steel Percussion Orchestra - arrived for the Festival of Britain celebrations in 1951[14] for which their performance received enthusiastic reviews in the British press.[15] The steel pan, or drum, was hailed, in 1958, as a "new folk instrument"[16] and it was predicted that:

> It seems probable that the steel drum is destined to spread through still other parts of the world than the West Indies, perhaps in each country adapting itself to local popular-folk traditions.[17]

The steel band and the Trinidadian carnival - its youthful energies, distinctive social dance customs and colourful expressions - provided the template for the development of the Notting Hill Carnival in London.[18] The Notting Hill Carnival achieved, in 2006, the status of an 'Icon of England' – "uniquely important to life in England and the people who live here"[19] - alongside such icons as Bonfire Night, morris dancing and the flag of St George.[20] However, while the steel band is Trinidad's unique gift to the musical world,[21] it has been formally recognized by the Trinidad government, since 1992, as the national instrument[22] and is a potent symbol of Creole cultural ingenuity.

Created in Trinidad's capital, Port of Spain, in the 1930s,[23] steel pans were forged and fashioned from old rusty American military oil drums by skilled metal workers called pan tuners.[24] The instruments are individually crafted and undergo a series of processes – pounding the head into a concave shape, grooving the position for each note, tempering the metal, cutting the barrel to the desired height and tuning pitch areas with a small hammer[25] - before the final product emerges. A recycled oil drum could take days - even weeks - to be transformed into a chromatic tuned steel pan. There is a wide variety of types of pans including tenor pan, guitar pan, cello pan, tenor bass pan and bass pan. Pans may be supplemented, in a steel band, by trap drums, congas and maracas to provide "a throbbing and harmonious accompaniment" to the melody of the pans.[26] The repertoire of a steel band is not confined to traditional calypso: many bands play transcriptions of demanding "European art music as well as other 'foreign' music".[27]

3. Steel Pans in British Schools

The introduction of the school pan into British schools coincided with a period – the 1960s and 1970s – when progressive educators advocated that music teaching should provide opportunities for children to express their feelings and thoughts and thus nurture their affective and cognitive facilities.[28] Moreover, this period witnessed a developing awareness of the importance of multicultural education, as expressed in a consultative document issued in 1977 by the Department for Education and Science:

> Our society is a multicultural, multiracial one, and the curriculum should reflect a sympathetic understanding of the different cultures and races that now make up our society.[29]

There were two related discernible reasons for the introduction of steel pans. First, steel pans gave credence to the cultural heritage of the black child in a multicultural environment, and provided opportunities for black children to explore this cultural heritage through performance. Inferences which could be drawn from this reasoning were that steel pans were solely for the benefit of black pupils, and that the instructors and music technologists - steel pan tuners - should also be black. However, second, steel pans would present the non-black child with positive elements of black culture which could supplement conventional notions of blackness and black culture. Thus, although the steel pan music classes were initially targeted at black children, the presence of the steel pan in schools introduced the instrument and music to non-black children.

The first school steel band was set up by Gerald Forsyth in Islington Green School, North London, in 1969. Forsyth later became the special Instrumental Organiser for the Inner London Education Authority [ILEA] with responsibility for the teaching of steel band music in all schools, the recruitment of steel pan teachers and setting the standards for steel pan classes and related activities in ILEA schools.[30]

A review of school instrumental services, in 1991, noted that steel pan tuition – while "most commonly taught in London Authorities" - "was provided by about a quarter" of local education authorities [LEAs].[31] A survey of LEAs' music services showed an increase in steel band ensembles from 12% in 1999 to 26% in 2002[32] while a recent estimate, in 2006, was that steel pan classes exist in over 15,000 schools in the United Kingdom.[33]

Most steel pan tuition and steel band direction is provided by peripatetic teachers as, rationally, "it is impossible for single schools and individual teachers to provide access to music-making involving, for example, the use of gamelan, steel pans, and standard Western orchestral instruments".[34] Peripatetic steel pan teachers, as a rule, teach steel pan in a number of schools - possibly across LEAs – and most are local steel band members - sometimes as leaders and/or musical arrangers – and may belong to the British Association of Steel Bands. These are musicians in the community whose contribution to school music programmes should "avoid perpetuating a separate musical sub-culture in schools, detached from music in the wider world".[35]

4. Special Education Needs, Music and Steel Pans

Historically, there has been a shortage of trained and experienced teachers of music in special education and, correspondingly, a lack of music provision.[36] These factors have restricted students in special education institutions from "engagement in music [which] promotes the growth of intellectual capacities and worthy dispositions".[37] One commentator has contended that:

> Music offers many different kinds of learning opportunities; more than any other domain. It can satisfy physically, intellectually, emotionally and spiritually and provides opportunities for developing a very wide range of skills which may be transferred to other domains.[38]

Students with special educational needs [SEN] should not be denied such learning opportunities. The National Curriculum Music Working Group, in 1995, recommended that the needs of students with SEN should be addressed by specific strategies, including adapting material appropriately and selecting and adapting instruments.[39] Students with SEN, for the purposes of steel pan tuition, are divided into two main categories: students with physical difficulties and students with learning difficulties. The responsibility of music teachers of students with SEN is to identify students' specific needs and adapt materials and instruments so that these are best suited to individual students. Some institutions enrol their students on one day steel pan workshops – a taster session – to see whether the instrument is suited to their specific learners. If successful, a one week – or even a six week – programme of workshops may consolidate and extend learning. Thereafter, the institution may decide to purchase a set of steel pans.

Teachers of students with SEN must alter their teaching styles to accommodate students with SEN: this may involve adaptive equipment for students with limited mobility or physical difficulties, augmentative devices for students with communication disorders and, generally, the use of conventional equipment in unconventional manners[40] (see Table 1). Steel pan performance conventionally requires an ensemble, and the tried and tested format would for a school steel band would include three single soprano pans, two sets of double-second alto pans, a pair of double guitar pans, a set of three pan cellos and one set of five drums. However, for students with SEN, it would be advisable to use single pan instruments, and a recommended adapted format would include four single soprano pans, two single second also pans, two single guitar pans, two single drum (five note) basses and some shakers and hand bells for percussion accompaniment.

The choice of an appropriate repertoire is extremely important. Most repertoires start with simple three chord melodies – e.g. *Hot Cross Buns*, *Old*

MacDonald, Twinkle, Twinkle Little Star – and advance to more challenging pieces, e.g. *Jamaica Farewell* and *Yellow Bird.* Repetition is the key to ensuring that learning takes place for students with SEN. The preferred repertoire for a steel band would be a mixture of old Negro spirituals, popular reggae classics and traditional English melodies that would be recognised by all.

Table 1: Recommendations for Steel Bands for Students with SEN

1.	Use simple tunes at all times, two/ three chord progression if necessary. This allows learners to build up a pattern which is easily transferred to another tune. The control of the learning process should reside with the teacher.
2.	Encourage rote learning. Repetition is the key for learners with poor motor skills or sensory impairment.
3.	Use tunes that the learners already know and will recognise. Learners are always intrigued when they can master a tune that is popular or relevant to their culture.
4.	When arranging a tune, use keys that are physically accessible. In the case of the steel pan, the 'C Major' key is best positioned for chord progression. This is because the chords are reachable, i.e. at the waist of the learner.
5.	Look for many ways to do the same thing. This may involve clapping, singing or even mixing the steel pans with traditional drums.
6.	Use colour coding on the notes of the pans. Colour stickers alert students to the notes of the chord and allow them to relate the different colours to different notes. The positioning of the hands then becomes a less challenging task.
7.	Be child-centred in your teaching approach, i.e. observe what each child can do and develop those skills.
8.	Use other teaching aids – recorded backing tracks to help them to progress.
9.	Use straightforward solutions, e.g. harnessing the pan stands to wheelchairs.
10.	Identify with and learn about various learning styles to make steel pan music teaching more appropriate for every child.

The institution needs to appreciate that there are maintenance issues that have implications for school budgets. If the instruments are treated with respect and carefully stored after use, they can remain repair-free for years However, the instruments will need to be serviced at least once a year: school steel pans often lose their sound earlier than steel pans in conventional bands, and may need to be tuned to their original pitch, requiring the services of a steel pan tuner.

It is important to ascertain what the institution hopes to achieve with steel pan tuition and steel band direction. Not uncommonly, head teachers expect a school steel band to be able to perform – e.g. at an assembly – after a short period, say three weeks, of preparation. Fortunately, school bands lend themselves to early performance, far earlier than most musical ensembles.

5. Case Studies

These case studies – of an institution for adults with SEN and an institution for children with SEN - draw upon documentary data, field notes and interviews with teachers of music and steel pans.

A. Woodbine Steel Band Project

The Woodbine Club is a day care centre – run by the Redbridge and Waltham Forest Learning Disability Partnership - that provides a daily service for adults with moderate learning difficulties from a wide, diverse and multicultural community in Wanstead, East London. The steel band was established in 2000 by one of the workers at the club who thought that steel pans would provide clubhouse attendees with a positive activity. Initially, the club hired steel pans and a venue for practice.[41] Later, a grant was provided to purchase steel pans and, initially, the club purchased a set of triple cellos (a set of three pans to be played by one player), a set of six drum basses, double guitar pans and double second pans: these, unfortunately, are not appropriate steel pans for students with SEN.

The clubhouse members had a succession of steel pan tutors - some of whom attended only once or twice – culminating with a tutor who returned to the Caribbean, leaving the group tutorless for a few months. When the current tutor took post, the steel band members had learnt some basic tunes – comprising two or three chords – but their new tutor had greater ambitions. He dealt first with the issue of the inappropriate steel pans.

> Steel pan tutor.
> I got rid of the triple cellos, and the six drum bass and introduced instead single pans in the band. I bought a single guitar pan and a single second pan. There was already a single tenor pan in the band. One of the learners purchased her own instrument - a five note single bass pan - and we began to look like a more adequate ensemble for the specific learners we had. We kept the double guitar pan and the double second pan, and introduced a policy where the same learners played these instruments - to build up a familiarity with the pans.

The current steel band has nine members whose ages range from early twenties to late thirties. The players rehearse on a regular basis and are enthusiastic about their classes. There are weekly sessions which each last three hours. Now, the steel band plays more challenging tunes and have a wider repertoire, directed by their tutor.

> Steel pan tutor.
> The learners do not play the soprano pan. I have found that to be a bit too challenging for them. I play the only soprano pan that carries the melody. The learners play the back ground rhythm pans and percussion. That way we all stay in time with the beat and there is some consistency

The steel band has been very successful, having being booked to perform for local councils - including Kent County Council's 'Celebration of Ability'[42] – and for festivals, events and corporate functions throughout the London area. A special achievement award was given to the Woodbine Steel Band at the Newham Steel Band Blockorama, 10th June 2007.[43]

B. Manor Primary School

Manor Primary School, Brent, has pupils with a wide range of special needs described as severe learning difficulties and autism with associated difficulties. An inspection report by the Office for Standards in Education [OFSTED] notes that:

> Only 16% of pupils are of White heritage and others represent a wide range of minority ethnic backgrounds, the largest group being from Black Caribbean or African and Asian backgrounds.[44]

OFSTED reports that, annually, there is a visit by steel bands.[45] The school provides steel pan tuition within a holistic approach: there is a steel pan programme that provides every child with the opportunity to play the instrument within their music sessions across the school. The school has established its own steel band with eight single pan instruments. An SEN primary teacher reports that training was provided for SEN and Music: "I went on a training day at the local educational centre. The training was geared towards Special Educational Needs."

Subsequently, the teacher was approached, by an advisor, to provide input to train others.

SEN primary teacher.
The Special Needs Music Advisor asked if I [could] give a talk on the benefits that children derive from steel pans in school and, maybe, do a session with staff on the course. I explained that, if they wanted to see the benefits that children got from the instrument, they needed to see the children working. We took a few of our children over and they played a piece that they knew well. I started teaching them a piece they did not know [*Brown Girl in the Ring*] so [that] staff were able to see how I taught the children. The nicest compliment that was made by the staff at that training session was that our children all looked so confident and happy within the lesson.

6. Discussion

Music, perhaps more than any other subject matter, can be experienced by everyone. It is often said that the music class is the setting where children with special needs function best.[46]

Music is a curriculum subject that can inspire. Most participants can experience a measure of success and self-esteem from playing a musical instrument. The findings of these case studies demonstrate that music – specifically steel pan tuition and performance in steel bands – can play a real part in the experience of adults and children with SEN and that social benefits can be derived.

Participation in music can contribute to learners' motivation and self-esteem,[47] and this is evidently applicable to receiving steel pan tuition and participation in steel bands. The motivation of the Woodbine Steel Band [WSB] is evident in the members' regular attendance of three hour weekly rehearsals, and their self-esteem will have been enhanced by their performances at festivals, events and corporate functions and the special achievement award bestowed at the Newham Steel Band Blockorama. Obviously, the WSB benefit from the direction of an experienced steel pan tutor who was able to provide the correct steel pans for the band and to provide musical direction.

Non-specialist teachers, by contrast, may experience insecurity and poor confidence when engaging in musical activities with their students[48] and these emotions may be communicated to their students. Thus, appropriate training is required in order that the non-specialist teacher feels secure and confident when teaching music. Notably, the non-specialist teacher in Manor Primary School [MPS] was suitably trained and - as evident in their account of the demonstration of steel pans to other teachers – the primary children with SEN who participated in the demonstration were evidently "confident and happy". The performance of the MPS ensemble would allow the performers to perceive correspondences between themselves and the steel bands that visit the school annually.

The adults and children of WSB and MPS have the opportunity to receive affirmation, not only as members of diverse multicultural communities but also as individuals with SEN included in musical activities that transcend culture and ability.

Notes

[1] Office for National Statistics, *Census 2001*, The Stationery Office, London, 2001.
[2] S Parker and D Goodhart, 'A city of capital', *Prospect*, no. 133, April 2007, pp. 22-27.
[3] K K Bhavnani and R Bhavnani, 'Racism and resistance in Britain', in D Coates, G Johnston and R Bush (ed), A Socialist Anatomy of Britain, Polity Press, Cambridge, 1985, pp. 146-159.
[4] House of Commons Culture Media and Sport Committee, 'Memorandum submitted by the Olympic Delivery Authority (Evidence 1), *London 2012 Olympic Games and Paralympic Games: Funding and Legacy*, Second Report of 2006-07, Volume II: Oral and written evidence, 24th January 2007.
[5] See R Lupton and A Sullivan, 'The London context', in *Education in a Global City – Essays from London*, T Brighouse and L Fullick (eds) Institute of Education, London, 2007, pp.8-39.
[6] J Solomos, *Race and Racism in Britain*, Palgrave, Basingstoke, 2003, 3rd ed, p. 246.
7 J Sparkes, *Schools, Education and Social Exclusion*, Centre for the Analysis of Social Exclusion [CASE] Paper 29, London School of Economics, London, 1999, p. 1
[8] P J F De Lima, 'Beyond place: ethnicity/race in the debate on social exclusion in Scotland', *Policy Futures in Education*, 1-4, 2003, pp. 653-666, p. 655.
[9] Social Exclusion Unit [SEU], *Preventing Social Exclusion*, Social Exclusion Unit, London, 2001, p. 11.
[10] Ibid., p. 28.
[11] Ibid.
[12] S Hallam and V Prince, *Research into Instrumental Music Services*, Department for Education and Employment [DfEE] Research Report No. 229, The Stationery Office, Norwich, 2000, p. 7.
[13] See P Fryer, *Staying Power: The History of Black People in Britain*, Pluto Press, London, 1984, and P Gilroy, *There Ain't No Black in the Union Jack:*

The Cultural Politics of Race and Nation, University of Chicago Press, Chicago, 1987.

[14] W R Aho, 'Steel band music in Trinidad and Tobago: the creation of a people's music', *Latin American Music Review*, 8-1, 1987, pp. 26-58, p. 46.

[15] S Dudley, Dropping the bomb: steelband performance and meaning in 1960s Trinidad', *Ethnomusicology*, 46-1, 2002, pp. 135-164, p. 138.

[16] P Seeger, "The steel drum: a new folk instrument', *The Journal of American Folklore*, 71-279, 1958, pp. 52-57.

[17] Ibid., p. 57.

[18] A Cohen, 'Drama and politics in the development of a London carnival', *Man*, 15-1, 1980, pp. 65-87, p. 68.

[19] Culture Online, *What is an icon?*, Culture Online, accessed 10th July, 2008 <www.icons.org.uk/theicons/copy_of_what-is-an-icon>.

[20] Culture Online, *Icons: A Portrait of England?*, Culture Online, accessed 10th July, 2008 <www.icons.org.uk/theicons/collection/view?mode=list>.

[21] J Stewart, 'Patronage and control in the Trinidad carnival', *The Anthropology of Experience*, V W Turner and E M Bruner (ed), University of Illinois Press, Urbana and Chicago, 1986, pp. 289-315, p. 305.

[22] P Manuel, 'Ethnic identity, national identity, and Indo-Trinidadian music', *Music and the Racial Imagination*, R Radano and P V Bohlman (ed), University of Chicago Press, Chicago, 2000, pp. 318-348, p. 327.

[23] Aho, op. cit., p.27.

[24] L McCalman, 'Steelbands in schools: the instructor dependency model vs. the teacher transferency model', *New Era in Education*, 84-2, pp. 42-50, p. 42.

[25] J M Svaline, "Why not start a steel band?", *Music Educators Journal*, 82-3, 1995, pp. 22-25, p. 22.

[26] Seeger, op. cit., p. 52.

[27] Dudley, op. cit., p. 135; see also Svaline, op. cit., p. 24.

[28] See J Paynter and P Aston, *Sound and Silence: Classroom Projects in Creative Music*, London, Cambridge University Press, 1970, R Witkin, *The Intelligence of Feeling*, London, Heinemann, 1974, and M Ross, *Arts and the Adolescent*, Schools Council Working Paper no. 54, London, Evans, 1975.

[29] Department for Education and Science [DES], *Education in Schools: A Consultative Document*, Cmnd 6869, The Stationery Office, London, 1977, p. 41.

[30] McCalman, op. cit., p.43.

[31] C Sharp, *When Every Note Counts: the Schools Instrumental Services in the 1990s*, National Foundation for Education Research, Slough, 1991, p. 42.

[32] S Hallam and L Rogers, *Survey of Local Education Authority Music Services*, Department for Education and Skills [DfES] Research Report RR478, Publisher? Place?, 2002, p. 67.

[33] R Gardiner, *Steelbands: Current Practice and Requirements for Sector Development*, report commissioned by the British Association of Steel Bands and the Arts Council England, London, 2006.
[34] C Plummeridge and K Swanwick, 'Music', in *Rethinking the School Curriculum: Values, Aims and Purposes*, J White (ed), Routledge Falmer, London, 2004, pp. 128-137, p. 134.
[35] Ibid., p. 135.
[36] S Hegarty, *Meeting Special Needs in Ordinary Schools*, Cassell, London, 1993, 2nd ed, p. 59; Y Packer, 'Music with emotionally disturbed children', G Spruce (ed), *Teaching Music in Secondary Schools*, RoutledgeFalmer, London, 2002, pp. 106-116, p. 106.
[37] C Plummeridge, 'The justification for music education', in C Philpott and C Plummeridge (ed), *Issues in Music Teaching*, RoutledgeFalmer, Abingdon, 2001, pp. 21-31, p. 21.
[38] S Hallam, 'Learning in music: complexity and diversity', in C Philpott and C Plummeridge (ed), *Issues in Music Teaching*, RoutledgeFalmer, Abingdon, 2001, pp. 61-75, p. 74.
[39] See G Pratt, 'Equal opportunities in music', in G Pratt and J Stephens (ed), *Teaching Music in the National Curriculum*, Heinemann, Oxford, 1995, pp. 39-46.
[40] M Humpal and J Dimmick, 'Special learners in the music classroom', *Music Educators Journal*, 81-5, pp. 21-23, pp. 21-22.
[41] W Kirk, 'Woodbine Steel Band', *Panpodium: The Official Magazine of the British Association of Steelbands*, issue 10, Winter 2004/5, pp. 6-7, p. 6.
[42] Ibid.
[43] Joseph, R, 'The Newham steel band blockorama, *When steel talks*, accessed 18th July, 2008 <www.panonthenet.com/articles/uk/2007newham-6-15-07>.
[44] Office for Standards in Education [OFSTED], *Manor School: Inspection Report*, Office for Standards in Education, London, 2006, p. 1.
[45] Ibid., p. 3.
[46] Humpal and Dimmick, op. cit., p. 23.
[47] See Hallam, op. cit., pp. 65-67.
[48] Packer, op. cit., p. 109.

Bibliography

Aho, W. R., 'Steel band music in Trinidad and Tobago: the creation of a people's music', *Latin American Music Review*, 8-1, 1987, pp. 26-58.

Bhavnani. K. K. and R. Bhavnani, 'Racism and resistance in Britain', in *A Socialist Anatomy of Britain*, D. Coates, G. Johnston and R. Bush (ed), Polity Press, Cambridge, 1985, pp. 146-159.

Cohen, A., 'Drama and politics in the development of a London carnival', *Man*, 15-1, 1980, pp. 65-87.

De Lima, P. J. F., 'Beyond place: ethnicity/race in the debate on social exclusion in Scotland', *Policy Futures in Education*, 1-4, 2003, pp. 653-666, p. 655.

Department for Education and Science [DES], *Education in Schools: A Consultative Document*, Cmnd 6869, The Stationery Office, London, 1977

Dudley, S., 'Dropping the bomb: steelband performance and meaning in 1960s Trinidad', *Ethnomusicology*, 46-1, 2002, pp. 135-164,

Fryer, P., *Staying Power: The History of Black People in Britain*, Pluto Press, London, 1984.

Gardiner, R., *Steelbands: Current Practice and Requirements for Sector Development*, report commissioned by the British Association of Steel Bands and the Arts Council England, London, 2006.

Gilroy, P. *There Ain't No Black in the Union Jack: The Cultural Politics of Race and Nation*, University of Chicago Press, Chicago, 1987.

Hallam, S., 'Learning in music: complexity and diversity', in C Philpott and C Plummeridge (ed), *Issues in Music Teaching*, RoutledgeFalmer, Abingdon, 2001, pp. 61-75.

Hallam, S. and V. Prince, *Research into Instrumental Music Services*, Department for Education and Employment [DfEE] Research Report No. 229, The Stationery Office, Norwich, 2000.

Hegarty, S., *Meeting Special Needs in Ordinary Schools*, Cassell, London, 1993, 2nd ed.

House of Commons Culture Media and Sport Committee, 'Memorandum submitted by the Olympic Delivery Authority (Evidence 1), *London 2012 Olympic Games and Paralympic Games: Funding and Legacy*, Second Report of 2006-07, Volume II: Oral and written evidence, 24th January 2007.

Kirk, W., 'Woodbine Steel Band', *Panpodium: The Official Magazine of the British Association of Steelbands*, issue 10, Winter 2004/5, pp. 6-7.

Lupton, R. and A. Sullivan, 'The London context', in *Education in a Global City – Essays from London*, T. Brighouse and L. Fullick (ed) Institute of Education, London, 2007, pp.8-39.

McCalman, L., 'Steelbands in schools: the instructor dependency model vs. the teacher transferency model', *New Era in Education*, 84-2, pp. 42-50.

Manuel, P. 'Ethnic identity, national identity, and Indo-Trinidadian music', *Music and the Racial Imagination*, R. Radano and P. V. Bohlman (ed), University of Chicago Press, Chicago, 2000, pp. 318-348.

Office for National Statistics, *Census 2001*, The Stationery Office, London, 2001.

Packer, Y., 'Music with emotionally disturbed children', G. Spruce (ed), *Teaching Music in Secondary Schools*, RoutledgeFalmer, London, 2002, pp. 106-116.

Parker, S. and D. Goodhart, 'A city of capital', *Prospect*, no. 133, April 2007, pp. 22-27.

Paynter, J. and P. Aston, *Sound and Silence: Classroom Projects in Creative Music*, London, Cambridge University Press, 1970.

Plummeridge, C., 'The justification for music education', in C. Philpott and C. Plummeridge (ed), *Issues in Music Teaching*, RoutledgeFalmer, Abingdon, 2001, pp. 21-31

Plummeridge, C. and K. Swanwick, 'Music', in *Rethinking the School Curriculum: Values, Aims and Purposes*, J. White (ed), RoutledgeFalmer, London, 2004, pp. 128-137.

Pratt, G. 'Equal opportunities in music', in G. Pratt and J. Stephens (ed), *Teaching Music in the National Curriculum*, Heinemann, Oxford, 1995, pp. 39-46.

Ross, M., *Arts and the Adolescent*, Schools Council Working Paper no. 54, London, Evans 1975.

Seeger, P., "The steel drum: a new folk instrument', *The Journal of American Folklore*, 71-279, 1958, pp. 52-57.

Social Exclusion Unit [SEU], *Preventing Social Exclusion*, Social Exclusion Unit, London, 2001.

Stewart, J. 'Patronage and control in the Trinidad carnival', *The Anthropology of Experience*, V. W. Turner and E. M. Bruner (ed), University of Illinois Press, Urbana and Chicago, 1986, pp. 289-315,

Witkin, R., *The Intelligence of Feeling*, London, Heinemann, 1975.

Lionel McCalman, who studied at Leeds University, University College London and the University of Hull, has been a teacher and lecturer for twenty-five years in London secondary schools, further education colleges and the University of East London. He has a doctorate in Educational Anthropology, is leader of Nostalgia Steel Band, a founder member of the British Association of Steel Bands and is currently researching carnival arts education, the anthropology of carnival and steel bands in schools.

Silent Voices: British Muslim Pupils in Mainstream Schools in East London

Nasima Hassan

Abstract

This chapter presents findings of a naturalistic study of Muslim pupils attending two mainstream secondary schools in London's East End. Their narrative accounts shed light on those elements which pupils claim influence their group identity whilst at school. Their perceptions of the curriculum as limiting and of educational policies as failing to acknowledge their diverse cultural and religious heritages are revealed as factors which give rise to resistance to schooling. The delivered curriculum is investigated in order to critique multiculturalism in one of London's most diverse boroughs. The students' voices disclose on-going struggles to re-negotiate identities within the mainstream schools in which they seek acceptance and inclusion.

Key Words: British, Muslim, identity, culture, ethnicity, race.

*****

1. Islamophobia – a New Word for an Old Fear[1]

Islamophobia, defined by the Runnymede Trust as an unfounded hostility towards Islam and, therefore, fear and dislike of all or most Muslims,[2] may have been heightened post '9/11'[3] and post '7/7'[4] but Muslims in Britain have been portrayed in derogatory terms – and vilified – for centuries. Although fear of Islam and Muslims has been a feature of European societies since the eighth century (common era),[5] the Muslim presence in Britain remained inconspicuous before the Second World War. However, the presence of Muslim communities became more perceptible when Britain recruited labour migrants – many of whom had British citizenship and passports as residents of the former colonies - to fill labour shortages in Britain.[6] There were, from the outset, fears expressed concerning the perceived social and racial problems that would arise with the influx of 'coloured' colonial labour migrants, even though they were British subjects.[7] Enoch Powell's infamous speech in 1968 - predicting that immigration would lead to "Rivers of blood" - contended that:

> "an Indian does not, by being born in England, become an Englishman. In law he becomes an Englishman by birth; in fact… he is… an Asian still."

Nevertheless, Muslims made considerable progress in achieving multiple forms of recognition[7] in Britain, to a certain extent comparable to the situations of Jews and Sikhs. However, when emphases on racial differences were superceded by emphases on religious differences - consistent with the reconceptualisation of the world as comprising seven or eight major civilizations - racial tensions were recast as the "clash of civilizations"[8] These religious fears have been exacerbated - post '9/11' in the United States of America and post '7/7' in Britain – by concerns that Muslim communities have not been integrated.[9] Daily media scrutiny and criticism of all matters related to the world of Islam cannot fail to have made an impression on the attitudes and feelings of Muslims. Consequently, Muslim pupils in British schools are facing trying times when confronted by the challenges of integration and Islamophobia.

2. British Muslims: An Emerging Identity

The multiplicity of cultural identities evident in the Muslim population of Britain adds further complexity to the formation of a unified identity. A report of the Commission on British Muslims and Islamophobia [CBMI] cites one interviewee who remarked that:

> 'Muslims have no common language and come from many cultures with their own traditions that have nothing to do with Islam. They will stand side by side in the mosque, but there are divisions... The Pakistani, the Nigerian, the black convert from Jamaica...'[10]

A contributory factor to this multiplicity of cultural identities is the number of Muslim diasporas. Bengali and Yemeni seamen (referred to as lascars) had established small communities in the ports of London and Cardiff by the end of the nineteenth century.[11] Predominantly South Asian labourers established communities around factories surrounding London and the textile towns of Bradford, Leeds and Manchester during the 1960s and 1970s.[12] East African Asians (mainly Gujeratis) – expelled from Kenya and Uganda – entered Britain in the 1970s.[13] Subsequently, waves of refugees – from Afghanistan, Bosnia, Iran, Iraq and Somalia – have arrived in Britain.[14] The cumulative effect of these diasporas is that Muslims have become the largest religious minority group in Britain,[15] but this group is not homogeneous. Moreover, this multi-ethnicity has prevented Muslims achieving the status of 'racial group' whereas such mono-ethnic religious groups as Jews and Sikhs are considered as 'racial groups' and afforded protection by anti-discrimination laws and policies in Britain.[16]

While Muslim diasporas have evoked islamophobias,[17] earlier instances of islamophobia were subsumed by debates concerning race.[18] Only later, in the 1980s, did the discourse on 'new racism' or 'cultural racism'[19] – the processes by which racialisation works through cultural rather than biological difference - move on the debate. More recently, in the 1990s, the identification of seven or eight meta civilizations – Western, Sinic, Orthodox, Latin American, Japanese, Islamic, Hindu and, possibly, African[20] – has further focused the debate on religion. The Islamic meta civilization is defined as embodying "acceptance of modernity, rejection of Western culture, and recommitment to Islam as the guide to life in the modern world".[21] The prediction that the Western and Islamic civilizations would clash in the twenty-first century[22] has compounded more recent instances of islamophobia.

Concurrently, research concerning the depiction of Muslims in the British media during the 1990s[23] indicated "gross under-representation and stereotypical characterization in entertainment genres" and "negative and problem-oriented portrayal with factual and news forms".[24] A study of the quality 'broadsheet' press in Britain contended that "Muslim communities are almost wholly absent from the news, excluded from all but predominantly negative contexts'.[25] Moreover, when Muslims did feature in the quality press, "they [were] included only as participants in news events, not as providers of informed commentary on news events":[26] their voices were silenced. The Muslim Council of Britain [MCB] – established in November 1997, and modeled on the Board of Deputies of British Jews[27] – challenges misrepresentations of Muslim communities and islamophobia in the media. The foundation of the MCB was due to the demand by the Home Office Secretary of State, in 1994, that Muslims form a single representative voice or he would not speak with Muslims.[28] Ironically, the most recent instances of islamophobia may have affected the self-perceptions of Muslims in Britain, as the CBMI interviewee remarked:

> 'In a strange way, Islamophobia is bringing us together… now we are the common enemy and that is fostering relationships... we are starting to see each other as brothers.'[29]

3. Exploring British Muslim Identity

Identities of Muslims in Britain are about, on the one hand, how Muslims have been represented - especially by the media in Britain - and, on the other hand, how those representations bear upon the ways in which Muslims in Britain might represent themselves.[30] The constructivist position on identity is that "identity is a construct and a creation from available social roles and materials".[31] But there are no essential materials – in terms of "ethnic, racial and national conceptions of cultural identity"[32] – from which Muslims in Britain might fashion a representation - a new ethnicity - of

British Muslim for themselves. Rather, to be Muslim in Britain requires an understanding that "identity must be anti-essentialist and capable of conceptualizing change and multiple forms of affiliations which can transcend national borders".[33] A formulation of *British Muslim* does not involve the fashioning of a stable identity that is binary but an identity that is hybrid requiring:

> a continuous [process]... that borrows and raids multiple economies of signs, that constantly reinterprets inherited traditions and formulates itself through complex, multiplex connections.[34]

Thus, identity need not be static: "one can choose and make – and remake – one's identity as fashion and life possibilities change and expand"[35] and children, in particular, "can be extremely fluid about their identifications with communities and collectives".[36] However, as one commentator remarks, there is a "countervailing pull where adults try to re-enculturate [young people]" and "differences emerge between elder and younger generation on the significance of culture and religion".[37] Moreover, the effects of education on the younger generation may mean that "being British is not simply about citizenship, as it is for the older generation, it is part of the cultural make".[38]

4. Methodology

There have been few accounts of identity creation amongst young Muslims in Britain, "with all the complexity, fluidity and contradictions these encompass".[39] This naturalistic study presents the accounts of pupils from two mainstream secondary schools, each with a predominantly Muslim intake, in East London. Both schools are located in racially diverse, socially disadvantaged community settings that are experiencing regeneration. School A is a single sex girls schools with a well-established selective schooling history. School B is a large mixed comprehensive which has specialist school status.

Twenty four Year 11 pupils from each school participated in the study. The forty-eight pupils comprised eighteen boys and thirty girls from a range of ethnic backgrounds including Gujarati Indian, Iraqi, Kosovan, Kurdish, Nigerian, Pakistani, Turkish and Somalian. All participants were second or third generation British Muslims - with well established extended family networks in London and throughout the British Isles – with the exception of three pupils: two pupils had recently relocated with their family to London (from India and Kuwait) as a result of employment opportunities; and the third pupil had joined his father (originally from Iran) following a second marriage to a British citizen.

Initially, two large buzz groups engaged in ice-breaker discussions of educational ambitions and family culture. Thereafter, smaller focus groups were organised according to gender and particular interests. Several distinct subgroups emerged amongst the participants. One group was the religious group, comprising individuals perceived as having a high level of Islamic education, and coming from families who were held to be steadfast in religious observance. Another group was labeled 'muslims' (with a small m), comprising individuals who were characterised as lacking religious engagement – e.g. with daily prayers - and as not attending rallies and influential lectures held in central London locations. Other groups were identified by core interests including Bollywood films, fashion, music and sport.

5. Findings

The data presented below are intended to allow the pupils' voices to be clearly heard. Pupils' names have been changed to ensure anonymity and confidentiality. Extracts from pupils' accounts are presented verbatim. The data are presented in categories – for accessibility - but these were not categorized by *a priori* criteria but by categories discernible in the data.

A. National identity

Discussions on Britishness occurred in focus groups. This is consistent with the centrality of this critically important issue for young people in the study. Pupils talked about the complex nature of belonging and how their self-selected identities were intended to nurture a greater sense of belonging. Despite diversity of ethnicities and cultures, some pupils affirmed a British identity.

> Noor (School B, 15, Bengali).
> We are all of us British. We live here. We were born here. Most of our parents were born in London, in the same area we all still live in. We are safe.

> Tehmina (School A, 16,Kurdish).
> I call myself British, because I am proud to say it. What else could I be? I was born here, so were my Mum and Dad and all my family. We have never lived anywhere else. It's our home.

However, some pupils' statements indicated some complexity to the issue of national identity, indicating "multiple forms of affiliation" which transcended national borders.[40]

> Suhjoon (School B, 16, Bengali).
> I'm not sure if I am British. I try not to call myself that. I am Bangladeshi but, when we go there for four weeks to see my grandparents, it does not feel like 'home'. More like, we are guests or visitors, even though it is my Dad's house. Usually, after a few days, I can't wait to get back. That's not our culture or even how we want to live in the future. Time has moved on.

Other pupils invoked a transnational identity related to religion, evoking an Islamic meta civilization.[41]

> Raheel (School B, 16, Pakistani).
> We are Muslim, first and last. That's all.

Still other pupils had experience of Muslims of different nationalities.

> Na'eem (School B, 16, Pakistani).
> I went on a retreat to a massive Mosque in Dewsbury with my brother. There were Muslims from all over England, loads of towns, and even different countries like Belgium and Canada. I was so impressed, 'cause they looked so different - the clothes, the hats, the languages. This boy was there - from my year - who got a tattoo. He got so much hassle about it, people telling him it's against Islam. It made me think about how, even though we look and maybe even act in different ways, well, we're different in how we live our life.

An instance – despite the censure of the tattoo - of "fostering relationships through Islam".[42]

B. Religious identity

Observance and prayer facilities - and time and space to for prayer – were recurrent concerns for the majority of pupils. Despite parental involvement, and informal support from some members of the teaching and non-teaching staff, pupils reported an on-going struggle to adapt arrangements of a non-Islamic school to Islamic pupils' requirements.

> Khalid(School B, 16, Indian Gujarati).
> All Muslims are not the same. Some try to pray on time. I know some parents really expect their kids to. But we are

together in a special way when we pray at school. Really powerful. And strong. It helps me to get through all my lessons. Our non-Muslim friends respect it too. Some of them watch, if the teacher gives them a pass. It's about living your whole life as a Muslim. Not just outside school.

There was perceived appreciation of pupils' religious identity on the part of teachers.

Iqbal (School B, 15, Pakistani).
Next year the Gym will be used for prayers. This has already been arranged because, the teachers, they know we won't give up on our prayer times. I told my English teacher that my prayers will help me do better in GCSE class. She said that's the same in her religion too. She is a Christian.

However, this appreciation was not necessarily the rule: there were instances of opposition to Islamic observance.

Wafa (School B, 16, Iraqi).
There were so many problems before we had the prayer room. Like one teacher asked why some Muslims have to pray at school and others don't. We are the same religion, not identical people. It's a very ignorant question, I told that teacher. She gave me a yellow card [part of the school discipline strategy].

Imran (School B, 16, Somali)
Some teachers understand, but most don't. It's the simple things like a separate prayer room for the girls. We were given the drama room in our school for prayers. Before Ramadan we did a petition and 468 pupils said they wanted to pray at lunchtime. About 60 can fit into the drama room. But we didn't give up until we had the whole first floor and some of our uncles and cousins came to help.

Related religious issues – such as fasting – were also concerns.

Hanna (School B, 15, Kuwaiti)
Every year another group of students argue with the welfare staff and even the teachers over fasting and why we want to and have to try very very hard to pray on time. It's like they think we might give up eventually. I lost it with our form

> teacher when he said, 'Let me remind you this is a school not a mosque'.

C. Islamic cultural representation in the curriculum

There had been some demand to introduce Arabic into the curriculum of both schools initiated by pupils, based on their supplementary schooling and their understanding that an additional qualification would enhance their further education choices. A lack of qualified teaching staff had prevented progress taking place for three years in one school. However, supportive staff and volunteer community teachers had enabled the implementation of Arabic as an intensive summer school project. Pupils reported the surprise of staff when over eighty Year 9 pupils applied for places at that summer school. Institutionally and personally, schools and teachers had been responsive to pupils' demands for greater Islamic representation in the curriculum.

> Shipon (School B, 15, Bengali).
> We talked to our teacher about Muslim scientists and inventors. She said she did not learn about them in her degree. But, when I brought in a box of books from home, she did include some information in our chemistry and maths lessons. She said she would ask the art teacher to do the same. She even wanted to know about the bookshop so she could have her own copy. The headteacher gave me a special mention in Assembly because of this.

Teachers' lack of knowledge did not prevent positive responses to Islamic cultural representation in the curriculum..

> Haroon (School B 15, Iraqi).
> There are no books about our culture in the school, not poetry or nothing. My mum has loads and loads at home. I don't get it. When I write about Arabic poetry my teacher always tells me its great and she never heard about that poet before.

However, reported responses were not always positive.

> Jamal (School B, 16, Kurdish).
> I complained about summer sport, that we only do cricket. Our teacher thinks we all love cricket. He even said once, 'The Pakistani nation is passionate about it [cricket]. What's

> wrong with you?' When I told him I am not from Pakistan he said that should not matter.

D. Islamic Cultural Identity

The wearing of Islamic dress in schools reinforced a sense of individual and group identity. Fashion was high on the agenda for the young people – especially the young women - who participated in this study. Exercise of choice in Islamic dress varied from the traditional – e.g. South Asian head-covering - to the political, e.g. scarves evoking the plight of the Palestinian people.

> Jamil (School B, 15, Somali).
> When I was eleven or twelve, I would never wear home clothes outside. Now, I wear it all the time. I want to show my religion and culture, how proud I am. It means we are not the same as the Muslims on TV who kill people, even if we wear the same clothes. Yes, it's my culture now: to wear my home clothes is so important.

But there were indications of generational tensions.

> Shaheena (School A, 16, Gujarati).
> No one can force you. You just wear it for the love of Allah. But I know loads of girl, they get forced, but that's not even their fault. I reckon it's their parents are scared they will run off or something so they make them wear it. I always ask a girl, 'Did your dad force you to wear it?' I tell 'em in Islam it says no one can force you.

The response of schools to expressions of Islamic cultural identity was not consistent. School B was perceived, by one pupil, as being fair.

> Kareema (School B, 15, Somali).
> Our school is fair about Islamic dress. There are so many Muslim kids and the parents want to make sure that, at school, we can cover in a respectful way. I feel safe at school because there are so many Muslims and we are a big, strong group.

However, there were reports of opposition to expressions of Islamic cultural identity, both institutional and personal.

Saima (School B, 16, Pakistani).
I did try to wear the jilbab [cloak] to school but the headteacher had a long talk to me and my Mum. 'It's not allowed,' she said. 'I didn't make a fuss because our teachers don't care what we wear as long as we get good exam results,' she said. In our school, lots of girls go to uni', then they come back and they still have the hijab [headscarf], in cool colours with nice pins and diamante. The teachers tell us all to be like them.

Hafiza (School A, 15, Gujarati Indian).
When I first started to wear the hijab, a teacher said to me, 'Are you sure you can hear me with that on?'

Kalillah (School B, 16, Iraqi).
My big sister told me that, at her unit, the teacher ignores the girls who wear the niqaab indaba [veil]. If they ask a question, the teacher pretends he can't hear who is asking the question. My sister said that some girls stay quiet because of his attitude. One student stands up and shouts out her question, so the whole world can see her. Not everyone is like that, I mean, that confident. I think the problems only get worse once you leave school.

Opposition to expressions of Islamic cultural identity was not confined to schools.

Yasir (School B, 16, Nigerian).
Girls who wear the hijab get a lot of hassle on the bus and stuff. Boys can get away with it. I admire women like my Mum who wear their hijab but also go out and work and care about everyone.

Such perceived opposition could lead to individual concessions concerning 'visible' Islamic cultural identity while not affecting Islamic values.

Salma (School A, 15, Turkish)
I don't wear a hijab, I like to straighten my hair. But it's what's in your heart that counts. I am still a Muslim, I pray. When I am older, say twenty-seven, I might start to wear it.

> Roxy (School A, 15, Kurdish).
> I don't wear hijab anymore. I did wear it for about two years. I still do all my prayers and fasting, which is more important than anything else, in my opinion. Some girls wear the hijab and get pregnant with their boyfriend. What's the point in that?

However, expressions of Islamic cultural identity could assert group identity.

> Shaeena (16, School A, Gujarati):
> At our school there is one main group of Muslims called the Hijabi Queens: we used to be called the Bling Queens. We have loads of girls support us. All you have to do is wear some bling. You don't have to wear a hijab.

> Tahir (School B, 16, Kurdish)
> Some girls wear Chanel hijabs, and similar styles, to show that they are in a group, all the same. It's great. It shows that Islam is important, but they are into fashion too. Most of all, they are strong about being Muslims. Girls who don't wear hijabs… I'm not sure. I think they are too Westernised and their parents let them get away with it.

E. 'Westernisation'

The issue of 'westernisation' disclosed possible generational conflict and heterogeneity in Islamic cultures.

> Mustakim (School B, 16, Turkish).
> Most Muslim parents are worried about their kids turning their backs on Islam, like drinking and getting married to non-Muslims and stuff. My parents are very modern because, in Turkey, they lived a free life, no hassles about clothes and going out. Here, all my mates think that's a good way to be. My culture is more modern and I'm sure that it will help me understand Islam better.

There was some ambivalence concerning 'westernisation': some participants were critical of Islamic culture as 'backward' while others, implicitly, argued for solidarity between Muslims and 'muslims'.

Sahim (School B, 16, Turkish)
The small 'm' group they are okay, really. They think it's a big deal to go out and get wasted. I could do it if I wanted to. I'm not going to show myself up. When I talk to those guys, they are having fun but they miss out on all our stuff. It's tough when all your mates are drinking and all I can say is, 'Don't do it, we are Muslims'.

Ummay (School B, 16, Kuwaiti)
Some girls go out and get drunk. They are Muslims too. Their parents probably suspect what they are up to. We try to be friends; no one wants to see Muslims get a bad name.

Esa (School B, 16, Indian Gujaraiti).
We do go out, clubbing, drinking. It's a laugh. Once we get married, that's it. Stay ay home. That happened to my sister and she tried to run a way twice. Our culture is backward like that.

F. Activism

Activism could be a reaction to the "negative and problem-oriented portrayal" of Islam in the British media.[43]

Sohail (School B, 15, Gujarati Indian).
We got to lectures and stuff on Islam and things in the news. It's our job to make sure that Islam is protected, like the beautiful religion it is. I know that some people think that Muslims in this country are a problem, like some go into terrorism, but that is just a few. I'm going to be a barrister when I leave university and I won't ever stick up for a terrorist. It's against Islam. What about the innocent people who get killed in the terrorist bombings, like in Madrid. That is wrong.

Thus, activism could be perceived as promoting a positive image of Islam.

Gazhaal (School A, 16, Bengali).
I started to go to a group in central London about what Muslims should do, like talk to neighbours, meet people of other religions, be a good role model. The school council is introducing some exchange with a Christian school now.

> We have to do lots of activities together so that they can see Muslim kids are just the same as they are.

Such activism could promote cross-cultural understanding.

> Habeeba (School A, 16, Iraqi).
> I went on a march and met loads of white girls, non Muslims. They were against the Israeli wall and supported Palestine. I was proud of them, they understand how Muslims feel. We are mates now. When we go to town we don't talk about my religion and stuff, we just have a laugh. If I did not go to the march outside 10 Downing Street, I would not have met them in my area, ever.

But there was wariness of the perils of activism.

> Fawaad (School B, 16, Iraqi).
> My parents told me not to get involved in any marches and stuff against the war in Iraq, 'cause that's how they [the organizers] find innocent boys to join their groups. I have seen it outside the mosque and even near our school. I still go to the demonstrations against the war because I believe that the war was wrong.

G. Aspirations

Tensions were apparent when participants – particularly girls – discussed their aspirations.

> Soheema (School B, 16, Bengali).
> Our group of friends will all go to uni' and try to make a different life. We won't marry someone from back home and hate them all our life. My life won't be a disaster like that. I want to be a barrister. I might work in Bangladesh for a bit, too, to see what their life is like out there.

These tensions could be due to 'traditional' expectations, but these expectations were not necessarily generational.

> Daniah, (School B, 16, Iraqi).
> At the community centre there is a talk about forced marriages and how Muslim girls can get help. I know it happens still for, like, some Bangladeshi girls and that. There should be talks about getting a good job, courses,

> becoming a paramedic or a midwife, becoming a translator. My mum works as a translator for three solicitors and the council. It's her first job ever. She started taking driving lessons last year. My aunty in Watford says she is a role model for loads of women now.

6. Discussion

This study offers insight into the construction of identity by young Muslims in mainstream secondary school in East London. Three factors recurred in the opinions voiced by participants: the issue of nationality; the issue of religious identity and the issue of generational tensions.

The heterogeneity of cultural antecedents of the young Muslims in this study meant that issues common to all were nationality and religious identity. Wherever the participants positioned themselves on a continuum between 'British' and 'non-British', the issue of nationality was key. Whether participants affirmed their British nationality – 'I call myself British... What else could I be?' (Tehmina - School A, 16, Kurdish) – or expressed multiple forms of affiliation – 'I'm not sure if I am British… I am Bangladeshi but…' (Suhjoon - School B, 16, Bengali) – or invoked a transnational identity related to religion – 'We are Muslim, first and last' (Raheel - School B, 16, Pakistani) – provisional identity bound the participants.

Similarly, wherever the participants positioned themselves on a continuum between observant Muslim and 'muslim' (with a small m), the related issues of religion and religious observance were key. Religious identity was consolidated by institutional and personal appreciation or opposition encountered in matters of observance – prayer facilities and Islamic dress – and Islamic representation in the curriculum. A complementary awareness of 'westernisation' and activism to ensure that 'Islam is protected' (Sohail - School B, 15, Gujarati Indian) confirmed this issue of religious identity.

Generational tensions were also reported. The young participants were aware of the concerns of the older generation - e.g. 'Muslim parents are worried about their kids turning their backs on Islam, like drinking and getting married to non-Muslims' (Mustakim - School B, 16, Turkish) – and perceived Islamic custom as being enforced by the older generation on the younger generation, e.g. 'parents want to make sure that, at school, we can cover in a respectful way' (Kareema - School B, 15, Somali) and 'parents are scared [their daughters] will run off or something so they make them wear [Islamic dress]' (Shaheena - School A, 16, Gujarati). The reported imposition of the older generation was generally attributed to concern for the younger generation, e.g. 'My parents told me not to get involved in any marches and stuff against the war in Iraq, 'cause that's how they [the organizers] find innocent boys to join their groups' (Fawaad - School B, 16, Iraqi). There was evidence of resistance, e.g. 'That's not our culture or even how we want to live in the future. Time has moved on' (Suhjoon, School B, 16, Bengali). However, there were instances of commonality in cross-generational aspirations - e.g. 'My mum works as a translator for three solicitors and the council… she is a role model for loads of women' (Daniah, - School B, 16, Iraqi) – not merely imposition and resistance.

These three factors affect the degrees to which young Muslims in Britain can choose and make their hybrid identity as *British Muslims* and "try to make a different life" (Soheema – School B, 16, Bengali).

Notes

[1] See Commission on British Muslims and Islamophobia [CBMI], *Islamophobia: Issues, Challenges and Action*, Trentham Books/Uniting Britain Trust, Stoke on Trent/London, 2004, p.7, and A Sajid, *Islamophobia: a New Word for an Old Fear*, paper presented at Organisation for Security and Co-operation in Europe [OSCE] Conference on Anti-Semitism and on other forms of Intolerance, Cordoba 8th and 9th June, 2005.

[2] Runnymede Trust, *Islamophobia: A Challenge for us All*, Commission on British Muslims and Islamophobia, London, 1997.

[3] '9/11' refers to the destruction by terrorist attack of the World Trade Centre in New York on 11th September, 2001.

[4] '7/7' refers to the terrorist attack in London on the 7th July, 2005.

[5] CBMI, ibid.

[6] P Bhachu, 'Disapora politics through style: racialized and politicized fashion in global markets', in C Alexander and C Knowles (ed), *Making Race Matter: Bodies, Space and Identity*, Palgrave Macmillan, Basingstoke, 2005, pp. 42-59, pp.43-44.

[7] J Solomos, *Race and Racism in Britain*, Palgrave Macmillan, Basingstoke, 2003, p. 52.

[7] S Vertovec, 'Islamophobia and Muslim recognition in Britain', in Y Y Haddad (ed) *Muslims in the West: From Sojourners to Citizens*, Oxford University Press, Oxford, 2002, pp. 19-35, p.19.

[8] See S P Huntington, 'The clash of civilizations?', *Foreign Affairs*, 72-4, 1993, pp.22-49.

[9] E Vasta, *Accommodating Diversity: Why Current Critiques of Multiculturalism Miss the Point*, Centre on Migration, Policy and Society [COMPAS], University of Oxford, Working Paper No. 53, 2007, COMPAS, Oxford, p. 19.

[10] CBMI, op. cit., p.4.

[11] Vertovec, op. cit., p. 19; Solomos, op. cit., pp. 44-45.

[12] Vertovec, op. cit., p. 19.

[13] Vertovec, op. cit., p.20; Solomos; op. cit., p. 60; K Reed, 'Comparing new migration with old: exploring the issue of asylum and settlement', in C Alexander and C Knowles (ed), *Making Race Matter: Bodies, Space and Identity*, Palgrave Macmillan, Basingstoke, 2005, pp. 76-89, p. 78.
[14] See T Modood, 'British Muslims and the politics of multiculturalism', in T Modood, A Triandafyllidou and R Zapata-Berrero (ed) *Multiculturalism, Muslims and Citizenship: A European Approach*, Routledge, Oxford, 2006, pp.37-56, p. 38.
[15] Vertovec, op. cit., p. 21.
[16] D McGhee, *Intolerant Britain: Hate, Citizenship and Difference*, Open University Press, Maidenhead, 2005, pp.97-97; Modood, op. cit., p. 38.
[17] Commission on British Muslims and Islamophobia [CBMI], op. cit., p.7.
[18] See T Modood and S May, 'Multiculturalism and education in Britain: an internally contested debate', *International Journal of Educational Research*, 2001, 35-3, pp. 305-317.
[19] M Barker, *The New Racism*, Junction Books, London.
[20] S P Huntington, *The Clash of Civilisations and the Remaking of World Order*, Simon and Schuster, New York, 1996, pp.45-47.
[21] Ibid., p. 110.
[22] Huntington, 1993, p. 35; Huntington, 1996, pp. 209-218.
[23] Commission for Racial Equality [CRE], *Stereotyping and Racism: Findings from Two Attitude Surveys*, CRE, London, 1998; S Cottle, *Ethnic Minorities and the Media: Changing Cultural Boundaries*, Open University Press, Buckingham, 2000; G Cumberbatch, S Gauntlet, M Richards and V Littlejohns, *Top 10 TV: Ethnic Minority Group Representation on Popular Television*, CRE, London 2001; J Richardson, 'British Muslims in the broadsheet press: a challenge to cultural hegemony?', *Journalism Studies*, 2-2, 2001, pp.221-242.
[24] R Bhavnani, H Safia Mirza and V Meetoo, *Tackling the Roots of Racism: Lessons for Success*, Policy Press, Bristol, 2005, p. 38.
[25] Richardson, op. cit., p. 221.
[26] Ibid.
[27] CBMI, op. cit., p. 1.
[28] Vertovec, op. cit., p. 22.
[29] CBMI, op. cit., p. 4.
[30] See S Hall, 'Who needs identity?' in S Hall and P du Gay (ed), *Questions of Cultural Identity*, Sage, London, 1996, pp. 1-17, p. 4.
[31] D Kellner, 'Popular culture and the construction of postmodern identities' in S Lash and J Friedman (ed), *Modernity and Identity*, Blackwell, Oxford, 1992, pp. 141-177, p. 143.
[32] Hall, p. 1.

[33] M Song, 'Global and local articulations of Asian identity', in C Alexander and C Knowles (ed), *Making Race Matter: Bodies, Space and Identity*, Palgrave Macmillan, Basingstoke, 2005, pp. 60-75, p. 64.
[34] Bhachu, op. cit., p.50.
[35] Kellner, op. cit., p. 142.
[36] S Ali, *Mixed-race, Post-race: Gender, New Ethnicities and Cultural Practices*, Berg, Oxford, 2003, p. 139.
[37] Y Samad, *Muslim Youth in Britain: Ethnic to Religious Identity*, paper presented at Muslim Youth in Europe conference, Edoardo Agnelli Centre for Comparative Religious Studies, Turin, 11th June 2004, p. 16.
[38] Ibid., p. 18.
[39] C Alexander, 'Re-imagining the Muslim community', in H Goulbourne (ed) Race *and Ethnicity: Critical Concepts in Sociology*, Routledge, London, 2001, pp. 42-57, p.42.
[40] Song, op. cit.
[41] Huntington, 1996, p. 45.
[42] CBMI, op. cit., p.4.
[43] Bhavnani et al, op. cit.
[44] Song, op. cit.

Bibliography

Alexander, C., 'Re-imagining the Muslim community', in H Goulbourne (ed) Race *and Ethnicity: Critical Concepts in Sociology*, Routledge, London, 2001, pp. 42-57.

Barker, M. *The New Racism*, Junction Books, London.

Bhachu, P., 'Disapora politics through style: racialized and politicized fashion in global markets', in C Alexander and C Knowles (ed), *Making Race Matter: Bodies, Space and Identity*, Palgrave Macmillan, Basingstoke, 2005, pp. 42-59.

Bhavnani, R., H. Safia Mirza and V. Meetoo, *Tackling the Roots of Racism: Lessons for Success*, Policy Press, Bristol, 2005.

Commission for Racial Equality [CRE], *Stereotyping and Racism: Findings from Two Attitude Surveys*, CRE, London, 1998.

Commission on British Muslims and Islamophobia [CBMI], *Islamophobia: Issues, Challenges and Action*, Trentham Books/Uniting Britain Trust, Stoke on Trent/London, 2004.

Cottle, S., *Ethnic Minorities and the Media: Changing Cultural Boundaries*, Open University Press, Buckingham, 2000.

Cumberbatch, G., S. Gauntlet, M. Richards and V. Littlejohns, *Top 10 TV: Ethnic Minority Group Representation on Popular Television*, CRE, London 2001.

Hall, S., 'Who needs identity?' in S. Hall and P. du Gay (ed), *Questions of Cultural Identity*, Sage, London, pp. 1-17.

Huntington, S. P., 'The clash of civilizations?', *Foreign Affairs*, 72-4, 1993, pp.22-49.

Huntington, S. P., *The Clash of Civilisations and the Remaking of World Order*, Simon and Schuster, New York, 1996.

Kellner, D., 'Popular culture and the construction of postmodern identities' in S Lash and J Friedman (ed), *Modernity and Identity*, Blackwell, Oxford, 1992, pp. 141-177.

McGhee, D., *Intolerant Britain: Hate, Citizenship and Difference*, Open University Press, Maidenhead, 2005.

Modood, T. *Multicultural Policies: Racism, Ethnicity and Muslims in Britain*, Edinburgh University Press, Edinburgh, 2005.

Modood, T., 'British Muslims and the politics of multiculturalism', in T. Modood, A. Triandafyllidou and R. Zapata-Berrero (ed) *Multiculturalism, Muslims and Citizenship: A European Approach*, Routledge, Oxford, 2006, pp.37-56,

Modood, T. and S. May, 'Multiculturalism and education in Britain: an internally contested debate', *International Journal of Educational Research*, 2001, 35-3, pp. 305-317.

Reed, K., 'Comparing new migration with old: exploring the issue of asylum and settlement' in C Alexander and C Knowles (ed), *Making Race Matter: Bodies, Space and Identity*, Palgrave Macmillan, Basingstoke, 2005, pp. 76-89.

Richardson, J., 'British Muslims in the broadsheet press: a challenge to cultural hegemony?', *Journalism Studies*, 2-2, 2001, pp.221-242.

Runnymede Trust, *Islamophobia: A Challenge for us All*, Commission on British Muslims and Islamophobia [CBMI], London, 1997.

Sajid, A., *Islamophobia: a New Word for an Old Fear*, paper presented at Organisation for Security and Co-operation in Europe [OSCE] Conference on Anti-Semitism and on other forms of Intolerance, Cordoba 8th and 9th June, 2005.

Samad, Y., *Muslim Youth in Britain: Ethnic to Religious Identity*, paper presented at Muslim Youth in Europe conference, Edoardo Agnelli Centre for Comparative Religious Studies, Turin, 11th June 2004.

Solomos, J. *Race and Racism in Britain*, Palgrave, Macmillan, Basingstoke, 2003.

Song, M., 'Global and local articulations of Asian identity', in C Alexander and C Knowles (ed), *Making Race Matter: Bodies, Space and Identity*, Palgrave Macmillan, Basingstoke, 2005, pp. 60-75.

Vasta, E., *Accommodating Diversity: Why Current Critiques of Multiculturalism Miss the Point*, Centre on Migration, Policy and Society [COMPAS], University of Oxford, Working Paper No. 53, 2007, COMPAS, Oxford.

Vertovec, S., 'Islamophobia and Muslim recognition in Britain', in Y. Y. Haddad (ed) *Muslims in the West: From Sojourners to Citizens*, Oxford University Press, Oxford, 2002, pp. 19-35.

Nasima Hassan, originally from Lancashire, worked in secondary schools as a Humanities curriculum leader and as a school-based professional mentor supporting initial teacher-trainees before moving to Liverpool Hope University as a subject tutor for secondary Religious Education. She has published chapters on themes of global education from the South African perspective and 'race' and is currently engaged in PhD fieldwork exploring the educational journeys of British Muslims.

Merely Gestural? Schools as a Site for Posturing against a Theatre of the Depressed

Namita Chakrabarty and John Preston

Abstract
Using a synthesis of Butler and Marx, this chapter argues that although sites are increasingly controlled, performative 'posturing' represents a form of resistance to this. The chapter defines posturing, then explores its use by students in two inner London secondary schools, against a 'theatre of the depressed', that is, an examinative performative culture. Posturing could present drama practitioners with the possibility of transforming supposedly neutral drama studios by harnessing the culturally disturbing elements of site-specific theatre. The chapter considers whether posturing disrupts the increasingly commodified nature of school drama.

Key Words: Posturing, performative culture, theatre.

*****

1. Introduction

> At the end of the twentieth century… elements of theatre have become an integral part of other spheres of activity. In politics, performance is increasingly become important; the drama in spectator sports is being enhanced and religion is becoming more of a live event as greater emphasis is put on creating conditions for a spiritual experience, rather than on dogma. The borderline between theatre and reality becomes more hazy as war becomes a media-spectacle… so theatre can move into new areas of performance.[1]

> It was a time of direct gestures, shameless discourse, and open transgressions, when anatomies were shown and intermingled at will, and knowing children hung about amid the laughter of adults: it was a period when bodies "made a display of themselves".[2]

> Words have no impact on you, therefore I'm going to talk to you in a language you understand.[3]

Gesture and 'gestural politics' have become seen to be increasingly important in terms of the ways in which we think about the political and dramatic possibilities of sites in the new century.[4] An implication of this is that the relationships between performance, site and self have become increasingly entangled, with major implications for our political agency. We are performing subjects, but this does not mean that what occurs in sites is open to transgression and the free play of identities. The 'performative' metaphor sometimes implies a liberatory and playful perspective on human agency. This is seducative but misleading. Sites are increasingly sites of performed (emotional, aesthetic) *labour* where human activity (including creativity and acting) is commodified. In terms of contemporary site-specific theatre, the importance of gestural politics and the commodification of public sites have been addressed to a certain extent.[5] In particular, there has been a recent pre-occupation with how site-specific drama might reveal the (psychoanalytically) 'hidden' features of sites[6] through the creation of dramatized walks and trails through cities. There have also been recent calls for a 'site unspecific' theatre as a direct challenge to the dynamics of globalisation.[7] Each of these approaches address the dramatic nature of (mundane) public sites and the political need to address that which is not commented upon. In this chapter, we show how, even within what is supposed to be non-site specific drama performances in schools, the posturing of pupils transgresses the commodified nature of performances, transforming them into particular forms of site-specific theatre. These are gestural, but political, acts in that they transgress the conventions of the performative.

We have never lived in a more performative public space but it is a performative that is highly scripted, pathologised and controlled. The concept that we use in this chapter, 'posturing', is not opposed to performativity and could not fail to be part of the performative. However, posturing represents both a codified control of the body, words and movement (hence it is a source of power) and a dislocation of circuits of power (through temporarily dislocating power structures - creating what anarchists such as Reclaim the Streets[8] refer to as a temporary autonomous zone of 'uncontrolled public space'). In terms of queer theory, posturing 'queers' the everyday performative of public space and may even form part of a resistant political project, particularly when coupled with insights from Marxist theory. As Joseph states, 'a Butlerian reading of Marx makes it possible to recognize the opportunities as well as the constraints available within production'.[9]

The starting point for our theoretical perspective on theatrical posturing is Butler's 'Merely Cultural'[10] in which she questions the distinction made between those political movements based on resisting material oppression and those based on overturning cultural distinction.[11] For Butler, the distinction between material and cultural life is not a stable one and queer politics is as concerned with the material as class politics:

> Why would a movement concerned to criticise and transform the ways in which sexuality is socially regulated not be understood as central to the functioning of political economy. [12]

Butler sees queer studies as an important component of Marxist critiques of the family and - to borrow concepts from critical race theory - the 'hidden backpack' of economic benefits of heterosexuality. Butler's paper 'Merely Cultural' has been criticised by materialist feminists[13] for ignoring the material basis of patriarchal structures of oppression, concentrating on capitalist forms. However, the strength of Butler's paper is that it places queer politics at the intersection of the dual systems of both patriarchy and capitalism offering if not an alternative based on overthrowing current social relations then a mode of resistance to those relations.

For us, Marx was writing a 'queer' political economy of one of those systems - capitalism. That is, not another political economy which aimed to describe capitalism - in the mode of Smith, Ricardo et al - but an alien political economy, written against political economy which subverted the essentialist notions of economic concepts such as labour, time and profit. Recent revisions of Marx pay attention to the notion of labour power - how such power is exploited by capital as a source of value and how this value creates an alienating and alien world of capitalist commodities.[14] Although some critics argue that Marx linked the theatre and theatricality with non-productiveness[15] in terms of what could be counted as labour power, Marx was extremely eclectic in his position that not only manual or mental labour could be included but also performative labour. In *Theories of Surplus Value*,[16] for example, Marx describes the labour of actors and clowns on the stage as being as more of a form of labour power than that of a tailor who mends the capitalists' trousers. In our modern capitalist economy notions of performative labour have become increasingly important - 'vanishing products are precisely what contemporary capitalism thrives on'[17] - and we find elements of performance in areas of work which might not have previously been considered as acting. Sites of production and consumption have become performative.[18] Increasingly, production requires 'acting' in terms of aesthetic and emotional labour. This may range from absolutely scripted communication to foster trust (in a call centre, in a fast food outlet), through more improvised performance (in a clothes shop, in a restaurant), to actual acting (as a character in a theme park or a play - this obviously has implications for the notion of an essentialist 'self' within performative labour). Capitalism is dependent and hungry for labour power of any form if it adds value to a commodity, so we should not be surprised that this most creative of human capabilities is increasingly plundered for profit. Indeed, 'race', 'gender' and 'sexuality' have become essentialised and commodified as performances, for example, the packaging and presentation of 'Black' culture for 'White' audiences in entertainment industries.[19]

If site and place are regulated, performative and commercial then it may seem that there is little space for resistance other than through formally constituted political movements or new social movements. However, to explore the Butler/Marx connection, there is another way in which performative labour (and, hence, performative sites) have a weakness. As Butler[20] suggests, in performance (production) there is the risk of failure, of misinterpretation and that the meaning of performance can be subverted, queered (in consumption). Marx reinforces this point in that, when there is human agency, labour has to be extracted from a thinking subject, so there is the possibility of resistance. This does not mean that all forms of what may appear, or what are performed as 'radical' performance (such as street theatre, youth drama) are potentially subversive of capitalism or other forms of oppression, and Joseph[21] has argued that supposedly subversive performative activities can be appropriated within capitalist production and consumption (as consumptive labour). However, there may be a subset of performative activities which are not appropriable by performative labour. Posturing is our term for these (temporary and contingent) resistances, queering performative labour or attempts to impose the production of commodified performances (such as in a classroom) more generally. Posturing represents a temporary seizure of space in terms of controlled bodily and linguistic gestures, operating outside the regulated performative. Posturing hails the performative from outside of what is being performed, making us aware that what we had been watching or engaged in was a performance.

Posturing also represents a transgression (or a reinforcement, or both simultaneously) of the capitalist performative in terms of the pulling of the everyday into the realms of both performance / live art and into the realm of the political. As Hill states, 'the most fundamental element of performance / live art is live presence, the presence of the performer and the live reception by an audience.'[22]

Thus the boundaries of performance permeate both life and political action and 'any number of works presented in gallery and theatre spaces could be dubbed performance art, but so would *certain* political demonstrations'[23] (our italics). Hill cites as examples of such demonstrations those by disabled protesters outside parliament and a number of activities 'performed' by the Suffragettes. We would extend Hill's analysis in that all political demonstrations are postural. We would also extend the realms of 'political' to other forms of resistance which are (for reasons of class-ism, racism or sexism) not considered to be 'political'. For example, Tracey Emin's *My Bed* and her performance on *Newsnight*[24] is posturing in that the everydayw w - whether a reconstruction of her bed or a conversation - is both performance and simultaneously political. There is, therefore, the potential for the 'everyday' postural to simultaneously be political, 'the subversive and parodic redeployment of power rather than on the impossible fantasy of its full-scale transcendence'.[25]

2. Researching 'Posturing' in School Drama

In researching 'posturing' in school drama we adopted a post-critical ethnography approach.[26] In particular, we were aware of the circuits of power which operate within the drama classroom. It is a common insight in ethnography that the act of observation effects what occurs in ethnographic sites[27] but post-critical ethnography moves beyond this in terms of its consideration of the operation of power within ethnographic sites. During our ethnography we observed that frequently 'terror' and 'fear' could be used to describe what was happening in the classroom. The term 'symbolic violence' - used by Bourdieu and Passeron to describe social control processes in the educational system[28] - is apt here. We observed pupils cowed by their teachers, teachers fearful of what we might be writing about them, and ourselves scared by the degree of power and control inflicted on all involved. However, power operated in all directions in a Foucauldian sense (between us, teachers and pupils). Adopting a participatory approach to research, research would not absent us from considerations of power (and according to Foucauldian analysis would open up new circuits of power relations). Therefore, we retain an awareness of ourselves as both the subjects and operators of power within the ethnography rather than 'neutral' observers (but also rather than as 'emancipators' or 'activists' within the ethnography).

We write the ethnography as a series of vignettes to illustrate tensions rather than as a straight ethnographic narrative. We consider ethnography to be a form of 'storytelling'[29] but that the verisimilitude of 'stories' may 'come very close to life as experienced'.[30] Our research focus is twofold: firstly, on the tensions between performance and posturing; and, secondly, how posturing transgresses performance. Obviously, there are ethical issues involved with the interpretation of our accounts. One technicist response to this, which we reject, would be 'respondent validation'[31] which would be to present each individual with a copy of the research findings pertaining to them and ask them to amend their interpretation accordingly. This procedure is sometimes followed for validity as well as ethics. We decided not to follow this route. A feature of many good ethnographies is discomfort and conflict. Humphrey's classic *Tearoom Trade*[32] is one example of a non-participant supposedly 'unethical' ethnography which reveals pertinent truths. The reporting of 'unpalatable' truths (such as the nature of power and commodification in drama classrooms) should be part of ethnography, particularly if this discomfort reveals something concerning the obscured nature of power relations. We concur with Epstein[33] who refers to the need for researchers to temper concerns with ethics with a concern for the political consequences of their research. We err on the side of politics rather than ethics in this research, and accept that although this may have consequences for the 'internal' validity of our findings we nevertheless reveal something of the contested power relations within drama classrooms in terms of tensions between performance / posturing.

We present here some initial results from what will be an extended ethnography of 'posturing' in educational sites. The schools which we have chosen to comment on here reflect different social characteristics. In both schools pupils were mainly non-white. However, in the first school there was a mixture of middle and working class students, whereas in the second students were predominantly from working class backgrounds.

3. Posturing and Peformativity in School Drama

Although it has become the convention in ethnography to choose pseudonyms for the participants, we have used numerical codes so that the reader is not lulled into a false sense of literary security which would be textual performance. We refer to schools as 1 and 2, teachers as T1, T2, T3 and students as S1, S2 and S3.

A. School 1

> Field Notes - The site…like a shopping centre from the setting for a dystopian science fiction movie… like an 'observation' of a New Labour project in terms of being looked at (by an elite panopticon) and isolated from the elite housing… the performance of harnessing black and urban culture towards empowering the school like the sixties adventure playgrounds, those urban spaces made by adults to appeal to young people but in their very makeshift qualities became rather quickly abandoned…. entering the school the analogy with shopping centre / car park continues with an underpass running through it… an urbanoid, rather than an urban site where sanitized and stereotyped features of supposedly 'urban' (often used as a euphemism for 'Black' or 'Black' as performed by dominant culture) life are used to enhance consumer (in this case pupil) experience. The 'urban' in this case was used as a symbol of that which is edgy, alien and desired, posturing, but employed in the form of regulation of student performance.

In the (non-uniform) school the students wore the uniform of the street: clother with 'labels', jeans and sweatshirts. The clothes produced the movement and gestures of urban music videos: the students stretching and altering shape under the sweatshirts, both hiding and exhibiting their bodies. This combination of clothing and gesture is de-gendered and translated well for the neutral mask work of Lesson 1. The stylized body work became an extension of the teenagers' body/street attitudinal style: the melancholic sagging shoulders, the druggy lolling head, the dragged feet and - the opposite extreme - the aggressive and confrontational. T1 pointed out the subject keywords on the board - body isolation, exaggerate, stylized - and stressed that the work was a commodity being developed for performance, to a specific audience (the group were developing work for performance to other young people). T1 talked about Sophocles' *Oedipus* when exploring the origins of the abusive phrase 'your mum'. Thus, the lesson drew on the pop video but also other popular and theatrical cultural narratives – the marionette and its master, *The Matrix*[34] fight scene and also drugs related crime scenes. The drama therefore is produced by the site and is a reflection of a growing culture which, like a magpie, takes the charismatic elements from others in the pursuit of safeguarding the status quo and denying authenticity. The visual product of this lesson, three scenes involving masks, was highly choreographed and self-contained, performative but, as the following three vignettes show, this performativity was always in a tension with posturing.

Vignette 1.

T1: If you're performing, the commitment is to your audience. What you want them to think, to feel.

S1: What if I just want to scare them?

T1: No, maybe what you're trying to teach someone is that murdering someone is bad…you don't actually do it. You can use suggestion, metaphor.

The tension for the drama teacher is a commitment to an aesthetic and democratic ethic in the tradition of twentieth century political theatre - which has the audience integral to the experience (a performance with value, laced with the emerging values of democracy) - in opposition to the student's playful posturing inquiry and to emotional labour. (Saturated with the narcotics of twenty-first century culture sex and gore, but also, we wonder, in line with Brechtian alienation, perhaps fear can be performative, challenging, educative?)

Vignette 2

S3: Hey, hey, remember, I'm the mad man with the mask
(He pretends to pick his nose through the mask.)

S2: That's deviant
(S3 pimp rolls across the classroom with mask.)

S2: You're not Darth Vader with the mask

Vignette 3
S1: First scene, between Morpheus and Neo
S2: He's going to be Smith
S1: You should have that kind of mask (a white one) (They re-enact one of the fight scenes from *The Matrix.*)
S3: Mortal Combat style
S1: MOR-TAL COM-BAT (intoned in style of the video game.)

In School 1, the performed scenes were well accomplished but lacking something without the posturing element of the rehearsal vignettes. It felt as though the tension between the performative and posturing arising from the site and time of London 2005 left an emptiness, a challenge for school drama which was not reflecting the feeling outside on the street in London 2005: Two months after the events of '7/7'- the coordinated suicide bombings - and the subsequent police shooting of Menezes, an innocent Brazilian, CCTV surveillance pictures are played and replayed, and we are all caught up within the performative: suspicion and counter-suspicion territories. Space seems to have disappeared and we are all cornered like billiard balls in a triangle, perhaps jostling to posture - along Old Compton Street, Soho, London's gay village, people continue to play with gender, body, and ownership of site twenty-four seven, while on the South Bank the National Theatre's 'Watch this Space' is a smorgasbord of site-specific outdoor street theatre at programmed times.

B. School 2

Field Notes - Our tension rises as we are recorded walking through the tube station along the corridors where the CCTV apparently wasn't working on 22/7 when Menezes was killed…we enter the school and a highly performative atmosphere….poster on notice board in reception 'The Streets Deserve Respect'… 'No hoodies or baseball caps'… traditional school, blazer and tie… walking into the drama room we are surprised that desks are arranged in a semi-circle around a whiteboard… we sit down and face outside through the window… looks like the flats where 21/7 suspects were arrested - T2 sees our faces and shuts the curtains, adjusting his tie and smoothing his suit… T2, male, soft but commanding voice… T3 female, louder but anxious voice: anxious to get the right words on the page…

> prompting key words in the performativity of written coursework for GCSE drama exam… teachers and students in perpetual cycle of examination and observation - terror.

Our feeling of tension-terror-performativity was undercut by the students' posturing use of props/objects during the work on a Bob Marley recording, 'Johnny Was',[35] introduced by T2 as one of a series of lessons for the EDEXCELL GCSE workshop paper. As instructed by T1 and T2, this melancholic song is the narrative of a young man caught within 'the system'. The students' were to produce three key scenes chosen from the song's narrative: they were asked to use mime with sparse speech to produce scenes to be performed to the timing of the recording. Counterposed to the melancholy-commodified examinative performance, posturing included a pen being tapped often, mobile 'phone play, and a pink umbrella. The latter was a girlish toy-like umbrella used by one of the boys to tap the floor whilst the others listened to the song. For us this was a Butler-esque queering of traditional masculinity, yet simultaneously reinforcing masculinity through this posture. The nearest analogy is the queer-culture androgyny in Gangsta Rap of dandyism. It was in this posturing that we found a tension with the performative.

This tension grated with the '70s song's atmosphere, reflected in the words of one student later:

> It's a vicious circle…it's the street, it's what happens… the dad thought he was Tupac, he got killed, the son has to avenge his death, then he gets killed [S4].

One group used a mobile as a pivotal object of power in their performance. The father's murderers witness Johnny's father on his mobile, talking to Johnny's mother. His murder is heard by Johnny's mother on her mobile phone. She recounts this to Johnny who later, using a mobile as a knife, kills his father's murderer, then Johnny himself is killed, enacted using mobiles as guns. The father's death, played in slow motion, was very moving and timeless in the manner of the destined-to-die gun-culture background of urban music videos. This death enactment was the site of the posture of what Foucault termed 'lyricism and religiosity'[36] in the amalgam of sound and stylised performance allied with dance in its fluidity, addressing the style and themes of the street entrapped by capitalist popular culture.

During evaluation, the teacher [T3] posed the students a question.

> T3: What are the connections between the dad and Johnny dying violent deaths?
>
> S5: (With a blank look.) What do you mean?

T3 presupposes that there is a catalyst to produce a violent event. The students, however, reflect the power of government and media discourses of the period following 7/7 - that everything is random (e.g. that 7/7 is disconnected from government policy on Iraq) - and that the concept of connections and causality is deemed to be an excuse for terrorism. Both T3 and T1 reminded the students before the end of the rehearsal period to make sure that they had an ending. All endings are a type of death and this we are terming a 'theatre of the depressed' - a theatre opposite in its intentions to that of Boal's Theatre of the Oppressed.

4. Discussion – Posturing against a Theatre of the Depressed

Both lessons, then, were promoting a kind of commodifed performative drama shaped by a cultural specificity of the examinative performative zones which schools have become, a school drama where stories have endings, that peoples' deaths can be explained, that there is a purpose to performance. There were many examples of posturing in both lessons but these were surplus to the performative for the teachers under exam-performative conditions. The inter-textual melancholia of these two lessons was situated in the mask. In the first lesson, students used physical masks and, in the second, the mask was the collective acceptance of a tragic trajectory, the pink umbrella a lone decorative accessory. Post-modernity sees no escape from this in that transgressions (postures) are decorative. Similarly, in contemporary sites, street theatre has become ornamental.[37] Mason notes that the 'radical nature' of work had 'been toned down to make it more "acceptable"' and he points out that 'site-specific work is currently becoming known and generally re-named as Environmental Arts'.[38]

Mason's thoughts, on the changes and future of street theatre, support our findings in that he indicates that young people, who may have been drawn to outdoor street theatre in the past, now feel a closer affinity with 'music, film and video'.[39] There is also the commercial issue at stake here: 'Commercial viability has become the dominant consideration in Britain'.[40] This was reflected in the school drama we witnessed - in terms of form, style, and the role of consumer objects - but also 'commercial viability' in terms of drama as a subject and how it is delivered as though to consumers within school. So that the posturing which we could see at work in some site specific theatre in London at that time (for example Sienta La Cabeza or the *Macbeth* of Friches Théâtre Urbain during 'Watch this Space', the National Theatre free performance space during the summer on the South Bank) was not available to students within the school performative zone, and it is this provocative ambiguity of posturing which was missing in school intentional performance.

The melancholic nature of the mini-drama in the two schools we find to be derived from the absence of a 'provocateur', 'communicator'

(Mason's terms) or, in our terms, a posturer working in opposition to the given. As Mason points out, communicators use popular culture to educate an audience, to challenge ideas, and he brings together the form this has traditionally taken - the use of cultural forms such as music hall and circus (as seen in London throughout the summer but specifically in the *Macbeth* of Friches Théâtre Urbain with its inter-textual references). There has been some really interesting use of site-specific and chorus work in London's youth drama work, for example the work of the Almeida outreach work with Islington schools using deserted buildings and community stories. However, what we are proposing are techniques to bring these site-specific elements into school specific sites. What we are wondering is how to get the clown with the pink umbrella to become the chorus/posturer, to transform the melancholic into something else, possibly utopian, a new theatre form perhaps which would take clown skills to poke fun at the nihilism of the gangsta rap cyclical story whilst embracing the posturing balletic forms of an ungendered and liberational space? What we are positing here is a theatre that takes on the powerful meta-postures of our times by posturing against the 'theatre of the depressed'.

Notes

[1] B Mason, *Street Theatre and other outdoor performance*, Routledge, London, 1992, p.207

[2] M Foucault, *A History of Sexuality Vol. 1: The Will to Knowledge*, Penguin, London, 1998, p.3.

[3] Mohammad Siddique Khan, the alleged leader of the 7th July 2005 suicide bombings in London, known thereafter as '7/7' – see Dodd, V. and R. Norton-Taylor, 'Video of 7/7 ringleader blames foreign policy', *The Guardian* [Online], 2.9.2005, accessed 29th January, 2008 <http://guardian.co.uk/alqaida/story/0,,1561384,00.html>.

[4] G Agamben (translated by V Binetti and C Casarino), *Means Without End: Notes on Politics*, University of Minnesota Press, Minneapolis and London, 2001.

[5] F Wilkie 'Mapping the terrain: a survey of site-specific performance in Britain', *New Theatre Quarterly*, vol.18-2, 2002, pp.140-160.

[6] C Turner ' Palimpset or potential space? Finding a vocabulary for site specific performance', *New Theatre Quarterly*, vol. 20-4, 2004, pp.373-390.

[7] D Rebellato, 'Playwriting and globalisation: towards a site unspecific theatre', *Contemporary Theatre Review*, vol.16-1, 2006, pp.97-113.

[8] 'Reclaim the Streets' is an informally situationist inspired group which organize such events as street parties to disrupt major roads.

[9] M Joseph, *Against the Romance of Community*, University of Minnesota Press, Minnesota, 2002, p.68.

[10] J Butler, 'Merely cultural', *New Left Review*, 227, 1998, pp.33-44.
[11] N Fraser and A Honneth, *Redistribution or Recognition: A Political-Philosophical Exchange*, Verso, London, 2003.
[12] Butler, op. cit., p.39.
[13] S Jackson, 'Why a materialist feminism is (still) possible – and necessary', *Women's Studies International Forum*, vol.34-3/4, 2001, pp.283-293.
[14] M Postone, *Time, Labor and Social Domination: A Reinterpretation of Marx's Critical Theory*, Cambridge University Press, Cambridge, 1993.
[15] For both an articulation and a rebuttal of that position, see Joseph, op. cit., p. 61.
[16] K Marx *Theories of Surplus Value*, Prometheus Books, New York, 2000.
[17] Joseph, op. cit., p.61.
[18] M Wickstrom, *Performing Consumers. Global Capital and its Theatrical Seductions*, Routledge, London, 2006.
[19] E Cashmore, *The Black Culture Industry*, Routledge, London, 1997.
[20] J Butler, 'Critically Queer', in *The Routledge Reader in Politics and Performance*, L Goodman and J de Gay (eds), 2000, Routledge, London, 2000, pp.167-171.
[21] Joseph, op. cit.
[22] L Hill, 'Suffragettes invented performance art', *The Routledge Reader in Politics and Performance*, L Goodman and J de Gay (eds), Routledge, London, 2000, pp.150-156
[23] Ibid., p. 152.
[24] Clare Longrigg commented on Emin's drunken comments on a television discussion programme after the Turner prize announcement that 'Tuesday's performance may be hailed as Tracey Emin's most significant, certainly her most entertaining, contribution to British art'. Longrigg, C., 'Sixty minutes, noise: by art's bad girl', *The Guardian* [Online] 4th December 1997, accessed 29th January, 2008 <http://arts.guardian.co.uk/turnerpeoplespoll/story/0,,1057896,00.html>.
[25] J Butler, *Gender Trouble*, Routledge, London, 1990, p.124
[26] K Gallagher, '(Post) critical ethnography in drama research' in *Research Methodologies for Drama Education*, J. Ackroyd (ed), Trentham Books, Stoke-on-Trent, 2006, pp. 63-80.
[27] M Hammersley, *Reading Ethnographic Research: A Critical Guide* (2nd ed), Longman, London, 1998.
[28] P Bourdieu and J Passeron, *Reproduction in Education, Society and Culture*, Sage, London, 1977.
[29] V Crapanzano, 'Hermes' dilemma: the masking of subversion in ethnographic description', in *Writing Culture: The Poetics and Politics of Ethnography*, J. Clifford and G. Marcus (eds), University of California Press, Berkley, 1984, pp.51-76.

[30] K Plummer, *Telling Sexual Stories: Power, Change and Social Worlds*, Routledge, London, 1995.
[31] M Hammersley and P Atkinson, *Ethnography: Principles in Practice*, Routledge, London, 1996, pp. 228-229.
[32] L Humphreys, *Tearoom Trade*, Aldine, Chicago, 1970.
[33] D Epstein, '"Are you a girl or are you a teacher?" The "least adult" role in research about gender and sexuality in a primary school', in *Doing Research about Education*, E Walford (ed), Falmer Press, London, 1998, pp. 27-41.
[34] A Wachowski and L Wachowski, *The Matrix* Warner Home Video, 1999.
[35] B Marley, 'Johnny Was', from *Rastaman Vibration*, Island Records, New York, 2001.
[36] Foucault, op. cit.
[37] Mason, op. cit.
[38] Ibid., p.205.
[39] Ibid., p.206
[40] Ibid.

Bibliography

Agamben, G. (trans. V Binetti and C. Casarino), *Means Without End: Notes on Politics*, University of Minnesota Press, Minneapolis and London, 2001.

Bourdieu, P. and J. Passeron, *Reproduction in Education, Society and Culture*, Sage, London, 1977.

Butler, J., 'Merely cultural', *New Left Review*, 227, 1998, pp.33-44.

Butler, J., 'Critically queer' in *The Routledge Reader in Politics and Performance*, L. Goodman and J. De Gay (eds), Routledge, London, 2000, pp.167-171.

Butler,J. *Gender Trouble*, Routledge, London, 1990, p.124

Cashmore, E., *The Black Culture Industry*, Routledge, London, 1997.

Crapanzano, V., 'Hermes' dilemma: The Masking of Subversion in Ethnographic Description' in *Writing Culture: The Poetics and Politics of Ethnography*, J. Clifford and G. Marcus (eds), University of California Press, Berkley, 1984, pp.51-76.

Dodd, V. and R. Norton-Taylor, 'Video of 7/7 ringleader blames foreign policy', *The Guardian* [Online], 2nd September,.2005, accessed 29th January, 2008 <http://guardian.co.uk/alqaida/story/0,,1561384,00.html>.

Epstein, D., '"Are you a girl or are you a teacher?" The "least adult" role in research about gender and sexuality in a primary school', in *Doing Research about Education*, E. Walford (ed), Falmer Press, London, 1998, pp.27-41.

Foucault, M., *A History of Sexuality Vol. 1: The Will to Knowledge*, Penguin, London, 1998.

Fraser, N. and A. Honneth, (2003) *Redistribution or Recognition: A Political-Philosophical Exchange*, Verso, London, 2003.

Gallagher, K., '(Post) Critical Ethnography in Drama Research', in *Research Methodologies for Drama Education*, J. Ackroyd (ed), Trentham Books, Stoke on Trent., 2006, pp. 63-80.

Hammersley, M., *Reading Ethnographic Research: A Critical Guide* (2nd Edition), Longman, London, 1998.

Hammersley, M. and P. Atkinson, *Ethnography: Principles in Practice*, Routledge, London, 1996.

Hill, L., 'Suffragettes invented performance art', in *The Routledge Reader in Politics and Performance*, L. Goodman and J. De Gay (eds), Routledge, London, 2000, pp.150-156.

Humphreys, L., *Tearoom Trade*, Aldine, Chicago, 1970.

Jackson, S., 'Why a materialist feminism is (still) possible – and necessary', *Women's Studies International Forum*, vol.34-3/4, 2001, pp.283-293.

Joseph, M., *Against the Romance of Community* (Minnesota, University of Minnesota Press, Minnesota, 2002.

Longrigg, C., 'Sixty minutes, noise: by art's bad girl', *The Guardian*, [Online] 4th December, 1997, accessed 29th January, 2008 <http://arts.guardian.co.uk/turnerpeoplespoll/story/0,,1057896,00.html>.

Marley, B. (2001) 'Johnny Was', from *Rastaman Vibration*, Island Records, New York, 2001.

Marx, K., *Theories of Surplus Value*, Prometheus Books, New York, 2000.

Mason, B., *Street Theatre and other outdoor performance*, Routledge, London, 1992.

Plummer, K., *Telling sexual stories: power, change and social worlds*, Routledge, London, 1995.

Postone, M., *Time,Llabor and Social Domination: A Reinterpretation of Marx's Critical Theory*, Cambridge University Press, Cambridge, 1993.

Rebellato, D., 'Playwriting and globalisation: towards a site unspecific theatre', *Contemporary Theatre Review*, vol.16-1, 2006, pp.97-113.

Turner, C., 'Palimpset or potential space? Finding a vocabulary for site specific performance', *New Theatre Quarterly*, vol.20-4, 2004, pp.373-390.

Wachowski, A. and L. Wachowski, *The Matrix*, Warner Home Video, 1999.

Wickstrom, M., *Performing Consumers: Global Capital and its Theatrical Seductions*, Routledge, London, 2006.

Wilkie, F., 'Mapping the terrain: a survey of site-specific performance in Britain', *New Theatre Quarterly*, vol.18-2, 2002, pp.140-160.

Namita Chakrabarty was born in Cheltenham, in the Cotwolds, spent her teenage years in the Midlands, and studied at Goldsmith's College in London. She has worked in the cultural industries – her work includes performance, video and writing, both creative and critical – and in education.

John Preston is originally from the Midlands and is Reader in Lifelong Learning, Competitiveness and Social Cohesion at the Institute of Education. His latest book is *Whiteness and Class in Education*.

Discover as a Learning Environment: Stimulating Creativity and Learning in Diversity

Joanne Kenworthy

Abstract
The late twentieth century saw the development of a new type of centre for children and families - popularly referred to as 'discovery centres' - designed to stimulate creativity and learning through exploration, play, and interaction. This chapter surveys the design, development, ethos and practice of one such centre in London's East End, *Discover*. The role of *Discover* as an advocate of children's rights is highlighted through a discussion of how children were consulted during its development phase. Current ideas and research on children's participation in decisions which affect them are briefly reviewed. This aspect of *Discover*'s work is further explored through a description of a project run by *Discover* in partnership with a local school and urban regeneration agencies to explore models of children's participation. Some findings on children's use of art forms to communicate their ideas about their environment, and the responses of adult regeneration professionals are discussed.

Key Words: Discovery centres, *Discover*, children's rights; diversity; regeneration

*****

1. Introduction: The Background to *Discover*

> Imagine expanding the possibilities for learning. Having more places where learners are engaged, enthusiastic, and motivated.[1]

In the late twentieth century, a new type of 'learning institution' began to evolve in the United States and Europe. The guiding principle of these institutions was that experience and exploration were powerful catalysts for learning. Focused on serving the needs of children, usually up to 12 years old, these institutions could be described as 'playspaces' but only if this term is used in a positive sense to convey spaces to play as 'powerful environments to enhance learning in people of any age and to stimulate rich adult/child interaction'.[2] The aim of such institutions was 'to encourage learning through discovery, through play, through fun, through hands on exploration, through interaction with things and with people.'[3] These new learning institutions were variously referred to as 'children's museums', 'children's discovery centres', or 'centres for curiosity and imagination'.

However, two features make these discovery centres distinct from other learning institutions. First, although child-focused, they are institutions for families. As well as being places for adults and children to learn together, they have a strong commitment to support families. The second feature is their aim to contribute to the social fabric of their local communities by responding to and reflecting the circumstances and needs, and cultural and ethnic traditions of those local communities.

An indication of the surge in activity and interest in discovery centres was the creation of the *Hands On! Europe Network.* In November 2001, *Hands On! Europe* held a conference in London on the theme of the educational role of children's museums. The conference - *'Playing to Learn? The Educational Role of Children's Museums'* - was an international event with a total of 203 delegates from 20 different countries. Over three days, conference presentations and workshops focused on descriptions of a wide range of new centres, on how children learn in museums, on issues of access, and on how children's museums should relate to other places where children learn.[4] It was against this backdrop of debates about designing places for children and their families to learn together that a plan for a children's discovery centre in east London was being developed.

2. The Beginnings of *Discover*

In 1997, a partnership was formed - under the auspices of the Stratford Development Partnership Ltd, a non-profit project management and development agency, with support from the Calouste Gulbenkian Foundation - with the aim of creating a centre for children and families in Stratford, east London. The Gulbenkian Foundation UK,[5] a charitable trust, was one of several organisations and groups that were concerned about the lives of children in the UK, including their increasing lack of freedom of movement and of opportunities for imaginative unstructured play activities. The lives of children in cities were of particular concern because 'urban environments seem to have evolved in ways which offered only moderate benefits to childhood.'[6] It was a board member of Gulbenkian Foundation UK who had initiated a research project and report that explored the operation of children's museums and their potential for development in the UK by community enterprises, development trusts and local authorities. Another partner was Community Links, a charity that runs community-based projects in east London and disseminates the local lessons nationwide. A company with charitable status was formed - the Children's Discovery Centre - and a steering committee was convened. In 2000, the London Borough of Newham donated two adjoining derelict buildings in central Stratford to house the centre (at a peppercorn rate).

The decision to locate the centre in Newham, in the heart of London's 'East End', was a strategic one. Newham and the neighbouring boroughs of Tower Hamlets and Hackney are among the poorest in the UK. Over 40% of the population of Newham is under 25 years old and more than 100 languages are spoken in the borough.[7] It is one of the most culturally and ethnically diverse boroughs in the UK. In all three boroughs, the proportion of households of lone parents with dependent children and households with no adult employment is higher than the UK average. As well as being economically deprived, this area of London has very few cultural venues, let alone any targeting young children.

3. The Planning and Design of *Discover*

In 1997, a part-time development officer was appointed and the steering committee began the planning, design, consultation and capital funding phase. This complex period took six years and involved many types and strands of activity. In order to explore and discuss *Discover*'s aims and ethos, a group of academics, teachers, and professionals with backgrounds in children's services and in museum design and management formed a Learning Advisory Group [LAG]. Through a series of meetings and informal seminars, the LAG discussed the themes of the centre and how the goal of interactivity would be achieved. A design consultant was appointed whose first task was to tour some of the existing centres in the United States and Europe. In discussions with the steering committee, she developed the concept of the building, and its adjacent outdoor space, as housing a flexible set of different interactive structures and spaces, each providing a variety of multi-sensory experiences created through the use of lighting, texture, colour, water, planting, sound and video images. The ideas of 'stories' and of 'making stories together' emerged as unifying themes for both the indoor and outdoor spaces. There would be listening and recording areas - where children and adults could listen to traditional stories in a range of languages and record their own stories to which others could listen - and performance areas, where puppets could be used to act out stories. An outreach programme was launched in order to pilot the technique of 'story-building'- groups of children working with adult facilitators - 'story builders' - would create original stories as they moved through the spaces and structures. The characters, setting, and plot twists and turns would be in the control of the children.

A central conviction of the steering committee was that children should participate in the development and design of the centre. To that end, a Children's Forum was established. In the summer of 1998, Save the Children was commissioned to carry out a consultation with children participating in summer play schemes in Newham. Approximately 125 children, the majority aged between 5 and 11, from three different play schemes, took part in a series of workshops and activities. The consultation had two aims: to find out what children would like to have in the centre and in what way the children would like to be involved in planning and running the centre; and to find out from the children the best ways in which adults could consult with children.

In carrying out the consultation, Save the Children was asked to mirror - as far as was possible - the culture planned for *Discover*: 'it was to be child centred…and exploit the ways that children express their meanings: …play, imagination, exploration, creativity.'[8]

Thus, right from the start, children - the 'end-users' of the centre - were involved in its planning and design. Following the consultation, the Children's Forum was relaunched for children, aged 4 to 13, recruited from local schools. Through workshops with sculptors, poets, visual artists and story-tellers, these children provided input for the logo, structures and spaces, accessibility, opening times, age limits (0 to 8 years) and crèche facilities. The character of Hootah - a baby space monster who has landed on earth to collect stories to take back to his planet - was conceived and designed in these workshops by the children. A vital outcome of this intensive period of discussion, consultation and planning was the establishment of the centre's mission and aims.

4. *Discover*'s Mission Statement and Aims

Discover's purpose is to provide creative play and learning opportunities to enable children, and their carers, to develop their potential: in particular, the purpose is to target families in circumstances of social and economic disadvantage and to ensure that children are listened to and participate in decisions that affect them.

Discover aims to:

- provide support and creative learning opportunities for children and families at crucial stages of their social and intellectual development;
- challenge disadvantage by providing quality resources and opportunities in one of the most deprived areas of London;
- work in partnership with the statutory and voluntary sectors to ensure that creativity, play and learning are at the heart of new and ongoing government initiatives;
- explore and pioneer new ways of consulting to and listening to children;
- pioneer story-building – a unique technique using words, language and imagination;
- provide training and support for artists, early years' practitioners, teachers and other adults who work with children; and

- develop new ways of engaging with diverse communities within a transient multi-lingual community.[9]

5. *Discover* in Operation

The funding to support the development and design phase, and for the renovation, refurbishment and fit-out of the building - to house the Story Trail and the outdoor space, the Story Garden - was considerable: over five million pounds was raised. In 2003, *Discover* - the UK's first hands on creative centre for children - opened to the public.[10] Children and their families come to explore the Story Trail and the Story Garden and to take part in the changing programme of events, workshops, community sessions, and projects.

Groups of school children have structured sessions designed to support language and creative development led by story builders. Admission costs are kept low[11] and there are special rates for Newham residents[12] and for schools and community groups. A Families Scheme ensures that some of the most vulnerable and disadvantaged families in the five east London boroughs are given free annual season tickets. Entry to the Story Garden is free and provides a vital playspace for children and families in an area that has very few safe outdoor play areas. Since its opening, *Discover* has worked with diverse groups including teenage parents, refugees and asylum seekers, parent and toddler groups, child-minders, and families whose children have special needs.

'Connecting Stories' is an example of one of *Discover*'s community and education projects. The aim of this three-year project is to produce a sound archive of stories, songs and poems performed by Newham residents who belong to some of the borough's diverse communities. Working with a sound artist, adults and children record their own choice of stories and songs and personal memories in their languages to produce CDs that can be used as a resource for others. Over the three years, the project has involved adults and children from six different groups: the Polish Roma community; the Somali Bravanese community; Albanian speaking people, mostly from Kosovo; members of the Bengali community linked to a local nursery school; members of the Pakistani, Sri Lankan, Phillipino and Bangladeshi communities linked to a local primary school; the white British community in the Canning Town area; and the Afro-Caribbean community.

When one participant was asked why she had contributed to the project, she replied:

> 'People need stories, it's how we are made. Human contact is essential and people don't want to feel on their own. Stories are a way of communicating to people we don't know.'

6. *Discover* as an Advocate for Listening to Children

In its mission and aims, *Discover* has positioned itself within the nexus of debate, policy and strategic initiatives that has developed, during the last ten to fifteen years, relating to children's rights. In reading *Discover*'s Mission Statement, two articles of the UN Convention of the Rights of the Child come to mind.

> Article 31
> …the right of the child to participate fully in cultural and artistic life and shall encourage the provision of appropriate and equal opportunities for cultural, artistic, recreational and leisure activity. [13]

The rationale for assuring this right has been articulated by Bernadette Duffy:

> 'Through the arts children can communicate their feelings in non-verbal and pre-verbal ways, express their thoughts, comprehend, respond and represent their perceptions. They can develop their understanding of the world, experience beauty and express their cultural heritage.'[14]

> Article 12
> Parties shall assure to the child who is capable of forming his or her own views the right to express those views freely in all matters affecting the child, the views of the child being given due weight in accordance with the age and maturity of the child.[15]

Lansdown emphasises the 'substantive'[16] nature of this right: children are entitled to be 'actors in their own lives, not merely passive recipients of adult care and protection.'[17] It is also 'procedural' in nature, in the sense that, when children's views are given due weight, other rights of children may be achieved. In the UK, we can recognise responses to UN Article 12 in such twenty-first century public policy as the Children's Act,[18] Every Child Matters: Change for Children[19] and The Children's Plan.[20] These policies have raised the profile of children and their rights. In London, one of the three strategic objectives for children and young people is 'ensuring we listen to and provide a voice for London's children and young people.'[21] Every London borough has a statutory duty to develop a children's and young people's plan, and each of these plans includes a duty to consult with children and young people.

The conviction that children have unique insights, perspectives and experiences underpins any commitment to listen to them. One of the theoretical starting points of many researchers and professionals involved in consulting with children is that childhood is a state of being, rather than one of becoming; that children are full citizens rather than citizens in training.[22] Those working within the discipline of the sociology of childhood, among others, emphasise the need to challenge assumptions about the incapacities of children.[23] Any tendency to underestimate children's ability to hold and express thoughtful opinions on a range of issues needs to be countered by recognising and valuing their views, through consulting with them and enabling their participation in decisions that affect them.

7. Definitions of Consultation and Participation

The terms 'consultation' and 'participation' are sometimes used interchangeably, but a distinction can be made between consultation as 'finding out views in order to inform decisions' and participation as direct inputs made into decision-making.[24]

Different 'degrees' of participation are discernible:[25] all are valid and require commitment but each category of participation creates different opportunities for children to be engaged. The boundaries between the categories of participation are not clear cut, and different initiatives and projects can bridge different categories. The factors that determine the degree of participation are the roles of adults and children as managers, initiators, facilitators, leaders, researchers, and designers of methodologies in the actual processes and mechanisms that are set up.

The first category is *consultation processes* which are generally adult initiated, adult led and managed, and lack any possibility for children to control outcomes: children's views and perspectives are elicited and then used to inform policies and practices. The second category is *participatory processes*: these are also adult initiated, but provide opportunities for children to be involved in activities such as identifying what the relevant questions or issues are, or helping to develop the methodology to be used. The third category is *self-initiated processes*: children are empowered to identify their own concerns and to take action as opposed to responding to an adult-defined agenda.

Empowerment has emerged as a key issue in the debate. One definition of 'real participation' foregrounds the outcomes of consultation - the decisions that are made:

> 'Real Participation includes the chance to express views and to contribute to shared decision-making. Participation in the fullest sense means not just taking part but having some influence.'[26]

Ownership of decision-making cannot be separated from corresponding responsibilities, nor from an acknowledgement that children's age, experiences and maturity - and their own preferences and interests - will determine how they participate. There is a need to recognise that, in the context of child participation, children are very diverse in their preferences.[27] For example, some shy children may not like communicating in groups, while others feel more supported in the company of their peers. Other children may prefer individual interviews or discussions because of their confidentiality and privacy.[28]

Within the debate about what counts as consultation or participation, there is agreement on a simple practical reason for children having a voice in matters that affect them: children are the experts in their own lives. When the first Children's Forum was consulted about the planned centre in Stratford, the question was posed, 'Is it a good idea for adults to consult with children?' The children said that it was. Two children expressed their reasons as follows: 'because they don't know what we like,' and 'because it would be better to have more people's opinion than one and we're the ones that are using it.'[29]

In the case of young children, consultation and participation require processes that are appropriate to them. If a dialogue is set up in a traditional consultation framework - with adults present who are experts in their fields and/or 'interested parties' - then young children will not receive the undivided attention they need. Although they may be given the opportunity to answer questions, they may not be encouraged to ask questions themselves. Young children have competences in many kinds of structured talk but, in a context where adult language skills of rationale discussion and argumentation are seen as the appropriate and ideal form of communication, they may be disadvantaged. For young children to participate effectively, adults must be prepared to interact in appropriate ways that play to children's strengths, e.g. drawing, role play, music, story-telling, workshops using games and imagined scenarios, voicing ideas through puppets, etc.

8. Developing Models and Methods for Listening to Children

The past decade has seen significant and accelerating innovation and critical enquiry into ways of giving children a voice. This has been fortified by several surveys, reviews and policy documents.[30] The Department for Education and Skills sponsored a review which was conducted, in 2003, by the Thomas Coram Research Institute[31] and, in 2007, The Children's Society began a two year inquiry, 'Good Childhood'.[32]

One method of giving children a voice is the 'Mosaic Approach',[33] a framework which combines traditional participant ethnographic observation and interviewing with an array of methods that play to children's strengths. Examples of these methods are:

- 'map-making': children make maps of a locality or building which are then used as a talking point;
- walking tours or 'place expeditions', where children take adults on a tour of a place (e.g. a nursery) while giving a running commentary to the adult; and
- a type of 'photo journalism' where children take photographs of 'important' or favourite places by which children to express their views.

As a child-centred organisation conceived and designed to stimulate creativity through play, imagination and the arts, and with a mission to ensure that children are consulted about their lives, *Discover* is ideally placed to contribute to the generation and investigation of approaches to children's participation.

9. 'Listening to Learn' – Exploring Children's Participation

When *Discover* opened in 2003, it had already become clear that Stratford was to be the site of the most significant redevelopment project in London in a generation. Plans to develop the 73 hectares of rail lands adjacent to Stratford were well-advanced. There would be a new 'Stratford City', with 4,000 housing units, a primary and secondary school, major commercial and retail areas, and a public park. The announcement, in July 2006, that the 2012 Olympics were to be held in the same part of London meant that the construction of an Olympic Park now overlapped with the Stratford City project.

Regeneration is seen as a solution to poor urban environments, but it presents a challenge to those who advocate the right of children to be consulted: what models of child participation are appropriate for complex urban regeneration projects? There was an opportunity for *Discover* to explore and develop methods and approaches that could be used by other culturally diverse communities in urban regeneration areas.

Previously, the challenges of children's participation in the regeneration of their area were highlighted by an exploratory case study conducted in 2002 in a deprived part of Edinburgh which was undergoing major housing redevelopment.[34] The study focused on the views of young people, aged 10 to 14, concerning their local environment and whether public policy and planning processes reflected their perspectives. The children conveyed their views to the researcher through informal group discussions, semi-structured interviews and a range of participatory methods.

When the young people were asked whether they thought that adults listened to what they said, there was a unanimous view that - apart from those close to them (e.g. parents and youth workers) - adults did not listen to them. The young people were sceptical about getting a positive response to requests for new parks or recreation areas.

Interviews conducted with officers from the local regeneration agency and the national agency for regeneration in Scotland revealed a recognition that traditional structures did not work for children and young people. Interviews with young people's organisations showed that their work focussed on particular 'youth specific matters' and was not integrated into the strategic or master planning processes.[35] According to representatives of local young people's organisations, a more creative and dynamic engagement with young people would be more effective.

A. The Design and Structure of 'Listening to Learn'

In designing a project to explore the voices of children in the context of regeneration, staff at *Discover* built on their growing experience and expertise gained through the activities of the Children's Forum and through working in partnership with other organisations concerned with children and the environment. *Discover*'s approach to the challenge of children's engagement in regeneration had two dimensions: first, working in partnership; and, second, the use of art forms as a way for children to communicate their ideas about public spaces and changes in their local area.

B. Working in Partnership

One of the partners is a local primary school. Located on the edge of the re-development, its pupils would be living next to a building site throughout their schooling. The school has a strong commitment to the arts. Its intake is highly diverse, with approximately 90% of children from ethnic minorities, with 75% of children having English as an Additional Language and over 50 languages being spoken by the pupils. Other partners are the agencies developing Stratford, and the Newham Local Authority regeneration team, who both agreed to identify key staff to work with *Discover*. They undertook to talk to the local children at their school and to attend key events to listen to the children's views and presentations concerning the plans for the new Stratford City. The third partner was the Cass School of Education at the University of East London, personnel from which would take on the role of evaluators and action researchers.

The project aims to investigate the potential of four different art forms as tools for communication for children of different ages, and the impact upon regeneration professionals of listening to and working with children in the context of regeneration.

With regard to the potential of art forms, the research questions focus on whether different art forms have different impacts on older/ younger children in terms of the quality of engagement, collaborative ways of working, and on children's ability to express their opinions about their environment. This aspect of the project would need to take into account the fact that the children themselves comprise diverse groups with different interests, talents, and artistic preferences, as well as preferences for different modes of action and interaction. The research questions relating to the regeneration professionals concerned whether - as a result of their contact and involvement with the children – these professionals would demonstrate and/or say that they experienced a less 'adult-filtered' understanding of children's competencies, a change in attitudes towards the benefits of children's participation, or any willingness to rethink priorities in their planning processes and procedures in order to enable children's participation.

Funding for a three year action research project was secured from the National Endowment for Science, Technology, and the Arts (NESTA) under the funding priorities of their current Learning Programme, specifically the Arts funding category of 'Understanding impact: projects to explore how we learn through 'the arts'.'[36] Further funding was provided by Sir John Cass's Foundation and the East Foundation.

The project was structured into three stages. During Stage One (the first year), 110 children from two year 4 and two year 5 classes at the participating primary school would work with a visual artist, a photographer, a film maker, and a drama artist. The children would explore a range of media and materials and drama techniques, and develop skills in the use of cameras. They would also learn about the changes planned for their local area. In Stage Two (the second year), the children - now in Years 5 and 6 - would work with younger children in two year 1 and two year 2 classes as 'art forms peer facilitators', supporting the younger children in expressing their ideas about their environment through the four art forms. In Stage Three (the third year), the findings of Stages One and Two would be disseminated.

The evaluation plan would use a wide range of methods, including participant ethnographic observation of the art forms sessions, semi-structured interviews with class teachers, and initial and follow-up structured interviews with the regeneration professionals. A wide array of participatory methods would be used with children, including questionnaires designed by the children for their classmates about what they had learned and what they liked/didn't like in the art forms sessions, journal entries written by the children after each weekly session, and video-conferencing.

Stage One of the project ran from September 2006 to August 2007. The following section will report on some of the findings during that period concerning the arts as a communication tool, and will outline some initial indications of the responses/impact on the regeneration professionals.

C. The Arts as Carriers of Meaning in the Context of Regeneration

Towards the end of Stage One - after twenty sessions, i.e. five sessions on each of the four art forms - the children and artists began to work on the displays, exhibits and performances that were to be presented at a public event, 'Listen to Our Stratford' in July 2007. Each artist worked with a group of children for a further six weeks to create a representation of their ideas concerning 'Stratford present and Stratford future'. The most straightforward manner in which this phase could have been organised would have been for the artists and project manager to allocate an art form and a topic to each of the four participating classes. But this was the children's opportunity to demonstrate their arts expertise and to communicate their ideas and views. The planning and preparation of the event was to be consistent with the culture of the project as a whole: the children would have an active role, and they would have the opportunity to take the lead in the decisions about the content of the event.

Organising the six weeks of work leading up to the public event in a manner that maximised the children's participation involved several preliminary stages. Firstly, the issues to be addressed had to be selected. Secondly, given that the working space available was four classrooms, these selected issues had to be organised into four themes. Each theme needed to be paired with an art form. Each child would then choose their preferred pairing of theme and art form, voting for a first and a second choice.

To decide on the issues that they wanted to cover, each class was asked to talk about the topic, 'What we need to tell the developers before they start all the work at Stratford'. In coming up with ideas, they were asked to remember that the rationale for their work was that developers wanted to know what children in Stratford do, the places and spaces they go to and use, and what children like and don't like about Stratford present and what they want for Stratford future. The four themes that emerged were 'Outdoor Spaces in Stratford', 'Children's Recreation', 'Our Neighbourhood' and 'Building the Future in Stratford'.

The next stage was to pair a theme with an art form. This stage was crucial, not only for the children but for the project managers and evaluators. It was important to capture as much information as possible about what notions, if any, the children had formed of the potential of each art form to convey their ideas about their local environment. A form was designed which asked each child to match themes with art forms and give reasons for their choices. The following table shows their decisions about the 'best' art form to communicate their ideas on the themes (see Table 1).

Certain matches of theme and art form were popular and other matches were less popular, from which the inference may be drawn that the matches were not made randomly but involved decisions concerning compatibility of medium and message. A content analysis of the reasons given for the pairings provided greater insight into how the children had been thinking about the art forms as communication tools. Some children wrote a comment explaining why they liked the art form, e.g. 'I chose filming because it's active'. Other children referred to the general potential of the form or its suitability for different people, e.g. 'I can use my imagination with colours' and 'If someone can't speak, they can act it out'.

Table 1: Themes and Art Forms for 'Listen to our Stratford'.

Theme	Art Forms			
	Drama	Film	Photography	Visual Arts
Outdoor Spaces	21	33	24	18
Children's Recreation	35	15	15	32
Our Neighbourhood	17	15	35	23
Building the Future	18	29	24	14

Table 2: Communicative Functions and Exemplary Reasons

Function	Exemplary reasons
Representative of the environment	I can show what a horrible park there is (Photography).
Representative of people's behaviour	We could act out how buses are crowded (Drama).
Promoting things to be changed (e.g. through identification)	When you film things people can see what needs to be done (Film).
Promoting designated change (e.g. through comparison)	[We] can show how people can be safer (Drama).
Expressive of attitudes, feelings, ideas and opinions	[We] can do a play about how we feel in Stratford… so people can see how we feel not just them (Drama).
Preserving personal experience or memory	[Children] can paint about the things they love now that are going to change (Visual Arts).
Supporting the act of design	We would be able to design or draw what it would look like (Visual Arts).

There were 142 reasons that showed the children's thinking about using art forms to communicate. Further analysis revealed seven types of communicative functions. Two of these functions were representative, i.e. representing the environment and people's behaviour. Two further functions promoted some kind of action, either by stimulating comparison or by identifying or designating things that need to be changed. Another function was expressive, i.e. expressing attitudes, feelings, ideas or opinions. A further function was linked to personal experience and memory, i.e. preservation of images of valued and important objects for the self and/or for others. The final function could be conceptualised as supporting the act of designing. Table 2 provides examples of reasons given by the children in these seven categories.

Table 3: Communicative Functions and Reasons for Art Forms

Function	Reasons for Art Forms			
	Drama	Film	Photography	Visual Arts
Representative of the environment	6	10	19	7
Representative of people's behaviour	4	5	1	1
Promoting things to be changed	7	14	13	9
Promoting designated change	-	8	6	-
Expressive of attitudes, feelings, ideas and opinions	10	2	-	5
Preserving personal experience or memory	-	-	3	1
Supporting the act of design	-	2	-	5

When the total number of reasons under each function was further analysed according to art form, some clear patterns in the children's notions of the potential communicative functions of drama, film, photography and visual arts emerged. Although all four art forms have the potential to represent the environment, photography was chosen most frequently. Film and drama can be used to represent the environment, but these two also have the potential to represent people's behaviour in places. Drama was most strongly associated with expressing feelings and attitudes. While visual arts can also serve this function, the number of links was half the number made for drama. All four art forms have the potential to promote change by showing people what needs to be changed, what children want, or images of a possible desirable future. However, film and photography were seen as having the greatest potential here. Film and photography can promote designated change by facilitating comparison - the old and the new, the clean and the dirty, etc - but visual arts and drama were never linked to this function. Photography and Visual Arts were linked to preserving personal experience or memory, albeit infrequently. The strongest link to the act of designing was visual arts with drama and photography not linked to this function at all (see Table 3).

10. Children and Adults Listening and Learning Together

The 'Listen to Our Stratford' event was an opportunity to gauge the responses of regeneration professionals to the displays, exhibits and performances that the children had created to express their ideas. The event was also conceived as a celebration of the work of the first stage of 'Listening to Learn' and as an opportunity for parents, carers, teachers and other people from the community to learn more about the project. What meanings would they construct from looking at the exhibits, watching the children's drama performance and their films? What impact would this type of contact have on the thinking of regeneration professionals about children's participation in regeneration?

Comments made by the adult professionals to the evaluators during the 'Listen to Our Stratford' event - and after the visits to the school - give an indication of their responses: 'I've suddenly become aware it is not just adults who are interested and have a view'; 'I've heard stuff I wouldn't otherwise have heard'; and 'It was great to hear children's ideas about a theme park'.

A response of one developer implied that he had reflected critically on the event. He commented that it was not just the 'instrumentality' of the messages that was significant but the 'process' - the fact that the children had developed such confidence through using art forms and were able to get up in front of an audience and to express themselves was so important, especially in the context of longer term benefits of participation.

'Listening to Learn' is expanding the possibilities of learning for all of its participants: the children are learning how to use art forms to express their views; regeneration professionals are learning about children's perceptions of their environment; the artists are honing their skills in working with primary aged children; the project managers are extending their expertise in working in partnership; the evaluators are exploring a wide range of participatory methods. The project is generating multiple learning curves that intersect as the participants interact in different ways. This project and other activities of *Discover* illustrate how a child-centred arts organisation can stimulate learning in diverse ways in the diverse community with which it works.

Notes

[1] B Jilk, 'Place making and change in learning environments', in M Dudek (ed) *Children's Spaces*, Elsevier, Oxford, 2005, pp.30-43, p. 30.

[2] J Pearce, *Centres for Curiosity and Imagination: When is a Museum not a Museum?*, Calouste Gulbenkian Foundation, London, 1998, p. 19.
[3] Ibid., p. 20.
[4] The *Hands On! Europe* conference - *Playing to Learn? The Educational Role of Children's Museums* - was hosted by *Discover* and organised in collaboration with Kids' Clubs Network and Centres for Curiosity and Imagination. It received support from the Calouste Gulbenkian Foundation, Department for Education and Skills, Sure Start Newham, Marks and Spencers, News International and the Stratford Development Partnership.
[5] http://www.gulbenkian.org
[6] M Dudek, 'Children's spaces', in M Dudek (ed), *Children's Spaces*, Elsevier, Oxford, 2005, pp.vii-xxii, p.xvi.
[7] Newham Council, Discover Newham, accessed 22nd June, 2008 <www.newham.gov.uk/Newham/DiscoverNewham/discovernewham>.
[8] J Miller, *A Journey of Discovery: Children's Creative Participation in Planning*, Save the Children, London, 1999, p.7.
[9] Discover, Trustee Recruitment Pack, 2007, accessed 22nd June, 2008 <www.discover.org.uk/cn/venue/documents/TrusteeRecruitmentpack>.
[10] *Discover* operates as a company, Limited by Guarantee registered in England No. 3479284, and is a Registered Charity No. 1070468. The Board of Trustees has overall responsibility for the strategic control and direction of *Discover* with day-to-day management delegated to the Director. *Discover*'s income comes from a variety of sources which include admissions, rental income from sub-letting space in the buildings, earned income through hiring of space in the buildings; community income from training courses; donations and grants from individuals, the corporate sector, trusts and charities; and income from the statutory sector for delivering services.
[11] Admission prices are £4.00 per adult/child with a Family Ticket for four costing £14.00.
[12] Admission price for Newham residents is £3.50 per adult/child.
[13] Committee on the Rights of the Child [CRC], Conventions on the Rights of the Child, United Nations High Commissioner for Human Rights, 1989, accessed 11th May, 2008 <www2.ohchr.org/english/law/crc.htm#art31>.
[14] B Duffy, *Ways into Creative Arts Training in the Early Years*, Discover, London, 2007, p.3.
[15] CRC, op. cit., accessed 11th May, 2008 <www2.ohchr.org/english/law/crc.htm#art12>.
[16] G Lansdown, 'Participation and young children', *Early Childhood Matters*, no. 103, 2004, pp.4-14, p.5.
[17] Ibid.
[18] Department for Education and Skills, [DfES], *The Children Act 2004 - Guidance*, 2004, accessed 11th May, 2008 <http://www.everychildmatters.gov.uk/strategy/guidance>.

[19] Department for Education and Skills [DfES], *Every Child Matters: Change for Children*, Department for Education and Skills, Nottingham, 2004.
[20] Department for Children, Schools and Families [DCSF], *The Children's Plan*, 2007, accessed 11th May, 2008 <http://www.dfes.gov.uk/publications/childrensplan>.
[21] Greater London Authority [GLA], *Making London Better for All Children and Young People: The Mayor's Children and Young People's Strategy*, Greater London Authority, London, 2004, p.7.
[22] A Clark, 'Talking and Listening to Children', in M Dudek (ed) *Children's Spaces*, Elsevier, Oxford, 2005, pp.1-13, p.2.
[23] H Penn, 'Spaces without children', in M Dudek (ed) *Children's Spaces*, Elsevier, Oxford, 2005, pp.178-194, p.184.
[24] M Hill, 'Children's voices on ways of having a voice: children's and young people's perspectives on methods used in research and consultation', *Childhood*, 3-1, 2006, pp.69-89, p.72.
[25] Lansdown, op. cit., pp.6-7.
[26] Miller, op. cit., p.7.
[27] Hill, op. cit., p.78.
[28] Ibid., p.82.
[29] Miller, op. cit., p.38.
[30] Some examples are: United Nations Children's Fund [UNICEF], *Children's Rights and Habitat: Working towards Child-FriendlyCities*, UNICEF, New York, 1997; R Hart, *Children's Participation*, Earthscan/UNICEF, London, 1997; P Kirby with S Bryson, '*Measuring the Magic*: *Evaluating and Researching Young People's Participation in Public Decision-making*, Carnegie Young People Initiative, UK, 2002. G Thomas and G Thomson, *A Child's Place: Why Environment Matters to Children*, Green Alliance/DEMOS, London, 2004. B Percy-Smith and N Thomas (eds) *Handbook of Children's Participation: Perspectives from Practice and Theory*, Routledge, London (forthcoming).
[31] A Clark, S McQuail, and P Moss, *Exploring the Field of Listening to and Consulting with Young Children*, Research report No 445, Queen's Printer, London, 2003.
[32] The Children's Society, *The Good Childhood Enquiry*, 2007, accessed 11th May, 2008 <www.childrenssociety.org.uk/all_about_us/how_we_do_it/the_good_childhood_inquiry/1818>.
[33] A Clark and P Moss, *Listening to Young Children: The Mosaic Approach*, National Children's Bureau, London, 2001.
[34] S Elsley, 'Children's experience of public space', *Children and Society*, 18-2, 2004, pp.pp.155-164.
[35] Ibid., p.162.

[36] National Endowment for Science, Technology and the Arts [NESTA] *Discover – Listening to Learn* www.nesta.org.uk/discover-listening-to-learn. [accessed 22nd June 2008].

Bibliography

Clark, A., 'Talking and Listening to Children', in M. Dudek (ed) *Children's Spaces*, Elsevier, Oxford, 2005, pp. 1-13.

Clark, A., McQuail S., and Moss, P., *Exploring the Field of Listening to and Consulting with Young Children*, Research report No 445, Queen's Printer, London, 2003.

Clark, A. and Moss, P., *Listening to Young Children: The Mosaic Approach*, National Children's Bureau, London, 2001.

Committee on the Rights of the Child [CRC], Conventions on the Rights of the Child, United Nations High Commissioner for Human Rights, 1989, accessed 11th May, 2008 <http://www2.ohchr.org/english/law>.

Department for Children, Schools and Families [DCSF], *The Children's Plan*, 2007, accessed 11th May, 2008 <http://www.dfes.gov.uk/publications/childrensplan>.

Department for Education and Skills [DfES], *Every Child Matters: Change for Children*, Department for Education and Skills, Nottingham, 2004.

Department for Education and Skills, [DfES], *The Children Act 2004 - Guidance*, 2004, accessed 11th May, 2008 <http://www.everychildmatters.gov.uk/strategy/guidance>.

Dudek, M., 'Children's spaces', in M. Dudek (ed), *Children's Spaces*, Elsevier, Oxford, 2005, pp.vii-xxii.

Duffy, B., *Ways into Creative Arts Training in the Early Years*, Discover, London, 2007.

Elsley, S., 'Children's experience of public space', *Children and Society*, 18-2, 2004, pp.pp.155-164.

Greater London Authority [GLA], *Making London Better for All Children and Young People: The Mayor's Children and Young People's Strategy*, Greater London Authority, London, 2004.

Hart R., *Children's Participation*, Earthscan/UNICEF, London, 1997.

Hill, M., 'Children's voices on ways of having a voice: children's and young people's perspectives on methods used in research and consultation', *Childhood*, 3-1, 2006, pp.69-89.

Jilk, B., 'Place making and change in learning environments', in M. Dudek (ed) *Children's Spaces*, Elsevier, Oxford, 2005, pp.30-43.

Kirby, P. with S Bryson, '*Measuring the Magic*: *Evaluating and Researching Young People's Participation in Public Decision-making*, Carnegie Young People Initiative, UK, 2002.

Lansdown, G., 'Participation and young children', *Early Childhood Matters*, no. 103, 2004, pp.4-14.

Miller, J., *A Journey of Discovery: Children's Creative Participation in Planning*, Save the Children, London, 1999.

Pearce, J., *Centres for Curiosity and Imagination: When is a Museum not a Museum?*, Calouste Gulbenkian Foundation, London, 1998.

Penn, H., 'Spaces without children', in M. Dudek (ed) *Children's Spaces*, Elsevier, Oxford, 2005, pp.178-194.

Percy-Smith, B., and N. Thomas, N. (eds) *Handbook of Children's Participation: Perspectives from Practice and Theory*, Routledge, London (forthcoming).

Thomas, G. and G. Thomson, *A Child's Place: Why Environment Matters to Children*, Green Alliance/DEMOS, London, 2004.

United Nations Children's Fund [UNICEF], *Children's Rights and Habitat: Working towards Child-Friendly Cities,*, UNICEF, New York, 1997.

Joanne Kenworthy, originally from Philadelphia, Pennsylvania, took her first degree in Boston, Massachusetts and her second in Edinburgh. She has worked at the University of East London for almost 30 years, and has been involved with Discover, an interactive arts organisation in Stratford, East London, since the early stages of its design and development.

The Commodification of British Higher Education: Trials and Triumphs of Massification in the Metropolitan University.

Patricia Walker

Abstract
By referencing the University of East London, this chapter recognises the work that is going on in the post-92 universities to open up higher education to those groups traditionally denied access. The implications for resourcing and work practice are discussed in relation to the wider changes taking place in higher education in the UK as a whole. It takes a historical perspective in charting the evolution of UK universities: from institutions with a privileged population in a system of minority participation with high completion rates to contemporary institutions with flexible access arrangements, mass participation and high dropout. The chapter recognises the life changing experience of higher education in the capital. The students (twice as many from the least affluent socio-economic groups, and marginally more Black and minority ethnic when compared to the average for the sector) are faced with a learning journey longer and more complex than some privileged peers in other universities in order to reach the economic and social outcomes for which they strive. It demonstrates how such institutions that embrace the Government's policies to widen - in addition to increasing - participation in higher education, are continuing the work of the erstwhile polytechnics in constructing universities for the people.

Key Words: Widening participation, access to higher education, massification, commodification, new universities.

*****

1. Introduction to the Discourse on Commodification

This chapter takes as a starting point the now ubiquitous notion of commodification in UK higher education [HE]. It charts the changes in UK HE from a privileged population system, characterized by minority participation and high completion rates, to one that typically features open access, mass participation and high dropout rates.

The notion of commodification is no longer a new one. The commodification of culture, for instance, as Shumar has pointed out, has 'come to be widely recognised as a ubiquitous process with profound implications for all aspects of life'.[1] Finding a convenient label for something, however, is not the same as fully understanding it. The changes taking place in British HE are complex and multi-faceted and the signs are that they will continue to be so. Notwithstanding, in order to shape an argument, it helps to visualise these multifarious issues in a central organising theme, one that can be perceived as the gradual and seemingly unstoppable commodification of the activities and outcomes of HE.

The very ubiquity of the term obscures its different interpretations. It is used by some as a synonym for that which they consider the privatisation of British education, by others to imply commodification and commercialisation. This writer uses the definition offered by Shumar and views commodification as the notion that such human activities as learning, teaching, writing and even thinking - which may in the past have been dedicated to God or to the service of humankind or to the celebration and fulfilment of human ability - are increasingly in the service of the marketplace. The products of education - ideas, research and publications - come to be valued in terms of their potential to generate income,[2] jeopardising other forms of value that may eventually be lost.

Education as product has not always been the case. Scott's examination of the changes which took place over time in the liberal universities that flourished throughout Europe provides an understanding of how the modern university came to be.[3] He demonstrates how universities stood slightly apart from society, in time and place, rising above what he describes as 'parochial intellectualoid preoccupations in the cause of a universal intellectual tradition'.[4] Universities' unworldliness and distance from society - a near-spirituality sustained by the superior authority of religion - was exemplified by the privileged nature of the participants, aristocratic in both financial and intellectual resources. The ancient universities of Britain were collegiate in nature: Oxford, Cambridge, Durham and the Scottish Universities, Edinburgh and St Andrews, their ecclesiastical architecture mirroring their origins in the Church. Teaching remained the primary focus for hundreds of years.

The emphasis on research came only after two world wars when there was a massive shift in the paradigm. In Britain, government and people were impatient to make progress - to re-build a new society led by technology: universities became the engines of production. Knowledge creation displaced the education of students at the heart of institutional endeavour. Universities began facing outwards towards the state and its interests, the economy and civil society. Technocratic enthusiasm for the knowledge society has continued unabated to the present day and was central to the political vision of the New Labour government (elected in 1997) discussed below.

2. The Evolution of Higher Education in Britain

It is worth remembering that the contemporary HE system has developed slowly over centuries: some of the Oxford colleges were founded in the eleventh and twelfth centuries. Later, the Victorians founded the huge civic universities - in wealthy northern and Midlands cities such as Manchester - as cathedral-like monuments to capitalism and progress. After the Second World War, universities' populations increased exponentially, driven in part by the technological revolution greedy for an educated workforce. In order to meet this demand, the White Paper 'Technical Education', in 1956, proposed the foundation of ten Colleges of Advanced Technology [CATs], later promoted to Technical Universities (Bradford and Salford are examples).[5] In the 1960s, when the number of 18 year-olds began to peak, a number of new universities - known variously as campus, green fields or plate glass - were established in cities like York, Lancaster and Norwich and in counties like Surrey, Sussex and Essex. The Robbins committee, however, saw that even this expansion would not be enough and, partly to address a perceived gap in vocational HE in the wake of the CATs' re-designation, the polytechnics were established towards the end of the decade.[6] The polytechnics were joined during the 1970s by more than 60 colleges of HE formed from the previous (and rapidly diminishing) system of specialist teacher-training institutions, as well as from some leading further education colleges.

A notable day in the history of the expansion of British HE is 18th October 1976, when James Callaghan's now famous speech from Ruskin College, Oxford, paved the way for a huge expansion in non-university institutions offering degree level courses and post-graduate degrees. This came to be known as the binary system of HE, over time bedevilled by problems many of which can be attributed to purpose and status. Both flanks of the binary divide offered bachelor's degrees, master's degrees and doctorates and the polytechnics - with unseemly haste - began to withdraw from vocational qualifications such as Higher National Certificates and Higher National Diplomas. This has been criticized as 'academic drift'[7] but it could be argued that the universities, in response to market forces, underwent a complementary 'vocational drift'. Other than the funding arrangements, which favoured the universities, increasingly there was little to choose in terms of course provision so that eventually, in 1992, the binary divide was dissolved when the polytechnics were re-designated as universities.

Before the paint was dry on the new logos, the former polytechnics - including those which had been in existence in one form or another since the 1800s - were being dubbed 'new' universities in order to distinguish them from the 'old' universities some of which had only come into being in the 1960s. Indeed, the University of East London is one such institution: a 'new' university, its roots stem from the West Ham Technical Institute, founded in 1892, which merged with the Walthamstow and Dagenham technical colleges in 1970 to become the North East London Polytechnic which was then re-designated as the University of East London [UEL] in 1992.

Using UEL as an example, the sections that follow seek to provide recognition of the pioneering work of the post-92 universities and its implications for resourcing and work practice. These achievements had been predicted by Eric Robinson, in 1968, when he contended that:

> The future pattern of higher education in this country can be set in the development of these [polytechnics] institutions as comprehensive people's universities.[8]

3. Stages on the Road to the Commodification of Higher Education

The modern university emphasised knowledge as product rather than process, and it was this view of education as a commodity that characterised the era of the Thatcher government (1979-1990). The 1980s will be remembered for, amongst other cuts, the erosion of funding to the public sector including to HE. With the advent of the so-called business culture, British universities accepted as inevitable that they and their social products would be viewed in terms of consumption. As an aid to a more complete understanding of the position of British universities in the early years of the twenty-first century, the historical development towards commodification and, perhaps as a consequence, massification must be traced.

The first sign of the Government's reluctance to continue funding increasing numbers of HE students was the decision to charge tuition fees to students from overseas. Students from abroad had been entering British universities in considerable numbers since the mid-nineteenth century (many from the former Empire and later, the Commonwealth) and the tuition fees for all students whether or not they had a connection with Britain had been heavily subsidised by the British taxpayer. Demand was well established, the numbers of overseas students rising year on year as the newly emergent nations endeavoured to educate their younger generation to meet the development needs of their respective countries. Successive governments struggled with the increasing financial burden until Shirley Williams, the then Minister of Education in Harold Wilson's Labour government (1966-70), took the decision, in 1969, to levy a differential fee for home and overseas students.

Home students were funded through their local authorities so were not personally responsible for meeting tuition fees at point of delivery. It was also the case that, while many overseas students were funded by their respective governments, it was feared that the increased fee would impact on the ability of overseas students from poorer countries to continue their education. The crucial issue was that the government demonstrated that HE was a valuable commodity and that non-UK domiciled students could not acquire it as a matter of right when they did not contribute through taxation.

This policy signalled a sea change in education policy insofar as a price tag was attached to a university education. Later, when Margaret

Thatcher was swept to power, one of her first measures was to deepen the policy: in May 1979, she imposed upon overseas students the full cost of their fees.[9]

From that point forward, HE was to be seen as a marketable asset and it followed inexorably that marketing universities was seen as axiomatic, inevitable, and legitimate. Initially it was the international markets that were prioritised. Notably, ten years on, in 1989, Reading University was awarded The Queen's Award for Industry for its income generation from international students (as they had come to be known). The commodification of HE had become a reality and it would be only a matter of time before fees were imposed on the home market.

4. Accelerating Massification: a Challenge of Widening Participation

According to Scott, the modern university - from its earliest days in the mid-twentieth century - was a mass institution in the sense of increased numbers of students (relative to the mediaeval or liberal universities) but also in the sense that knowledge was henceforward to be mass-produced as opposed to the 'artisanal production of knowledge.'[10] It would seem that, if the education system is the expression of the nation, the university is, as Flexner observed many years before, 'an expression of the age'.[11]

With the change in international students' status from guest to client, they acquired a degree of what might be considered as consumer power and, thus, universities became increasingly student-focused as policies and practices evolved to meet the new clients' needs. Demand factors came to influence HE planning, organisation and development and, as time passed, a climate developed in which innovation and flexible responses to diversity became commonplace.

As a result of New Labour's victory in 1997 - with Prime Minister Tony Blair's apophthegm, 'Education, education, education' - demand for HE intensified. Central to Blair's maxim was widening participation in HE for the under-30 age cohort. This was to include non-traditional learners, including minority ethnic groups who previously had failed or declined to participate in HE. The government set a target of 50% of all young people in Britain to experience some form of HE.

As the erstwhile polytechnics embraced the post-Ruskin Speech agenda to extend participation by increasing provision – especially, initially, in technical and vocational degrees – so the post-92 'new' universities have led the way in accepting the challenge to act as agents of social mobility for non-traditional learners. Paradoxically, those very skills in pro-active marketing that had been honed in the international marketplace to recruit international students in their thousands were recalibrated to reach out to home students not only under-30 but also women returning to learn, mid-career professionals and, especially in London, potential home students from the successive waves of immigrants from the enlarging European Union. Moreover, the post-92 universities had an enabling curriculum - featuring flexible programs and e-learning to optimize learning opportunities - that had been developed for orienting overseas students into the culture of HE but which now could ease a new non-traditional home student population into the culture of HE.

Although the practice of charging fees directly to the overseas client had been deemed a success, the announcement by the Labour government of tuition fees for home students, in July 1997, was deeply unpopular with students and, initially, with universities. Universities were expected to raise revenue by fees - and other means - whilst their grant from the government was proportionally eroded. It became incumbent upon universities to encourage increasing numbers of students – overseas and home, traditional and non-traditional - to participate in HE. This led to a charge from some quarters that the access agenda was actually supply driven and not the altruistic policy it had seemed at its inception although, in public policy, both explanations were valid and not mutually exclusive.

The Oakes Report of 1978 had warned that, due to the decline in the number of 18 year olds in the early 1980s, existing recruitment policies might need to change, that 'the system itself might reach out to embrace different types of students and to meet fresh needs, such as that of recurrent or continuing education'.[12]

The National Institute of Adult Continuing Education, in 1989, had observed that:

> The traditional market for HE courses, eighteen and nineteen year old school leavers, has been declining for some years. The fall in live births from the mid sixties to the late 1970s meant a decline in the potential student population in this age group to the mid 1990s with only a marginal increase predicted to the end of the century.[13]

5. Consumer Behaviour in Higher Education

The HE system at the start of the twenty-first century is vastly different in purpose and nature from early liberal universities. The formerly professionally-oriented, producer-led system – with an immutable curriculum and a single-mode delivery pattern - has been transformed into a consumer-led and market-driven industry – with flexible entry and multi-mode delivery – in which undergraduates have morphed from students, through clients, into customers. Moreover, as the numbers of consumers have increased exponentially, so has there been an explosion in the number of providers thus creating a buyers' market.

In business, there is a maxim that the customer is always right, and paying customers are within their rights to demand the service and quality of service for which they are paying. In the buyers' market of HE, where supply equals or exceeds demand for places, providers are placed in the position where they have to woo the purchaser: universities do not select students so much as seduce them. In this context, as I have commented elsewhere, the Japanese HE system, which features not mass but universal HE, has much to teach us.[14] So that, in the 1990s and 2000s, *widening* participation - as opposed to *increasing* participation which was the movement in the 1970s and 1980s - has resulted in a diverse study body - as was the objective – but, in many respects, an adverse learning and teaching environment, which was not.

6. Higher Education, Social Class and Social Capital

One of the consequences of the widening participation agenda is that there have been tremendous pressures - on students, academic staff, administrators and support staff - created by a learning environment which, for myriad reasons, is unpredictable.

Some of these pressures relate to the social composition of the student body and the extent to which students possess appropriate social capital to benefit from the environment in which they find themselves. A succession of government reports - from Robbins to Dearing - underline the fact that university study has conventionally been, and remains, a middle class occupation and, indeed, pre-occupation. Although working class participation has increased slowly since the 1950s, middle class participation has grown exponentially. Not until the New Labour government was the under-representation of working class participants seriously challenged. Ross has commented that:

> Within the five years 1991-95, those in socio-economic class I had increased their participation rate from 55% to 79% - a growth of 43%. The growth of other socio-economic groups was also great – the increase for socio-economic class V from 6% to 12% was a doubling in size, for example. In terms of expectations, higher education had now become the normal rite of passage of a social class I young person, and was still only the exceptional route for just an eighth of those in social class V.[15]

On 1st October 2004, the Times Higher identified the 'Working Class Heroes' of HE, the ten universities with the highest participation rates from the lower social class groups. All were post-92 universities, and half were in and around the London region: Luton (44.8%), South Bank (44%), Westminster (44%), London Met (43.9%) and UEL (43.3%).[16]

Assigning social class to students, however, is fraught with inaccuracies, since it is customarily calculated on parental occupation: these days young people tend to be self-sufficient or, at least, without recourse to parental financial support. A more accurate picture of social deprivation and uncertain economic outcomes can be estimated by reference to residence. At UEL, 50% of students reside in the surrounding six boroughs which are known to be areas of serious social deprivation. Indeed, the London Borough of Newham - in which the UEL Stratford Campus is located - is currently the most deprived borough in the country, although that may change with the advent of the Olympics. A further 37% of UEL students come from other areas across London, a pattern common to other London institutions. Arguably, the most potent statistic is that, compared to the average for the sector, there are twice as many students from the least affluent socio-economic groups.

Students from social classes III–V Manual, who gain admission to a university - even one like UEL with a reputation for inclusivity - can find themselves, in many ways, in an alien landscape, where the organizational culture is unfamiliar, even hostile. These entrants need to understand that there are certain accepted, 'normal' ways of going about things within the framework, or systems and rules, and that any nonconformity is likely to be seen as deviant. Trying to reconcile and manage students' expectations of staff and staffs' expectations of students requires considerable cultural shifts on both sides and the potential for emotional and organizational stress is profound.

7. The Student Voice

In the following sections the student voice can be heard through written testimonies volunteered after a group discussion on first year students' perceptions and impressions. Whilst the exercise was conducted, a number of oral comments were made, one or two of which are included. In all cases speech is reported verbatim.

There are a number of ways in which students come to terms with this situation: some integrate and learn the rules of the game, seemingly naturally; others feel they need to make an effort to adapt. One student commented:

> Do you think I could learn to talk posh? Maybe I'll end up talking like you. Oh what would my husband say? (laughter).

Other students feel alienated by the way staff relate to them, and the language of lectures and tutorials baffles many: 'I don't know what he's going on about!' is a common cry. There is an awareness that their own idiolect is lacking. One student remarked, 'Some [academic staff] expected you to speak in a way they want and think that if you can't speak like them you are not intelligent'. Some students reject outright the trappings and paraphernalia of academia - operating an entirely instrumental approach: 'I just wanna get my degree and get outta here.'

Culturally determined inter-personal styles can be a source of potential conflict between students and staff as in the complaint, 'Lecturer A is so disrespectful to me – she should not treat me like a kid when I'm a mature student'. Equally, academic staff can be somewhat taken aback to be addressed as 'Hi Ange', or similar, by students whom they have never met, in an e-mail on an ostensibly academic topic. These seemingly petty miscommunications, when multiplied across semesters and years, build up a pervading atmosphere of frustration. It could be argued that, with the prevailing culture of (faux) intimacy across all aspects of English society, it is the university that is out of step in the degree of formality with which it conducts its business. Notwithstanding, discordance continues to exist in certain aspects of staff/student discourse.

Students often express grievances against the university administration: 'This place is so unorganized'. A range of problems originate from a lack of robust data on student enrolment and choices of programme and modules, attributable in no small measure to the inner city London universities' late admission of considerable numbers of students through Clearing. Students who cannot - or neglect to - officially enrol on a programme or register for modules prior to the start of the semester risk being unable to find their assigned room, building or even campus on the first day of classes. Furthermore, given that entry to HE is largely dependent upon previous qualifications, students admitted through Clearing will tend to be those with lower than expected grades or with non-standard entry qualifications. Many students, therefore, begin their university studies with the fear that they are only barely acceptable, implying emotional setbacks before they are ever tested in the academic arena. This increases further the likelihood of stress and contributes to the perceptions of some academic staff that certain students are very 'needy' and demand help in the wrong way - i.e. lacking in autonomous behaviour – with reciprocal criticisms by students of unsympathetic tutors and unhelpful administrators.

More problematic is that academic staff in such universities cannot take for granted the knowledge base and learning experiences with which their students enter the degree programme, making lecture and tutorial preparation - not to mention individual student academic guidance - most burdensome. Whilst a lecture may go over the heads of some students, other students will be frustrated at the slow pace and frequent explanations. One student remarked, 'Unhappy with peer group – support of like-minded students. Feel drained – dragged down.' Yet students lacking confidence in their academic preparedness are often operating at the very limits of their competence and experiencing high levels of anxiety. This is turn can lead to a blame culture: 'It must be someone's fault I feel so bad.'

There are also significant issues relating to institutional status. Many working class students with an imperfect understanding of the hierarchy of universities, and the indicators on which the league table are based, perceive the HE options available to them as being of a lower quality than that available at the 'Middle class preserves'[17] with whom the Times Higher contrasted the 'Working Class Heroes' remarked upon above:

> 'A lot of friends who ask me what Uni I attend don't respect UEL - they always encourage me to change to other Unis that they feel is better, for a lot of reasons.'
>
> 'No confidence in the selection procedures. Does the university accept students who may have the necessary intelligence but not the necessary skills to cope with study at this level?'
>
> 'Does the university accept students on a cash basis?'

Sadly, these remarks echo the findings of Archer whose respondent volunteered:

> 'Because anyone can get into [university name], it's an inner city polytechnic for God's sake! Like you don't have to be academically elite to get into [university] because that's why I'm here. Because I live locally and I am stupid basically'.[18]

The financial burdens believed to be experienced by students from social classes III-V (53.8% of the student body) are commonly considered to contribute to the high drop-out rate of 28% - close to that of the UEL's comparators, though far from that of Cambridge which has only 1.3%.[19] The explanation for this is that students who are 'returning to learn' as mature students, or who are young students unable to rely on financial support from parents, cannot afford to give up their paid work to study full-time. While such students are officially full-time, the reality is that many work full-time and, therefore, actually spend only a fraction of the week on campus, whether in lectures, the libraries and computer centres. These students, therefore, suffer the double blow of having barely sufficient time to cover the basics of study and are physically exhausted in the process.

8. Ethnicity and Higher Education

Students at UEL, and at other post-92 London universities, have a significantly different profile from those in the sector as a whole. At UEL, in 2006/7, the student population comprised 20,722 of whom 7,539 were white - constituting 36% - whereas across the sector white students made up about 77% of the student body nationwide. Similarly, if so-called ethnic minority students are considered, they constituted 52% at UEL yet made up only 14.6% of the sector nationwide. At UEL, 4,787 (23%) are Black compared to 1.3% for Black Caribbean and 3% Black African across the sector. In respect of Asian students the university had 4,541 (22%) whereas Asian students made up only 7% across the sector.[20]

Universities UK (UUK) – the voice of universities in the UK – has reported that there is no problem with Black and minority ethnic [BME] participation in HE and, on the contrary, it is one of the success stories of the sector.[21] However, this claim was refuted by Trevor Phillips[22] who commented on the inability of many Black students to gain entry to any but such inner-city post-92 universities as UEL. There are more Black Caribbean students in one post-1992 institution, London Metropolitan University, than there are in the entire Russell Group, Phillips claimed, consequently creating the possibility of Black ghettos in the capital's new universities. Interestingly, one UEL student commented:

> This School [of Education] is mainly made up of Asians and Africans and even though I come from one of these ethnic minorities I would like to attend a Uni' where the competition is high. Even if I am the bottom of the class, I will aim to climb and complete my education at a well respected university (Black mature woman student who subsequently withdrew from her course).

These comments, and others above, clearly indicate a movement toward commodification in HE, common elsewhere, e.g. as noted above in respect of Japan.[23] Paying for education leads to a consumer approach of 'shopping around' for the best deal going and the aspiration to purchase certain 'top brands' and 'designer labels'.

9. Retention and Persistence

Amongst other issues, drop-out rates are of interest to policy makers, practitioners, statisticians, politicians and ultimately, funding councils. There is pressure on universities to plan for low dropout rates and high retention by supporting students in persisting with their programmes.

It is recognized that students entering university with non-traditional academic qualifications are more likely to demand frequent academic guidance than their peers who have a high level of preparedness both in terms of intellectual experience and earned qualifications. Additionally, such students tend to be unfamiliar with the conventions governing academic writing, including referencing and other features of written assignments. Moreover, they will be more difficult to help: students without a meta-language for talking about linguistic issues do not find it useful to have their errors defined or emendations recommended, for instance, 'This essay should be re-written using passive voice' or 'Try to establish some academic distance here'. Non-traditional students need practical help such as modelling, i.e. in being given examples from which to work, an approach to feedback unfamiliar to many tutors. Students commonly expect tutors to proof read their work and to write corrections in the text – clearly an unrealistic expectation fated to fuel frustration on both sides. Many academics become dispirited by an organizational culture that seems to infantilise students and fails to hold them accountable for their own actions. Yet subsequent and continuing government funding requires that the customers should be retained in the system and cash-strapped universities have to work desperately hard to ensure they are.

Despite the commodification metaphor providing a useful argument around which to organize ideas on the current state of UK HE, there are fundamental problems in viewing education as a commodity to be bought and sold. Firstly, education is both process and product and, arguably, it is the latter for which students pay, together with the environment in which the activities embedding the process take place. The idea that the product - as in certificate, degree, or diploma - cannot be purchased *per se* but still needs to be earned, even after cash has exchanged hands, is not always understood by students. Secondly, universities are not comfortable about students going home empty-handed after having paid for years of tuition, especially in an increasingly litigious society, so put pressure on academic staff to create opportunities for students to succeed. This generates a remorseless round of re-sitting and re-taking which leaves academics with a virtually unbroken cycle of assessment: assessment boards; setting of re-sit papers and assignments; re-assessment of re-submissions; re-submission boards; and final award boards. And, threaded through all this, is a continuous process of student guidance and feedback, counselling and one-to-one tuition.

It is demonstrable that those universities that have embraced the government's agenda of widening participation are fated to be in the lower reaches of the league tables. These institutions may further extend their remit by accepting the Leitch[24] proposal to raise the proportion of the working population with a level 4 qualification from 29% to 40% - thus increasing their skills development and employability – and this will require yet more new thinking and resourcefulness. There are league tables that measure retention levels, the numbers of first classification degrees awarded, income for research through performance in a Research Assessment Exercise (RAE), and time taken to obtain awards. These are difficult hurdles to clear when over half the student body is less qualified, older and poorer than the average, and spending only a fraction of time on campus due to family and work commitments.

It is incontestable that universities like UEL articulate the affirmation of HE as an agency for social mobility. Cohorts of students testify to the life changing power of their experience. It is reported that Bill Rammell, the Minister for Lifelong Learning and Employment, agrees: 'For many people, going to university is a life-changing experience, and the best route to a secure future'.[25]

UEL's annual graduation ceremony at the Barbican illustrates this life-changing experience: a joyously triumphant occasion yet a humbling and poignant experience. The packed auditorium contains more children, including babies, than are usually seen at such ceremonies. Many of the graduands are the first in the family ever to walk across a stage wearing a mortar board and flowing gown. Some graduands have four generations of their family present to cheer them on. These are the very people that the government wants to encourage in their bid to widen the range of entrants into HE, as the Minister for Lifelong Learning explained:

> I want a broader proportion of people to be able to enjoy the benefits that going to university brings and as the first person in my family to go to university, I know that doing so transformed my life chances.[26]

But UEL's mission extends beyond creating life chances and greater economic outcomes for individuals. It is rising to the challenge of maintaining the UK's economic global position by educating as many people as possible to the highest levels despite our currently having one of the worst drop-out rates at age 16 in the industrialised world. Our competitors - India, China and some European countries - are pushing ahead in graduate numbers whilst our tomorrow's workforce is currently in jobs and not in education upskilling themselves: this trend must be reversed lest the UK begins to lose the competitive edge which has been enjoyed for decades.

UK universities such as UEL are driving the expansion of HE, whilst the privileged universities continue to do what they have always done: preserve the benefits of HE for the traditional students. This is wrong, probably immoral, definitely not in the national interest and, axiomatically, not what our society and the economy needs. These post-92 universities are operating in the most difficult and complicated territories yet are being judged against the same performance indicators as those preserves of middle class privilege whilst struggling with the additional demands of a diverse student population. There needs to be recognition of the in-built tensions in balancing the requirement to educate (in the same timeframe as other institutions) those non-traditional students who have a learning journey that is longer and harder. It is time that this effort was recognised and rewarded, not only be public investment but by demonstrable confidence – indeed, trust – in the universities by politicians: political will to match institutional commitment.

Notes

[1] W Shumar, *College for Sale: A Critique of the Commodification of Higher Education*, Routledge, London, 1997, p.142.
[2] Ibid., p.5.
[3] P Scott, *The Crisis of the University*, Croom Helm, London, 1984.
[4] Ibid., p.4. It is from the adjective 'universal' that the word 'university' is derived.
[5] Ministry of Education, *Technical Education*, Cmnd 9703, Ministry of Education, 1956.
[6] Lionel Robbins was chair of the Royal Commission on Higher Education which published its report in 1963.
[7] J Pratt and T Burgess, *Polytechnics: A Report*, Pitman, London, 1974, p.50.
[8] E Robinson, *The New Polytechnics*, Penguin, Harmondsworth, 1968, p.193.
[9] It should be understood that the original policy marked a fee differential between home and overseas tuition. However, it was claimed that the British taxpayer still subsidized students from overseas. The Thatcher government calculated the true cost of educating a student in higher education and charged that in full to all students from overseas. Those who were already in the system were allowed to continue to pay the differential fee.
[10] Scott, op. cit., p.54
[11] A Flexner, *Universities: American, English, German*, Oxford University Press, Oxford, 1930.
[12] Ministry of Education, *Report of the Working Party on the Management of Higher Education in the Maintained Sector*, Cmnd 7130, London, HMSO, 1978, p.3.
[13] National Institute of Adult Continuing Education [NIACE], *Adults in Higher Education*, NIACE, Leicester, 1989, p.7.
[14] P Walker, 'System transition in Japanese short-term higher education', *Compare*, vol. 37-2, 2007, pp. 239-255.
[15] A Ross, 'Access to higher education: inclusion for the masses', in L Archer, M Hutchings and A Ross (eds), *Higher Education and Social Class*, Routledge, London, 2003, pp.45-74, p.70.
[16] P Hill, 'Old institutions fail on access targets', *Times Higher Education Supplement*, 1st October 2004, pp.8-9.

[17] Ibid.
[18] L Archer, 'The value of higher education' in L Archer, M Hutchings and A Ross (eds), *Higher Education and Social Class*, Routledge, London, 2003, pp. 119-136, p. 129.
[19] Hill, op. cit.
[20] HESA 2004-5 contrasted with statistics supplied by the university, November 2007.
[21] Universities UK [UUK] 2005 National BME Education Strategy Group Review of Black and Ethnic Participation in Higher Education, a summary report for conference 21st June 2006.
[22] P Curtis, 'Black students failing to get into top universities', *The Guardian*, 3rd January, 2006, p. 4.
[23] Walker, op. cit.
[24] HM Treasury, *Prosperity for All in the Global Economy: World Class Skills*, HM Treasury/HMSO, 2006.
[25] J Marston, 'Investing in student life will pay off', *Evening Star 24*, 1st June, 2006, accessed 17th February, 2008 <http://www.eveningstar.co.uk/content/eveningstar/features/story.aspx?brand=ESTOnline&category=Features&tBrand=ESTOnline&tCategory=Features&itemid=IPED24+May+2006+14%3A03%3A45%3A503>.
[26] Marston, ibid.

Bibliography

Archer, L., 'The value of higher education' in L. Archer, M. Hutchings and A. Ross (eds), *Higher Education and Social Class*, RoutledgeFalmer, London, 2003, pp. 119-136.

Curtis, P., 'Black students failing to get into top universities', *The Guardian*, 3rd January, 2006, p. 4.

Flexner, A., *Universities: American, English, German*, Oxford University Press, Oxford, 1930

HM Treasury, *Prosperity for All in the Global Economy: World Class Skills*, HM Treasury/HMSO, 2006.

Hill, P., 'Old institutions fail on access targets', *Times Higher Education Supplement*, 1st October 2004, pp. 8-9.

Marston, J., 'Investing in student life will pay off', *Evening Star 24*, 1st June 2006, accessed 17th February, 2008

<http://www.eveningstar.co.uk/content/eveningstar/features/story.aspx?brand=ESTOnline&category=Features&tBrand=ESTOnline&tCategory=Features&itemid=IPED24+May+2006+14%3A03%3A45%3A503>.

Ministry of Education, *Technical Education*, Cmnd 9703, Ministry of Education, 1956.

Ministry of Education, *Report of the Working Party on the Management of Higher Education in the Maintained Sector*, Cmnd 7130, London, HMSO, 1978.

National Institute of Adult Continuing Education [NIACE], *Adults in Higher Education*, NIACE, Leicester, 1989.

Pratt, J. and T. Burgess, *Polytechnics: A Report*, Pitman, London, 1974.

Robinson, E., *The New Polytechnics*, Penguin, Harmondsworth, 1968,

Ross, A., 'Access to higher education: inclusion for the masses', in L Archer, M Hutchings and A Ross (eds), *Higher Education and Social Class*, Routledge, London, 2003, pp. 45-74.

Scott, P., *The Crisis of the University*, Croom Helm, London, 1984.

Shumar, W., *College for Sale: A Critique of the Commodification of Higher Education*, Falmer, London, 1997.

Walker, P., 'System transition in Japanese short-term higher education', *Compare*, vol. 37-2, 2007, pp. 239-255.

Patricia Walker has lectured in English Language and Education, and conducted research into higher education, in Japan, Nigeria and the United Kingdom. She was awarded her PhD, by Oxford Brookes University, for her study of the political economy of higher education, and she is interested in metropolitan higher education institutions as engines of social change.

The SENDA Agenda: The Vision for Inclusive Higher Education

Helen Masterton

Abstract
Government initiatives in higher education in England and Wales intended to widen participation include commitment not only to substantially increasing student numbers but also to facilitating access for students who were not traditionally considered to be higher education students. The Special Educational Needs and Disability Act (2001), it was anticipated, would play a key role in realizing these initiatives for widening participation and inclusion. Despite this legislation, higher education has been - and continues to be - one of the least inclusive sectors of education. Issues of disability have been addressed in statutory education sectors but, thus far, seem not to have significantly impacted on practice in higher education. This chapter explores the impact of disability legislation on higher education, drawing on evidence from a staff development training programme on inclusivity in a higher education institution in London. It argues that legislation is crucial if inclusion is to feature prominently on the agenda for higher education and that this prominence will only be achieved by strategic planning and training for the development of understanding of the concept of entitlement. Current attitudes will have to be challenged in order for genuine inclusion to become a reality.

Key Words: Inclusion, disability, special educational needs, higher education, support.

*****

1. Integration and Inclusion in Education

The statutory education sectors in England and Wales have been subject to considerable policy development in respect of children with disabilities and special educational needs [SEN] since the recommendations of the Warnock Report[1] were published in 1978. The Warnock Report was pivotal in the reassessment of educational provision for children with disabilities and SEN: the report advocated that such children – who were customarily placed in special school, separate and distinct from their peers - should be integrated into mainstream schools. Many of the recommendations made in the Warnock Report became legislation - under the Education Act (1981)[2] – and local authorities and schools developed the integration of pupils with disabilities and SEN through the active engagement of dynamic individual teachers and officers. However, an early review of integration schemes, in 1981, found that many staff considered that integration affected only those children who previously had been segregated in special schools.[3] Moreover, there was a tendency for this integration to become too narrowly interpreted as placement without any regard to the quality of that placement[4] and, furthermore, there was evidence that the social aspects of integration became privileged over educational aspects and goals.[5] The Fish Report, in 1985, responded to these tendencies by advocating that all pupils with disabilities and SEN who were integrated in schools of the Inner London Education Authority should be provided with equal opportunities for education.[6]

These factors contributed, during the 1990s, to the emphasis on integration being superseded by an emphasis on inclusion, a term which has two implications: "first, that it embraces the needs of all pupils but, second, that for some of them there is a risk of exclusion to be redressed".[7] While the terms integration and inclusion may still have currency in educational discourse – and the terms may be used interchangeably - each signifies a distinct approach with 'real differences of values and practice between them'.[8]

The participation of higher education [HE] in this early debate of 'integration versus inclusion' tended to be restricted to those academics who concentrated on those contributions that research might offer to professionals working with children with disabilities and SEN in other sectors. The HE sector was not required to directly address the inclusion of students with disabilities and SEN and has demonstrably remained the most exclusive sector of education during a period when significant changes were occurring in statutory sectors of education in England and Wales.

However, two decades after the introduction of the legislation that concerned the integration/inclusion of children with SEN into mainstream schools, in 2001, the government passed a law relating to students with SEN in HE, the Special Educational Needs and Disability Act [SENDA].[9] An amendment of the Disability Discrimination Act (1995),[10] this legislation came into effect in September 2002 and was groundbreaking insofar as, for the first time, it afforded civil rights to all people with SEN in England and Wales. Furthermore, SENDA provided the baseline against which the HE sector was required to measure its ability to address issues relating to SEN within HE institutions. This involved a shift from conducting research about SEN in schools to addressing SEN practice within HE institutions.

SENDA covers the whole range of education provision - from Early Years to post-sixteen further education [FE] and HE - and there are indications that, since the introduction of SENDA, there have been moves towards more inclusive provision and practice in the statutory sector. While the Audit Commission has remarked the "lack of robust research evidence [which] makes it impossible to say whether there have been increases or decreases… in terms of demand for specialist provision",[11] the decrease in appeals registered with the Special Educational Needs and Disability Tribunal [SENDIST] would provide grounds for cautious optimism. Appeals registered with SENDIST in 2002/3 – when SENDA was implemented - totaled 3,532, while appeals registered with SENDIST in 2006/7 totaled 3,110,[12] a decrease of 12%. While the President of SENDIST conceded that the factors contributing to this decrease were not exactly clear,[13] such a decrease would be consistent with compliance of schools in the statutory sectors with their duties under SENDA. However, these schools have had the experience of two decades of compliance with previous legislation: for HE institutions, compliance with SENDA has involved more radical changes in institutional culture.

2. Inclusivity and Higher Education

The Warnock Report had estimated, in 1978, that some 20% of children were likely to have special educational needs and, subsequently, the accuracy of this estimate has been demonstrated. The Audit Commission, in 2001, noted that:

> Schools in England and Wales currently identify one in five children (1.9 million) as having difficulty learning, such that they need some form of help in class. These children are said to have special educational needs. One child in thirty (275,000) is considered to need more help than their school can provide.[14]

More recently, the Department for Education and Skills noted that pupils with statements of SEN in mainstream statutory education constituted 17.5% of primary pupils and 15.4% of secondary pupils, noting that the proportions of such pupils peaked in year 6, at primary/secondary sector transition, and in year 10, at the onset of study for General Certificate of Secondary Education examinations.[15] Notably, the Disability Rights Commission [DRC] remarked that statistics reported by the Higher Education Statistics Agency indicated that participation of students with SEN and disabilities in the post-compulsory sector had increased from 4.1% to 5.8% during the period 2001 to 2007.[16]

The implementation of SENDA constituted one initiative to increase inclusivity in all sectors of education. However, the New Labour government's agenda for the HE sector, in 1997, had envisaged inclusivity as entailing a substantial increase in student numbers. Correspondingy, the government set a target to increase participation in HE towards 50% of those aged 18-30 by 2010.[17] Thus, inclusivity for students with SEN and disabilities was one aspect of initiatives intended to increase participation and success in HE of those representing groups traditionally excluded on the basis of age, gender, disability, ethnicity and socio-economic status.[18] It is not the intention to consider the broad remit of the widening participation agenda - addressed elsewhere in this book[19] - other for one observation: whereas widening participation generally targeted for recruitment those who were socially disadvantaged, the initiative tended to recruit students with SEN and disabilities from the most socially advantaged sectors of society.[20]

While widening participation initiatives were seen as enhancing provision in HE, there was a perception - among governors and managers in the HE sector - of barriers to inclusivity which inhibited this provision: a decrease in overall institutional funding, an increase in workloads and the prioritization of research activity.[21] Governors and managers were accountable for compliance with SENDA, and were conscious of the potential for students to resort to litigation to ensure that their rights to equal access and treatment were met.[22] An increase in complaints from HE students was anticipated,[23] concurrent with an increase in student expectations and financial commitments through the payment of fees for study:[24]

> the premium attached to a good degree in the jobs market, the evidence that graduates will generally have a more highly remunerated career than non-graduates… and the cost of attendance since the introduction of variable fees… all of which have raised the stakes for students when provision or assessment are perceived to be inadequate.[25]

These factors were perceived as potentially fostering an Americanesque "culture of complaint"[26] and this led to the development of a pre-emptive "culture of complaint management" which centred on "greater systematicity, broader transparency, early resolution and linkage with service" and quality control procedures.[27] These systematic and transparent procedures tended to involve 'evidence based' outcomes for students which were amenable to being audited to demonstrate appropriate institutional responses. However, this is a needs driven approach, more akin to integration than inclusion. Arguably, this 'service-dominated approach' is likely to result in limited change in practices:[28]

> In such a legislative environment, the interactions between institutions and organisations as well as individual players would be minimal, keeping the existent status quo rather than creating enforceable civil rights to be enforceable by disabled students and a number of specialised governmental organisations.[29]

Consistently, evidence indicates that the support provided in HE institutions for students with SEN and disabilities[30] has been predicated on the notion of individualised needs and 'progress towards an inclusive environment has been hampered by a lack of senior management support and under-resourcing of disability specialists.'[31]

Moreover, there was some ambiguity in the wording of SENDA which was open to interpretation. SENDA stated, for instance, that:

> a responsible body discriminates against a disabled person if for a reason which relates to his disability, it treats him less favourably than it treats or would treat others to whom that reason does not or would not apply.[32]

However there was no clear definition of what might constitute 'less favourably'. Institutions were understandably concerned, therefore, that definitions would be determined in law as a result of individual casework which would then set precedents for the sector as a whole. Institutions could not afford to attract negative publicity - whether from legal action or performance indicators in the national press – and the need for positive publicity was paramount – in the context of increasing competition between institutions for student numbers. The increase in transparency and the publication of performance data in 'league tables' that compared HE institutions meant that relevant data on SENDA compliance could be accessed by prospective students.

3. Implications for Academic and Administrative Staff

Governors and managers in HE institutions - in addition to concerns for accountability and procedures – were conscious of the resource implications of compliance with SENDA and, moreover, the implications of this legislation for the customary practice of academic and administrative staff. The implementation of SENDA should have achieved inclusivity in HE but there was evidence that inclusivity was not readily achieved. A survey of providers of staff development in HE institutions concerning provision for students with disabilities, in 2001, had found that non-specialist staff not only lacked awareness of disability access – including curricular access and inclusion – but also focused on disability-specific difficulties rather than attempting to address the issue of inclusion *per se*.[33] Moreover, a survey of staff in HE institutions, conducted for the DRC in 2002,[34] disclosed that only 6% of staff felt that their institution could be described as being fully inclusive.

Not least, there were concerns for individual interpretations of 'inclusivity' as either liberal or critical. Liberal inclusivity would focus on "broadening access to opportunity for enculturation and reproduction of particular professional knowledge bases and practices" with success determined by "benefits to the individual".[35] This liberal inclusivity would be akin to integration insofar as it would be:

> largely to do with manipulating the inputs and processes and little to do with challenging outcomes that perpetuate unequal or oppressive social and economic structures and relations.[36]

Critical inclusivity, by contrast, would have a more radical focus, not merely on those factors directly affecting access, participation, success and the benefits to the individual but also on the outcome that all students "operate in more inclusive ways for the betterment of society".[37]

This dichotomy between the liberal and the critical is illustrated by a hypothetical scenario provided by one commentator. A tutor is responsible for a popular course with three hundred students of whom twenty students have a disability:

> This could result in the tutor having to make as many as twenty individual adaptations. [But] with forethought and advance planning it is possible to avoid making lots of adaptations… The needs of all of these students can be meet with one simple action on the part of the tutor – the provision of lecture notes and their availability in different formats.
> This example shows how tutors can make courses accessible, and learning and teaching inclusive – and in ways that benefit all students.[38]

This 'mainstream' framework of standard common provision[39] would benefit a range of students: those who may be unaware of the availability of support and fail to access the support to which they are entitled; and those who may be reluctant to disclose a disability and assume a disabled identity[40] - only a minority of students are aware of disability politics and the disabled people's movement.[41] Research would indicate that students with a disability which could be described as 'hidden' – for instance, dyslexia or epilepsy, with no physical impairments - often choose to reject the label of disability in the broadest sense, using it only when absolutely necessary to access academic or pastoral support.[42] Failure to disclose a disability would render student specific procedures toward liberal inclusivity ineffectual, but could be addressed by procedures toward general critical inclusivity.

Nevertheless, disclosure of disability by a student to a member of academic or administrative staff should instigate a specific 'specialist' framework of learning support provision.[43] The legislation states that:

> a responsible body does not discriminate against a person if it shows that, at the time in question, it did not know and could not be reasonably expected to know, that he was disabled.[44]

If a student has disclosed a disability to a member of academic or administrative staff, this may pose a dilemma for the institution as to whether this disclosure constitutes a reasonable expectation that the institution should be aware of the student's disability. Generally, once a student has disclosed a disability, early resolution of difficulties are pursued, often through a central support system and key actors, such as a learning support service and learning support staff. However, there is research that would indicate that such central support systems are potentially more consistent with integration than inclusion[45] as such systems are specifically for students with disabilities. Staff awareness of disability issues is fundamental to effective disability provision.

4. Investigating Staff Awareness

A case study was conducted in a London HE institution to gauge administrative staff awareness of disability issues. All staff, both academic and administrative, had previously participated in disability awareness training and had evaluated their perception of the training in terms of their own understanding of the requirements of SENDA. Evaluation data were gathered by questionnaire on completion of the training. Without exception, these questionniare data indicated that staff felt that their awareness of disability and of their responsibilities towards students with disabilities within the institution had increased as a result of the training that they had received. Staff reported that they had found the opportunity to unpack the implications of SENDA useful but that problematic issues had been raised, particularly concerning the availability of funding for additional support.

Subsequently, a year after the disability awareness training, a second questionnaire was distributed to key members of administrative staff responsible for such services as finance, learning resources and learning support. The questionnaire comprised ten open-ended questions: while most questions concerned general disability-related issues, particular questions concerned the relative merits of 'mainstream' and 'specialist' provision. Responses were analysed - by reading and re-reading – to identify issues.

Generally, responses indicated awareness of disability issues and respondents cited instances of those ways in which this awareness had made an impact on practice and provision: specific changes to the physical environment; guidance materials; and appointment of academic staff to provide learning support.

Concerning 'mainstream' and 'specialist' provision, there tended to be consensus that the most effective support for students was provided by a combination of learning support services and staff providing support in the individual faculties. The respondent from learning support services maintained that:

> I think a combination... is important and I also think that it is important that central services give support to the lecturers/staff in schools.

However, respondents tended to emphasise the individuality of each student's needs: "each individual's needs are different and [the institution should try] to tailor the support from the centre and the schools to meet that requirement" (Finance); and "the balance that should be aimed for really depends on the student and their disability" (Learning Support Services). This emphasis on individual needs would tend to favour 'specialist' learning support provision[46] over 'mainstream' standard common provision.[47]

The responses indicated an awareness of obstacles to readily meeting individuals' needs - "our location hinders support" (Finance) and "space and money constraints" (Learning Resources) – and a conviction, best expressed by the respondent from learning support services, that "we are working towards improving our support".

5. Discussion

Findings from a small scale case study in one HE institution cannot be applied across the entire HE sector, but it is interesting to note the impact that SENDA has had on practice in this one HE institution over a relatively short period of time. Moreover, there is a discernible willingness on the part of HE staff to change to meet students' needs. Unquestionably, in a sector which is becoming more customer focused, it is important to pay due attention to students' voices and legislative rights to equal treatment throughout their educational experiences. Furthermore, in a sector which is required to review practice in an environment of increased accountability, it is essential to demonstrate professional standards. Disability awareness and inclusivity constitute areas in which HE can be seen to be 'catching up' with the compulsory sector of education. Irrespective of whether the pursuit of improvements in these areas is driven by a change in the hearts and minds of HE staff, or due diligence concerning legal requirements, or a fear of litigation, the success of students with disabilities will be facilitated.

One commentator, in 2007, remarked that, 'until recently, the university has contributed relatively little in terms of nurturing our understanding of social citizenship for disabled people'.[48] It is incumbent on those working in the HE sector to identify those principles which should be adopted by the HE community. Obviously, the notion of inclusion rather than integration should be adopted. Thereafter, the preferable form of inclusion has to be considered: should HE favour liberal inclusivity, concerned with manipulating inputs and processes, or favour critical inclusivity, concerned with challenging the perpetuation of inequalities?[49] The preferable form of inclusion has to be complemented by consideration of learning support provision: should HE favour specific 'specialist' learning support provision or 'mainstream' standard common provision?[50] This study would indicate a tendency among administrative staff to favour liberal inclusivity and 'specialist' learning support provision.

The principles of inclusion need to be identified and embedded within the culture of HE institutions if inclusion is to become a reality for students rather than being imposed on institutions through government initiatives. In order for this to be achieved, there needs to be clearer understanding and agreement within the academy of what constitutes inclusion and how this is to be delivered as provision.

Notes

[1] Department for Education and Science, *Special Educational Needs: Report of the Committee of Inquiry in to the Education of Handicapped Children and Young People (The Warnock Report)*, Her Majesty's Stationery Office, London, 1978.
[2] Department of Education and Science [DES], *Education Act*, Her Majesty's Stationery Office, 1981.
[3] S Hegarty, K Pocklington and D Lucas, *Educating Pupils with Special Needs in the Ordinary School*, National Foundation for Educational Research [NFER]-Nelson, Windsor, 1981, p. 15.
[4] L Florian, 'Inclusive practices: what, why and how?', *Promoting Inclusive Practice*, C Tilstone, L Florian and R Rose (eds) Routledge, London, 1998, pp. 13-26, p. 14.
[5] S Beveridge, 'Foreword', *Promoting Inclusive Practice*, C Tilstone, L Florian and R Rose (eds) Routledge, London, 1998, pp. xiii-xvi, p. xiv.
[6] See L Barton, 'The politics of special educational needs' *Disability Studies: Past, Present and Future*, L Barton and M Oliver (eds) Disability Press, Leeds, 1997, pp. 138-159, p. 153, re Inner London Education Authority [ILEA], *Educational Opportunities for All (The Fish Report)*, Inner London Education Authority, London, 1985.

[7] S Beveridge, *Special Education in Schools*, 2nd ed., Routledge, London, 1999, p. 59.

[8] F Lennon, 'Organization and management in the secondary school', *Scottish Education*, T Bryce and W Hume (eds), 2nd ed., Edinburgh University Press, Edinburgh, 2003, pp. 419-428, p. 426.

[9] Department for Education and Skills [DfES], *Special Education Needs and Disability Act*, Stationery Office, London, 2001.

[10] Department of Employment [DoE], *Disability Discrimination Act*, Stationery Office, 1995.

[11] Audit Commission, *Special Educational Needs: A Mainstream Issue*, Audit Commission, London, 2002, para. 15.

[12] Special Education Needs and Disability Tribunal [SENDIST], *Special Education Needs and Disability Tribunal: President's Annual Report 2006-2007*, SENDIST, Darlington, 2008, p.5.

[13] Ibid, p. 2.

[14] Audit Commission, op. cit., para. 11.

[15] Department for Education and Skills [DfES], *Statistics in Education: Special Educational Needs in England: January 2003*, Statistical Bulletin 09/03, Stationery Office, London, 2003, p. 6.

[16] Disability Rights Commission, *Understanding the Disability Discrimination Act*, Disability Rights Commission, Stratford upon Avon, 2007, p. 6.

[17] Department for Education and Skills [DfES] The Future of Higher Education, Stationery Office, Norwich, 2003, p. 57.

[18] See T Nunan, R George and H McCausland, 'Inclusive education in universities' *International Journal of Inclusive Education*, vol. 4-1, 2000, pp. 63-88, p. 64.

[19] See P Walker, 'The commodification of British higher education: trials and triumphs of massification in the metropolitan university', this volume.

[20] S Riddell, T Tinklin and A Wilson, *Disabled Students in Higher Education*, Routledge, London, 2005, p. 148.

[21] J Goode, 'Managing disability: early experiences of university students with disabilities', *Disability and Society*, vol. 22-1, 2007, pp. 35-48.

[22] D Gosling, 'Supporting student learning', *A Handbook for Teaching and Learning in Higher Education*, H Fry, S Ketteridge and S Marshall (eds), Routledge, Abingdon, 2003, pp. 162-181, p. 178.

[23] See N Harris, 'Resolution of student complaints in higher education institutions', *Legal Studies*, vol. 27-4, 2007, pp. 565-603, at p. 571.

[24] National Committee of Inquiry into Higher Education [NCIHE], *Higher Education in the Learning Society [The Dearing Report]*, Stationery Office, London, 1997, para. 15.58.

[25] Harris, op. cit., pp. 570-571.

[26] See R Hughes, *The Culture of Complaint: The Fraying of America*, Oxford University Press, Oxford, 1993.
[27] P McGhee, *The Academic Quality Handbook*, RoutledgeFalmer, 2004, p. 119.
[28] O Konour, 'Creating enforcable civil rights for disabled students in higher education: an institutional theory perspective', *Disability and Society*, vol. 15-7, 2000, pp. 1041-1063.
[29] Ibid., p. 1042.
[30] J Goode, 'Managing disability: early experiences of university students with disabilities', *Disability and Society*, vol. 22-1, 2007, pp. 35-48.
[31] Ibid., p.36
[32] Department for Education and Skills [DfES], *Special Education Needs and Disability Act*, Stationery Office, London, 2001, p.26.
[33] V Parker, 'Staff development and curricular inclusion in higher education', *Research in Post-Compulsory Education*, vol. 6-1, 2001, pp.105-112.
[34] I Clunies-Ross, *Raising Staff Awareness: Report 2 - Further and Higher Education*, Disability Rights Commission, London, 2003.
[35] Nunan et al, op. cit., p.65.
[36] Ibid.
[37] Ibid.
[38] A Hurst, 'Inclusive learning in higher education' the impact of policy changes', *Enhancing Teaching in Higher Education: New Approaches for Improving Student Learning*, P Hartley, A Woods and M Pill (eds), RoutledgeFalmer, London, pp. 178-186, pp. 178-179.
[39] E Avramadis and D Skidmore, 'Reappraising learning support in higher education', *Research in Post-Compulsory Education*, vol. 9-1, 2004, pp. 63-82, p. 79; B Wright, 'Accommodating disability in higher education: a closer look at the evidence for a mainstream framework of learning support', *Research in Post-Compulsory Education*, vol. 10-1, 2005, pp. 121-144, p. 142.
[40] C Panting and K Kelly, *Barriers to Success? Disability Identity in Higher Education.* Conference paper presented at Pedagogical Research in Higher Education: Enhancing Student Success, Hope University, Liverpool, 2006.
[41] See C Barnes, 'Disability, higher education and the inclusive society', *British Journal of Sociology of Education*, vol. 28-1, 2007, pp. 135-145, p. 142.
[42] See M Olney and K Brockelman, 'Out of the disability closet: strategic use of perception management by select university students with disabilities', *Disability and Society*, vol. 18-1, 2003, pp. 35-50.
[43] Wright, op. cit.
[44] Department for Education and Skills [DfES], op. cit.
[45] A Houghton, 'Getting through the gate is only the first hurdle: a review of disabled students' support needs', *Diversity and Difference in Lifelong*

Learning, P Coare, P Armstrong, M Boice and L Morrice (eds), 35th Annual Conference of the Standing Conference on University Teaching and Research in Education of Adults, University of Sussex, 2005, pp. 163-171.
[46] Wright, op. cit.
[47] Wright, ibid.; Avramadis and Skidmore, op. cit.
[48] Barnes, op. cit., p. 140.
[49] Nunan et al, op. cit.
[50] See Wright, op. cit. and Avramadis and Skidmore, op. cit.

Bibliography

Audit Commission, *Special Educational Needs: A Mainstream Issue*, Audit Commission, London, 2002.

Avramadis, E. and Skidmore, D., 'Reappraising learning support in higher education', *Research in Post-Compulsory Education*, vol. 9-1, 2004, pp. 63-82.

Barnes, C., 'Disability, higher education and the inclusive society', *British Journal of Sociology of Education*, vol. 28-1, 2007, pp. 135-145.

Barton, L., 'The politics of special educational needs' *Disability Studies: Past, Present and Future*, L Barton and M Oliver (eds) Disability Press, Leeds, 1997, pp. 138-159.

Beveridge, S., *Special Education in Schools*, 2nd ed., Routledge, London, 1999.

Beveridge, S., 'Foreword', *Promoting Inclusive Practice*, C Tilstone, L Florian and R Rose (eds.) Routledge, London, 1998, pp. xiii-xvi.

Clunies-Ross, I., *Raising Staff Awareness: Report 2 - Further and Higher Education*, Disability Rights Commission, London, 2003.

Department of Education and Science [DES], *Special Educational Needs: Report of the Committee of Inquiry into the Education of Handicapped Children and Young People (The Warnock Report)*, Her Majesty's Stationery Office, London, 1978.

Department for Education and Skills [DfES] *The Future of Higher Education*, 2003, Stationery Office, Norwich.

Department for Education and Skills [DfES], *Statistics in Education: Special Educational Needs in England: January 2003*, Statistical Bulletin 09/03, Stationery Office, London, 2003.

Disability Rights Commission, *Understanding the Disability Discrimination Act*, Disability Rights Commission, Stratford upon Avon, 2007.

Florian, L., 'Inclusive practices: what, why and how?', *Promoting Inclusive Practice*, C. Tilstone, L. Florian and R. Rose (eds) Routledge, London, 1998, pp. 13-26.

Goode, J., 'Managing disability: early experiences of university students with disabilities', *Disability and Society*, vol. 22-1, 2007, pp. 35-48.

Gosling, D., 'Supporting student learning', *A Handbook for Teaching and Learning in Higher Education*, H Fry, S Ketteridge and S Marshall (eds), Routledge, Abingdon, 2003, pp. 162-181.

Harris, N., 'Resolution of student complaints in higher education institutions', *Legal Studies*, vol. 27-4, 2007, pp. 565-603.

Hegarty, S., K. Pocklington and D. Lucas, *Educating Pupils with Special Needs in the Ordinary School*, National Foundation for Educational Research [NFER]-Nelson, Windsor, 1981.

Houghton, A., 'Getting through the gate is only the first hurdle: a review of disabled students' support needs', *Diversity and Difference in Lifelong Learning*, P. Coare, P. Armstrong, M. Boice and L. Morrice (eds), 35th Annual Conference of the Standing Conference on University Teaching and Research in Education of Adults, University of Sussex, 2005, pp. 163-171.

Hughes, R., *The Culture of Complaint*, Oxford University Press, 1993.

Hurst, A., 'Inclusive learning in higher education' the impact of policy changes', *Enhancing Teaching in Higher Education: New Approaches for Improving Student Learning*, P Hartley, A Woods and M Pill (eds), RoutledgeFalmer, London, pp.178-186.

Inner London Education Authority [ILEA], Educational Opportunities for All (The Fish Report), Inner London Education Authority, London, 1985.

Konour, O., 'Creating enforcable civil rights for disabled students in higher education: an institutional theory perspective', *Disability and Society*, vol. 15-7, 2000, pp. 1041-1063.

Lennon, F., 'Organization and management in the secondary school', *Scottish Education*, T Bryce and W Hume (eds), 2nd ed., Edinburgh University Press, Edinburgh, 2003, pp. 419-428.

McGhee P., *The Academic Quality Handbook*, RoutledgeFalmer, 2004.

National Committee of Inquiry into Higher Education [NCIHE], *Higher Education in the Learning Society [The Dearing Report]*, Stationery Office, London, 1997.

Nunan, T., R. George and H. McCausland, 'Inclusive education in universities' *International Journal of Inclusive Education*, vol. 4-1, 2000, pp. 63-88.

Olney, M. and K. Brockelman, 'Out of the disability closet: strategic use of perception management by select university students with disabilities', *Disability and Society*, vol. 18-1, 2003, pp. 35-50.

Panting, C. and K. Kelly, *Barriers to Success? Disability Identity in Higher Education.* Conference paper presented at Pedagogical Research in Higher Education: Enhancing Student Success, Hope University, Liverpool, 2006

Parker, V., 'Staff development and curricular inclusion in higher education', *Research in Post-Compulsory Education*, vol. 6-1, 2001, pp. 105-112.

Riddell, S., T. Tinklin and A. Wilson, *Disabled Students in Higher Education*, Routledge, London, 2005.

Special Education Needs and Disability Tribunal [SENDIST], *Special Education Needs and Disability Tribunal: President's Annual Report 2006-2007*, SENDIST, Darlington, 2008.

Wright, B., 'Accommodating disability in higher education: a closer look at the evidence for a mainstream framework of learning support', *Research in Post-Compulsory Education*, vol. 10-1, 2005, pp. 121-144.

Helen Masterton, originally from Essex, worked for Essex Social Services with 'looked after' children and, after qualifying as a teacher at Hull College of Higher Education, taught in special schools in Kingston and London and in an inner city further education college. She has lectured and conducted research on inclusion in universities in and around London, and is currently Associate Dean at the Cass School of Education.

Undergraduate Autonomy and Diversity: Perspectives from a Post-1992 University

Ratha Perumal

Abstract
Since the introduction of the widening participation agenda in higher education, student diversity in higher education has manifested itself in a variety of ways. Age, employment status, ethnicity and gender are some of the variables in which the diversity of students in higher education has increased. There is much that students themselves can tell about this diversity, and how this influences the way that they engage in higher education learning contexts. To investigate this phenomenon, a survey was conducted, at the University of East London, to investigate students' propensity to engage in certain identified self-initiated - or autonomous - learning behaviours deemed essential for success in higher education. This survey is a phase of a longitudinal three year research project to trace the development of learner autonomy among undergraduates during their years at university. The findings suggest that concurrent employment and ethnicity are reliable indicators of students' potential for autonomous behaviours in their learning, possibly leading to future academic achievement. These findings can inform tutors in the use of strategies to support and foster students' perceptions of their own competence, motivation and locus of control, all of which are strong indicators of success in higher education, and beyond. Tacit in the discourse is the notion that the university degree is much more than an academic qualification, and that undergraduate study is inherently empowering to the individual, equipping him/her with the knowledge and capability to challenge and overcome barriers to achievement.

Key Words: Learner autonomy, higher education, student diversity, collaborative learning and teaching strategies.

*****

1. Introduction

The ability to think and behave independently in the context of learning is a fundamental skill in higher education (HE). It is a skill that is sought-after by graduate employers, and has become a key learning outcome in the HE curriculum. Despite these clear acknowledgements, certain aspects of this concept are not explicated in contemporary academic literature, particularly in relation to British HE contexts, such as the propensity of individuals to be autonomous, how that potential may be converted into actual independent behaviour, and the environmental factors that may exert an influence on that development.

As a response to the recommendations in the Dearing Report[1] in 1997, the widening participation agenda gained new prominence in the government's HE strategy. In the years since then, student diversity in HE – and at the University of East London (UEL) - has continued to manifest itself in many ways, extending beyond conventional intersections of culture and ethnicity, to include variables such as age, previous qualifications and/or experience, as well as concurrent employment status.

At UEL, a research study was undertaken to investigate this student diversity, and to examine its influence on individual autonomy. This project provided an opportunity to measure the potential for autonomy of a sample of university students at the outset of their undergraduate careers. To trace the development of their autonomy, a series of surveys of that sample are planned during their years at university. The data in this study provides an opportunity to inform changes to teaching and learning strategies to meet and support the continuing development of self-initiated behaviours among entry-level undergraduates at UEL.

2. Learner Autonomy in Higher Education

The development of learner autonomy is the process by which the individual student gradually takes greater responsibility for his/her learning, an innate interest in the subject being the catalyst for increasing levels of self-determination in engagement with curriculum, with appropriate tutor support. Central to this process is the student, and the autonomy-supportive relationships with him/her that can be nurtured in the classroom: these have the potential to take students beyond the written or spoken word, long after the conclusion of formal teaching.[2] The ways in which learner autonomy can be fostered in undergraduate classrooms is, to some extent, determined by the students themselves, by their individual and general characteristics. The changing demographic profile of undergraduate students today - distinct from earlier generations of students - presents a new challenge to teachers in HE.[3] Students manifest diversity in a variety of ways: age, concurrent employment status, culture and ethnicity, gender and previous academic experience.

This new demography is observable in the profile of students at UEL and is consistent with its situation in an urban region of a metropolis. However, UEL has a long-standing tradition of encouraging and welcoming the participation of students from under-represented groups that predates the introduction of the government's widening participation initiatives. In many post-1992 institutions, the most pronounced shift in student profile, in the last decade or so, has been the increasing numbers of female mature students.[4] Such diversity in undergraduate classrooms presents a new challenge to educators in HE, requiring additional teaching and learning strategies to ensure appropriate engagement with the undergraduate curriculum.

This study examines the potential of entry-level undergraduates to think and act autonomously in the context of learning in HE. The concept of autonomy is disaggregated into its three psychological constructs, discussed in the following section, and measured against the aspects of student diversity noted earlier. This information will be used to construct classroom strategies that can more effectively support teaching and learning. Researchers and practitioners engaged in teaching in these diverse and 'non-traditional' HE contexts advocate a variety of research-based practical strategies, which encompass the quality of teacher-student classroom interaction, issues in the devolution of certain decision-making processes to students, and a general classroom ethos that is 'autonomy-supportive'.[5] Such strategies are considered below.

3. Learner Autonomy: a Review of the Literature

One of the fundamental definitions of learner autonomy states that 'autonomy is the ability to take charge of one's own learning'.[6] Implicit in this definition is the notion of the devolution of the responsibility for learning from the teacher to the learner, succinctly expressed as the move from 'directed teaching' to 'self-directed learning'.[7]

However, learners can be reluctant to take charge of their own learning, seemingly defaulting to the passive role assigned to pupils in school and distrustful of the idea that they should make decisions about their own learning targets, learning materials and activities, and make evaluations of their achievement of learning outcomes. Notwithstanding this assumption of a passive role, experience of parenting suggests the contrary of children:

> they are hardly passive creatures to be easily moulded by the actions of others… they make their active presence, their wilful agency, their demands and protests, very vividly felt. In every household that has children, negotiations must be made with young family members: their personal agendas must somehow be accommodated.[8]

It is in our nature to be autonomous, to be proactive in exploring and responding to our environment and to persist in following the agendas that we set for ourselves.[9] This model of human behaviour chimes with constructivist theories of learning which place the individual at the centre of the learning process. Implicit in this paradigm is the notion of an active, enquiring learner, one who formulates hypotheses, constructs new ideas, and selects information that is integrated into existing knowledge and experience.

The capacity for 'reflective intervention' is a defining characteristic of the autonomous learner.[10] This is the learner's sense of self that is premised on the ability to control and select knowledge as needed, thus enabling him/her to become a member of a culture creating community.[11]

The suggestion is, therefore, that the individual's innate propensity to think and behave autonomously may be constrained during the school years, consolidating a model of the passive learner within a transmissive process of education.[12] These roles can then serve to perpetuate the inappropriate expectation of some entry-level undergraduates that learning in HE will involve the reprisal of passive learner-teacher relationships that existed in earlier learning contexts.

Therefore, it is asserted that fostering learner autonomy in HE requires the encouragement of some learners to rediscover and apply their innate abilities to self-regulate and to behave with a sense of volition and choice in the context of learning in HE.

One model of learner autonomy in HE comprises three psychological constructs which identify behaviours associated with autonomy: the individual's perception of their own competence to meet the academic challenges of HE; the individual's sense of overall control over their learning; and the individual's levels of motivation.[13] Self-perceived competence denotes the extent to which a student holds an expectation that he/she is competent to meet the challenges of learning at university.[14] Perception of control refers to the extent to which a student perceives that success or failure in studying is contingent upon personal characteristics and behaviour – i.e. internal control - or factors outside their control, i.e. external.[15]

Motivation is generally regarded as the driver of volitional, self-initiated behaviours:[16] however, motivation for studying in HE may be categorised as self-initiated, and therefore intrinsic, or initiated externally and therefore extrinsic. Intrinsic motivation is apparent when an individual engages in an activity for its inherent satisfaction rather than for some separable consequence. When intrinsically motivated, the individual is moved to act for the fun or challenge entailed in the activity rather than because of external pressures or rewards. This is a critical element in human cognitive, physical and social development because, through acting out of their own interests, the individual grows in knowledge and skills. Extrinsic motivation is conventionally regarded as unvaryingly non-autonomous: however, extrinsic motivation can vary considerably in the degree to which it is self-determined, and a taxonomy of extrinsic motivation has been proposed that ranges from forms of extrinsic motivation that are least autonomous to those which are more self-determined.[17]

Finding strategies that encourage students' motivation presents a pedagogical challenge for educators. It would be difficult to ensure that all activities in the classroom would be intrinsically motivating to all students, particularly in the light of research that suggests that, beyond early childhood, the freedom to be intrinsically motivated becomes increasingly curtailed by social demands and roles that require individuals to assume responsibility for non-intrinsically interesting tasks.[18] In the HE context, an appropriately modified objective would aim to achieve levels of extrinsic motivation among students that are more self-determined (or autonomous) in nature.

4. Learning and Teaching for Autonomy

A practical consequence of the widening participation agenda in post-1992 universities is the emergence of a "skills curriculum" across some undergraduate programmes. Comprising a range of academic support embedded in every level of undergraduate study, this curriculum could be construed as an acknowledgement that some new undergraduates may not have had opportunities to hone their academic skills in the years leading up to HE, opportunities which may have been afforded to their more conventional undergraduate peers elsewhere. However, the provision of support can be said to tacitly assume disempowerment among students, and could have the unanticipated effect of perpetuating a "culture of dependence" among some learners, producing a disabling effect when these provisions of support were intended to empower. It is in this context that the following discussion should be considered.

When considering those factors that can contribute to learner autonomy in HE, the literature supports the view that the quality of student motivation and, in turn, autonomy is determined in part by the nature of the teacher's motivating style.[19] Research has indicated that a teaching style that is "autonomy-supportive" is characterised by listening more to students, encouraging student initiative in relation to learning materials, asking questions about student preferences, responding to student queries and offering empathetic statements that reflect the learner's perspective.[20] Other appropriate approaches would be teaching strategies that provide rationales for aspects of learning/teaching, use positive feedback where appropriate, offer encouragement during tasks, and provide hints to facilitate completion of those tasks.[21] Research has shown that teachers who were found to be more autonomy-supportive were observed to be more enthusiastic during instruction than their counterparts who used less autonomy-supportive, e.g. controlling, strategies.[22] The study concluded that autonomy-supportive teachers tend to differ from their so-called controlling counterparts not in the nature of the information that they convey to their students but in the "quality of their instructional style".[23]

These strategies can approach teaching and learning in a flexible and student-centred manner, enabling students to gain an accurate appreciation of their academic strengths and weaknesses. This appreciation would be facilitated by early formative assessment of academic tasks, with recommendations of any appropriate remedial steps to be taken prior to any summative assessment process. This measure could also facilitate the devolution of control over students' learning by enabling independent adjustments to be made to their learning techniques. Such devolution could enhance individual student's perceptions of their competence to meet the challenges of HE. Moreover, this devolution of control over certain procedural or administrative aspects of their studies could enhance students' sense of control over their learning in HE. Research has found that increasing students' sense of, and actual, control over the learning environment and curriculum content - subject to the appropriate learning objectives and outcomes - had a positive influence on their perceptions of their role and influence in the learning process, as well as increasing enthusiasm (motivation levels) for learning and participation in the classroom.[24] The enhancement of students' sense of control by such classroom strategies, could have a positive influence on their engagement with the academic subject.

Locating effective strategies to encourage learners' motivation presents a challenge for educators for two interrelated reasons: student heterogeneity and the fundamentally subjective nature of human motivation. Student motivation could be enhanced by strategies considered previously in this section: the forms of teacher-student interaction that are autonomy-supportive, and the strategies to enhance locus of control and perception of competence constructs which could achieve the indirect effect of developing and supporting student motivation. In addition, efforts to make the undergraduate curriculum relevant to students' lives and perspectives could achieve the practical effect of enhancing their motivation to learn.

The introduction, and current widespread use, of virtual learning environments have made the HE experience even more student-focused by facilitating flexible opportunities to learn and to engage in formative assessment through the use of online tests and other resources. This is particularly useful for students with multiple demands on their time, whether through concurrent employment or extra-mural responsibilities.

5. Embedding Empowerment in the HE Curriculum

An emancipatory aspect of autonomy is that students should free themselves from the constraints under which they are already thinking and acting.[25] Correspondingly, the affective and cognitive dimensions of learning should accompany opportunities to develop 'critical' skills, including the ability to reflect on ones place in the broader socioeconomic context.[26] The attribute of "critical autonomy" can be developed:

> By engaging with established bodies of thought, being able to participate in associated conversations, seeing new possibilities for understanding and being able to go beyond conventional insights and wisdom…where learners can develop new knowledge from old or participate in determining the content of learning…or what counts as educational knowledge'.[27]

Teaching strategies to foster the development of autonomy among less autonomous students could include Cummins' collaborative classroom relations that can enable students to analyse and understand the social realities of their own lives and that of their communities.[28] These ideas are, in part, an amplification of Cummins' earlier theoretical framework for the empowerment of minority ethnic students, which asserts that the acknowledgement of students' cultures and home environments in the classroom and the use of interactive reciprocal discourse in the classroom can have a positive and enabling influence on their learning.[29] Intended for use in primary and secondary education contexts, the framework has the potential for modification for HE curricula, particularly when it is considered in the context of "autonomy-supportive" classroom strategies.[30]

More generally, the nature of power relations in society could form part of HE classroom discourse. These discussions, as a strategy to foster self-initiated attitudes and behaviour, could occur within an autonomy-supportive learning environment, and be combined with previously articulated strategies, to enhance students' own perceptions of competence, sense of control and motivation to learn.

Cummins' framework for the empowerment of minority students additionally proposes that the teacher's role should encompass that of advocate for students, in ensuring the fairness of teaching and assessment strategies in place.[31] This assertion gains empirical support from an unexpected quarter: research on the low retention rates of indigenous HE students in Alaska. This work focused on the disengagement from HE of Native American and Canadian students in tertiary education at the University of Alaska.[32] When investigating the possible reasons, most students were found to have been adequately prepared academically by the reservation schools that they attended, but that they encountered:

> Racism, impersonal classes, dysfunctional counselling, and the lack of interaction with their teachers and their mainstream classmates.[33]

It was these factors that corresponded with disengagement and poor retention among indigenous students in HE. An intervention to re-engage twenty-three failing students - of whom twenty were Native American or Canadian First Nation - early morning 'breakfast' tutorial sessions were provided. During these sessions, it emerged that students wanted and needed open and comfortable communicative relationships - with their classmates and tutor - much more than they wanted or needed support with academic work. In the light of this, the tutorials continued to focus on interpersonal relationships within the group, paying less attention to academic issues. Despite this apparent neglect of academic work, virtually all the students performed well on their course, leading to the conclusion, after further research interviews, that the nature of the relationship students have with their teachers can have a significant impact on their educational success: "What matters most to these students is the personal and human contact they have with the [tutor]".[34]

6. The Study, its Aims and Method

A survey of entry-level (Level One or First Year) undergraduates' potential to engage in volitional acts in the context of their learning was conducted, the first phase of a longitudinal three-year study intended to trace the development of students' ability to think and behave autonomously during their undergraduate studies. The focus of this study is to measure the potential of undergraduates to be autonomous in their learning.

The respondents to the survey were 105 entry-level undergraduates in the School of Education at UEL: each participant was required to complete a questionnaire, comprising 20 statements, to which they expressed their responses (strongly agree, agree, neither agree nor disagree, disagree and strongly disagree) on a five-point Likert scale. The questionnaire gauged participants' propensity for autonomous behaviour with items which were adapted from previous research: psychological constructs of individual autonomy, i.e. perceptions of their own competence to meet the academic challenges of HE, the sense of overall control over their learning; and levels of motivation;[35] incremental scales of learner autonomy;[36] and measures of intrinsic and extrinsic motivation.[37] The veracity of participant responses was tested by the random inversion of several questionnaire statements.

An index of autonomy was compiled from the items in the questionnaire and mean ratings of autonomy were used for the purposes of analysis by such factors as gender, age, previous qualifications, concurrent employment and ethnicity.

7. Findings

There was a high overall return rate of questionnaires in the survey - 105 completed questionnaires in total. The response rate to individual items was also high, in most cases 100%. The lowest rate was 92% (97 responses) for one statement. This elevated rate of response to individual items in the survey complemented the relatively high rate of overall participation of respondents approached.

A. Autonomy and Gender

The sample of 105 students was split unevenly by gender, with 91 female participants (86.7%), 12 males (11.4%) and 2 unknowns (1.9%). The demographic pattern apparent in this survey is consistent with the general trend at UEL - and in higher education generally - which has seen male enrolment increasingly outstripped by female enrolment in the last decade. An examination of the mean ratings for autonomy for the sub-samples demonstrated no correlation between autonomy and gender.

Table 1: Gender and Mean Ratings for Autonomy

Gender	Mean Rating for Autonomy
Female (n = 91)	3.7
Male (n = 12)	3.7

Further analysis of the data by gender was considered to be potentially unfruitful due to the skewed demographic pattern in favour of females.

B. Autonomy and age

The ages of respondents ranged between 19 and 51 years, with only 24.8% of the sample group coming within the conventional post-‘A’ level age group (see Table 2).

Table 2: Distribution of Respondents’ Ages

Age range (in years)	Percentage of overall sample
19-21	24.8%
22-30	31.7%
31-40	24.8%
41-50	17.8%
51-60	1.0%

When mean ratings for autonomy were examined against participants’ ages, no significant correlations were evident, n = 105, correlation coefficient 0.16.

C. Autonomy and Concurrent Employment

Mean ratings for autonomy for all respondents were examined against concurrent employment - which initially included participants not in employment – and there were no correlations evident. However, when respondents not in concurrent employment were removed from the statistical analysis, a positive relationship between hours worked and ratings for autonomy was found, n = 51, 0.38, significant at the 5% level.

Thus, participants whose responses indicated an ability to engage in autonomous behaviours tended to be those who were concurrently employed. These participants' agreement with such statements as 'I am able to find the answer to most questions I am asked' and 'The person with the greatest influence over my success or failure at university is me' tended to increase with hours spent in concurrent employment.

D. Autonomy and Previous Academic Qualifications

Data relating to the highest prior qualifications of respondents was differentiated into four broad categories, with each category examined against mean ratings for autonomy (see Table 3).

Table 3: Autonomy and Prior Qualifications

Prior Qualifications	Mean Ratings for Autonomy
'A' Levels	68.5 (sd 6.6)
BTEC/HNC	67.7 (sd 6.8)
Diploma	64.2 (sd 8.5)
AS Level/NNEB/Access	69.1 (sd 5.5)

There were no significant differences found by two sample t-tests between the mean ratings for autonomy for sub-samples differentiated by prior qualifications.

E. Autonomy and Ethnicity

Data from the survey were differentiated by perceived ethnicity of the participants (see Table 4). It can be observed that the mean rating for autonomy for the Asian sub-sample was significantly lower than those for the three other sub-samples, and as much as five points lower than its nearest cohort (see Table 4).

Table 4: Autonomy and Perceived Ethnicity

Perceived Ethnicity	Mean Ratings for Autonomy
Black-African	68.3 (sd 8.1)
Black Caribbean	68.7 (sd 5.4)
Asian	63.3 (sd 7.7)
White European	70.4 (sd 6.2)

These differences in magnitude were confirmed by a series of two sample t-tests between mean ratings for autonomy which established that the mean of the Asian sub-sample was significantly smaller than those of the other sub-samples (see Table 5).

Table 5: Comparisons of Sub-samples by Ethnicity

Sub-Samples Compared	Two-sample t-test Results			
	t	p	df	Significance
Asian/Black-African	2.124	0.0438	25	< .05
Asian/Black Caribbean	3.398	0.0014	45	< .01
Asian/White European	3.590	0.0012	28	< .01

Further analyses were undertaken within the sub-sample of Asian students, i.e. by geo-ethnic groups (Bangladeshi, Indian and Pakistani). No significant differences were found between mean ratings for autonomy for these geo-ethnic groups, thus indicating that the conflation of these groups had not adversely affected the integrity of the analysis. Further exammination of the students in this sample disclosed that all were women – but the sample was predominantly female – and that all were in the younger age categories.

8. Interpretation

The findings from the first phase of this longitudinal research project suggest that entry-level undergraduates at UEL generally tend to perceive themselves as being autonomous: on a range of ratings for autonomy from 1-5, students' mean ratings achieved 3.7, i.e. towards a rating of 4 indicating agreement. Notably, there were no discernible effects upon autonomy by a number of factors: age, gender and previous qualifications – factors that have become markedly more diverse – did not discernibly affect mean ratings for autonomy. However, more detailed analyses of the survey data raise issues concerning two factors - concurrent employment and ethnicity – which appeared to affect students' mean ratings for autonomy.

First, those students who were engaged in concurrent employment were discerned to have a more developed ability to think and behave in an autonomous manner. Whether the ability to think and act autonomously is a pre-existing characteristic - enabling some individuals to contemplate, initiate and sustain multiple demanding pursuits - or whether it is engagement in those multiple demanding pursuits that facilitates the development of greater autonomy is an issue that remains to be examined in later phases of the study.

Second, ethnicity was found to be a factor in determining autonomy insofar as the Asian sub-sample had the lowest ratings of all participating sub-samples by ethnicity. Apparently, these students had a lower self-perception of their own competence to meet the demands of HE, a sense that their own success or failure was contingent on factors beyond their control; producing a low mean rating of autonomy. The presence of three geo-ethnic groups within the Asian sub-sample – all three with similar tendencies - would tend to support the interpretation that the influencing factor is more likely to be cultural than religious. While a plausible rationale for this low autonomy was offered by the relative youth of respondents in the Asian sub-sample, this phenomenon raises important questions about the effects of culture on the development of individual autonomy which will be examined in later phases of this study.

Similar tendencies have been reported by studies of entry-level undergraduates at the University of Alaska and the University of Wales[38] and, in order to respond to these tendencies in student self-perception, it has been believed appropriate to offer entry-level undergraduates open and comfortable communicative relationships with their peers and teachers and early opportunities to increase their self-perception of academic competence.

The UEL students' attitudes and perceptions revealed by the data in this study are encouraging. The survey data discloses that students arrive at UEL with considerable potential to be autonomous in their learning. The students participated in the survey possess many of the essential traits critical to success in higher education, but it is the task of educators to recognise this potential, and to harness and support its development during the years of undergraduate study.

Notes

[1] National Committee of Inquiry into Higher Education [NCIHE], *Higher Education in the Learning Society [The Dearing Report]*, Stationery Office, London, 1997.

[2] See P Freire and D P Macedo, *Literacy: Reading the Word and the World*, Routledge, London, 1987, in which the empowerment of students is an overarching theme.

[3] See P Walker, 'The commodification of British higher education: trials and triumphs of massification in the metropolitan university', this volume.

[4] R Johnston and B Merrill, *Learning in HE: Improving Practice for Non-traditional Adult Students*, SOCRATES Grundvig Project: University of Warwick, 2005, accessed 30th July, 2007 <www2.warwick.ac.uk/study/cll/research/lihe/national_contexts.pdf>.

[5] See 1) R Reeve, E Bolt, and Y Cai, 'Autonomy-supportive teachers: how they teach and motivate students', *Journal of Educational Psychology*, vol. 91-3, 1999, pp. 537-548. 2) R Reeve and H Jang, 'What teachers say and do to support students' autonomy during a learning activity', *Journal of Educational Psychology*, vol. 98-1, 2006, pp. 204-218.

[6] H Holec, *Autonomy and Foreign Language Learning*, Oxford, Pergamon, 1981, p. 3.
[7] D Little, 'Language learner autonomy: some fundamental considerations revisited', *Innovation in Language Learning and Teaching*, vol. 1-1, 1998, pp. 14-29, p. 16.
[8] P Salmon, Life at School: Education and Psychology, Constable, London, 1998, p.24.
[9] Little (op. cit..).
[10] See J S Bruner, 'The language of education', in J S Bruner, *Actual Minds, Possible Worlds*, Cambridge, Mass., Harvard University Press, 1986, pp. 121-133, p. 132.
[11] Ibid.
[12] See P Freire, *Pedagogy of the Oppressed*, London, Routledge, 1970.
[13] D M A Fazey and J E Fazey, 'The potential for autonomy in learning: perceptions of competence, motivation and locus of control in first year undergraduate students', *Studies in Higher Education*, vol. 25-3, 2001, pp. 345-361.
[14] Ibid.
[15] J Heckhausen and R Shultz, 'A life-span theory of control', *Psychological Review*, vol. 102-2, 1995, pp. 204-384.
[16] E L Deci and R M Ryan, *Intrinsic Motivation and Self-determination in Human Behaviour*, Plenum, New York, 1985.
[17] R M Ryan and E L Deci, 'Intrinsic and extrinsic motivations: classic definitions and new directions', *Contemporary Educational Psychology*, vol. 25-1, 2000, pp. 54-67.
[18] Deci and Ryan, op. cit., report research undertaken in American schools which demonstrates that intrinsic motivation becomes weaker with each advancing year in the formal learning environment.
[19] See 1) B Weiner, 'A history of motivation research in education', *Journal of Educational Psychology*, vol. 82-4, 1990, p. 616-622. 2) E L Deci, R J Vallerand, L G Pelletier and R M Ryan, 'Motivation in education: the self-determination perspective', *Educational Psychologist*, vol. 26-3/4, 1991, pp. 325-346. 3) Reeve, Bolt and Cai, op. cit.
[120] Ibid.
[20] See 1) E L Deci, N H Spiegel, R M Ryan, R Koestner and M Kauffman, 'Effects of performance standards on teaching styles: behaviour of controlling teachers', *Journal of Educational Psychology*, vol. 74-6, 1982, pp. 852-859. 2) C Flink, A K Boggiano, and M Barrett, 'Controlling teaching strategies: undermining children's self-determination and performance', *Journal of Personality and Social Psychology*, vol. 59-5, 1990, pp. 916-924.
[22] Reeve, Bolt and Cai, op. cit.
[23] Ibid., p. 549.
[24] Fazey and Fazey, op. cit.

[25] R Barnett, *The Limits of Competence*, Buckingham, Open University Press, 1994.
[26] See P Hodkinson, 'Technicism, teachers and teaching', *Journal of Vocational Education and Training*, vol.50-2, 1998, pp. 193-209, and K Ecclestone, 'Assessment and critical autonomy in post-compulsory education in the UK', *Journal of Education and Work*, vol. 13-2, 2000, pp. 140-162.
[27] Ecclestone, ibid., p. 15.
[28] J Cummins, *Biliteracy, Empowerment and Transformative Pedagogy*, 2003, accessed 1st September, 2007 <http://www.iteachilearn.com/cummins/biliteratempowerment.html,>.
[29] Ibid.
[30] Reeve and Jang, op. cit.
[31] Cummins, op. cit.
[32] P Wilson, 'Key factors in the performance and achievement of minority students at the University of Alaska, Fairbanks', *American Indian Quarterly*, vol. 21-3, 1998, pp. 535-545.
[33] Ibid., p. 536.
[34] Ibid., p. 537.
[35] Fazey and Fazey, op. cit.
[36] Ecclestone, op. cit.
[37] Deci and Ryan, op. cit.
[38] Wilson, op. cit. and Fazey and Fazey, op. cit.

Bibliography

Barnett, R., *The Limits of Competence*, Buckingham, Open University Press, 1994.

Bruner, J. S., 'The language of education', in J. S. Bruner, *Actual Minds, Possible Worlds*, Cambridge, Mass., Harvard University Press, 1986, pp. 121-133.

Cummins, J., *Biliteracy, Empowerment and Transformative Pedagogy*, 2003, accessed 1st September, 2007 <http://www.iteachilearn.com/cummins/biliteratempowerment.html,>.

Deci, E. L. and R. M. Ryan, *Intrinsic Motivation and Self-determination in Human Behaviour*, Plenum, New York, 1985.

Deci, E . L., N. H. Spiegel, R. M. Ryan, R. Koestner and M. Kauffman, 'Effects of performance standards on teaching styles: behaviour of controlling teachers', *Journal of Educational Psychology*, vol. 74-6, 1982, pp. 852-859.

Deci, E.L., R. J. Vallerand, L. G. Pelletier and R. M. Ryan, 'Motivation in education: the self-determination perspective', *Educational Psychologist*, vol. 26-3/4, 1991, pp. 325-346.

Ecclestone, K., 'Assessment and critical autonomy in post-compulsory education in the UK', *Journal of Education and Work*, vol. 13-2, 2000, pp. 140-162.

Fazey, D. M. A. and J. E. Fazey, 'The potential for autonomy in learning: perceptions of competence, motivation and locus of control in first year undergraduate students', *Studies in Higher Education*, vol. 25-3, 2001, pp. 345-361.

Flink, C., A. K. Boggiano, and M. Barrett, 'Controlling teaching strategies: undermining children's self-determination and performance', *Journal of Personality and Social Psychology*, vol. 59-5, 1990, pp. 916-924.

Freire, P., *Pedagogy of the Oppressed*, London, Routledge, 1970.

Freire, P. and D. P. Macedo, *Literacy: Reading the Word and the World*, Routledge, London, 1987.

Heckhausen, J. and R. Shultz, 'A life-span theory of control', *Psychological Review*, vol. 102-2, 1995, pp. 204-384.

Hodkinson, P., 'Technicism, teachers and teaching', *Journal of Vocational Education and Training*, vol. 50-2, 1998, pp. 193-209.

Holec, H., *Autonomy and Foreign Language Learning*, Oxford, Pergamon, 1981.

Johnston, R. and B. Merrill, *Learning in HE: Improving Practice for Non-traditional Adult Students*, SOCRATES Grundvig Project: University of Warwick, 2005, accessed 30th July, 2007 <www2.warwick.ac.uk/study/cll/research/lihe/national_contexts.pdf>.

National Committee of Inquiry into Higher Education [NCIHE], *Higher Education in the Learning Society [The Dearing Report]*, Stationery Office, London, 1997.

Reeve, J. and H. Jang, 'What teachers say and do to support students' autonomy during a learning activity', *Journal of Educational Psychology*, vol. 98-1, 2006, pp. 204-218.

Reeve, E., E. Bolt and Y. Cai, 'Autonomy-supportive teachers: how they teach and motivate students', *Journal of Educational Psychology*, vol. 91-3, 1999, pp. 537-548.

Ryan, R. M. and E. L. Deci, 'Intrinsic and extrinsic motivations: classic definitions and new directions', *Contemporary Educational Psychology*, vol. 25-1, 2000, pp. 54-67.

Salmon, P., *Life at School: Education and Psychology*, Constable, London, 1998.

Weiner, B., 'A history of motivation research in education', *Journal of Educational Psychology*, vol. 82-4, 1990, p. 616-622.

Wilson, P., 'Key factors in the performance and achievement of minority students at the University of Alaska, Fairbanks', *American Indian Quarterly*, vol. 21-3, 1998, pp. 535-545

Ratha Perumal is a lecturer in Education at the Cass School of Education. Her research into learner autonomy in higher education - which forms the basis for this chapter - is a three year longitudinal study examining the influence of the university experience on the development of autonomy in undergraduates.